PRIVATEERS AND PRIVATEERING

From a drawing by Commander E. P. Statham, R.N.

THE "INVENTION," A REMARKABLE FRENCH PRIVATEER, CAPTURED BY A BRITISH FRIGATE JULY 27, 1801. (See p. 263.)

Frontispiece]

PRIVATEERS AND PRIVATEERING

With Eight Illustrations

by
Commander
E. P. Statham, R. N.

HERITAGE BOOKS
2012

HERITAGE BOOKS

AN IMPRINT OF HERITAGE BOOKS, INC.

Books, CDs, and more—Worldwide

For our listing of thousands of titles see our website
at
www.HeritageBooks.com

A Facsimile Reprint
Published 2012 by
HERITAGE BOOKS, INC.
Publishing Division
100 Railroad Ave. #104
Westminster, Maryland 21157

Originally published
New York
James Pott & Company
1910

International Standard Book Numbers
Paperbound: 978-0-7884-2286-7
Clothbound: 978-0-7884-9422-2

PREFACE

A FEW words of explanation are necessary as to the pretension and scope of this volume. It does not pretend to be a history of privateering; the subject is an immense one, teeming with technicalities, legal and nautical; interesting, indeed, to the student of history, and never comprehensively treated hitherto, as far as the present author is aware, in any single work.

The present object is not, however, to provide a work of reference, but rather a collection of true stories of privateering incidents, and heroes of what the French term " la course "; and as such it is hoped that it will find favour with a large number of readers.

While the author has thus aimed at the simple and graphic narration of such adventures, every effort has been made to ensure that the stories shall be truly told, without embroidery, and from authentic sources; and it has been found necessary, in some instances, to point out inaccuracies in accounts already published; necessary, in view of the fact that these accounts are accessible to any one, and probably familiar to not a few possible readers of this volume, and it appears to be only fair and just that any animadversions upon these discrepancies should be here anticipated and dealt with.

It has not been considered necessary, save in rare instances, to give references for statements or narratives ; the book is designed to amuse and entertain, and copious references in footnotes are not entertaining.

It will be noticed that the vast majority of the lives of privateers and incidents are taken from the eighteenth century ; for the simple reason that full and interesting accounts during this period are available, while earlier ones are brief and bald, and often of very doubtful accuracy.

Some excuse must be craved for incongruities in chronological order, which are unavoidable under the circumstances. They do not affect the stories.

There remains to enumerate the titles and authors of modern works to which the writer is indebted, and of which a list will be found on the adjoining page.

LIST OF MODERN AUTHORITIES

" History of the American Privateers and Letters of Marque in the War of 1812," etc. By George Coggleshall. 1856.

" Mann and Manners at the Court of Florence." By Dr. Doran. 1876.

" The Naval War of 1812." By T. Roosevelt. 1882.

" Studies in Naval History." By Sir John K. Laughton. 1887.

" The Corsairs of France." By C. B. Norman. 1887.

" Life Aboard a British Privateer in the Reign of Queen Ann." By R. C. Leslie. 1889.

" Robert Surcouf, un Corsaire Malouin." Par Robert Surcouf, ancien Sous-préfet. 1889.

" The British Fleet." By Commander C. N. Robinson, R.N. 1894.

" The Royal Navy." By Sir W. Laird Clowes, etc. 1894.

" Old Naval Ballads," etc. The Navy Records Society. 1894.

"A History of the Administration of the Royal Navy," etc. By M. Oppenheim. 1896.

" History of the Liverpool Privateers," etc. By G. Williams. 1897.

" Naval Yarns, Letters, and Anecdotes," etc. By W. H. Long. 1899.

" A History of American Privateers." By E. S. Maclay. 1900.

" Sea Songs and Ballads." By C. Stone. 1906.

" Les Corsaires." Par Henri Malo. 1908.

CONTENTS

SOME FRENCHMEN

SOME AMERICANS

Contents

LIST OF ILLUSTRATIONS

INTRODUCTORY

CHAPTER I

INTRODUCTORY

THE privateersman, scouring the seas in his swift, rakish craft, plundering the merchant vessels of the enemy, and occasionally engaging in a desperate encounter with an opponent of his own class, or even with a well-equipped man-of-war, has always presented a romantic and fascinating personality. Many thrilling tales, half truth, half fiction, have been written about him; and if he has not infrequently been confounded with his first cousin the pirate, it must be admitted that for such confusion there is considerable justification. The privateer is a licensed, the pirate an unlicensed, plunderer; but plunder, not patriotism, being, as a rule, the motive of the former, it is not perhaps surprising that, failing legitimate prey, he has sometimes adopted, to a great extent, the tactics of the latter.

Before proceeding to give an account of some of these licensed rovers and their adventures, let us consider for a moment or two the origin and development of privateering; this will assist us in forming an appreciation of the advantages and drawbacks of the system, and also of the difficulties which presented themselves to an honest and conscientious privateer captain—for such there have been, as we shall see, though there are not too many who merit such terms.

It is not very easy to say when privateering was first inaugurated, though it is pretty certain that the term "privateer" did not come into use until well on in the seventeenth century; licensed rovers, or private men-of-war, were known previous to this period by some other title, such as "Capers"—from a Dutch word, "Kaper"—or "letters of marque," the latter a very incorrect term, adopted through a loose manner of speech, for a "letter of marque" is, strictly speaking, a very different affair from a privateer; indeed, the application of such a term to a ship is obviously absurd : to convert a piece of paper or parchment with writing on it into a seaworthy vessel would be a considerably more marvellous piece of conjuring than turning a pumpkin into a carriage, as the good fairy did for the accommodation of Cinderella.

There is no doubt that the employment of private vessels for the purposes of war, and the granting of letters of marque, went on side by side for a great number of years. From the earliest times, before the Norman Conquest, there were hordes of sea-rovers who, entirely on their own account, and solely for the purpose of plunder, infested the seas, robbing without scruple or distinction every defenceless vessel they encountered, and in many instances wantonly slaughtering the crews ; they would also, on occasion, make a descent upon the coast either of their own or some adjacent country—they were quite impartial in this respect—and sack the farms and dwellings within easy reach, retiring to their vessels before any force could be assembled to deal with them. The Danes, as we know, were particularly handy at this kind of thing, and gave us no little trouble.

Nobody appears to have made any great effort to put down this piracy; but sometimes it was convenient to enlist the services of some of these hardy and adventurous ruffians against the enemies of the sovereign. In the year 1049, for instance, that excellent monarch, Edward the Confessor, finding the Danes very troublesome on the south coast, sent a force, under Godwin, to deal with them; and we are told that it was composed of " two king's ships, and forty-two of the people's ships "; these latter being, no doubt, a collection of—let us hope—the less villainous of these sea-rovers, hardy and skilful seamen, and desperate fighters when it came to the point.

Nearly two hundred years later, in 1243, King Henry III. issued regular patents, or commissions, to certain persons, seamen by profession, " to annoy the king's enemies by sea or land wheresoever they are able," and enjoined all his faithful subjects to refrain from injuring or hindering them in this business; the condition being that half the plunder was to be given to the king, " in his wardrobe "—that is, his private purse—and it is quite probable that both the king and the recipients of his commission made a nice little profit out of it.

This is a genuine instance of what was known later as privateering; and it will be noticed that the " king's enemies " are specified as the only persons against whom the commission holds good ; in other words, such a commission can have no significance, nor indeed can it be issued, in time of peace or against any friendly Power. This is an essential characteristic of privateering : it can only be carried on when a state of war exists, and the fitting out of a privateer to attack the subjects of any sovereign would in itself be an act of war.

Now let us see what is meant by a letter of marque ; there is a good instance on record at the end of the thirteenth century, in the reign of Edward I.

One Bernard D'Ongressill, a merchant of Bayonne— at that time a portion of the realm of the King of England—in the year 1295, was making a peaceful, and, as he hoped, a profitable voyage from Barbary to England, in his ship the *St. Mary*, with a cargo of almonds, raisins, and figs ; unfortunately he encoun-tered heavy weather, and was compelled to run into Lagos—a small sea-port at the south-west corner of Portugal which affords secure shelter from westerly gales—and, while he was waiting for the weather to moderate, there came from Lisbon some armed men, who robbed D'Ongressill of the ship, cargo, and the private property of himself and his crew, and took the whole of their spoil to Lisbon. The King of Por-tugal very unscrupulously appropriated one-tenth of the plunder, the remainder being divided among the robbers.

The unhappy victim at once applied for redress to the king's representative, Sir John of Brittany,

Lieutenant of Gascony, representing that he had lost some £700, and requesting that he might be granted letters of marque against the Portuguese, to take whatever he could from them, until he had made up his loss. This was conceded, and authority bestowed to " seize by right of marque,[1] retain, and appropriate the people of Portugal, and especially those of Lisbon and their goods, wheresoever they might be found," for five years, or until he had obtained restitution. This was dated in June : but the king's ratification was necessary, and this caused some delay, as Edward was at that time shut up in a Welsh castle ; however, he was able in October to confirm the licence ; but he added the proviso that if D'Ongressill took more than £700 worth from the Portuguese, he would be held answerable for the balance.

This is an excellent example of the form and import of a letter of marque ; and it will be noticed that

---

[1] Sir Harris Nicolas, in his " History of the Royal Navy," interprets the Latin word *marcare* (or *marchare*) " to mark," and, in referring to this incident, says that Bernard was accorded the right of " *marking* the men and subjects of the King of Portugal," etc. It is curious that so diligent and accomplished a chronicler should have fallen into this error. The verb *marcare*, as he would have discovered by reference to the " Glossarium " of Du Cange, the learned French archæologist, was in fact a bit of " law Latin," coined for a purpose ; that is, to express in one word the rights conceded by a letter of marque ; it will not be found in any ordinary Latin dictionary. The grant of a licence to " mark " the subjects of some monarch, and their goods, is, indeed somewhat of an absurdity—clearly, the " marker " would first have to catch the men and their possessions !

England was not at war with Portugal, nor did the issue of this letter of marque constitute an act of war ; it was, in fact, a licence to a private individual to recover by force from the subjects of another sovereign the goods of which he had been despoiled ; the practice dates back, certainly, to the early part of the twelfth century, and probably further ; and it was in use in England until the time of Charles II., or later. The one condition, not mentioned in the case of D'Ongressill, was that letters of marque should not be granted until every effort had been made to obtain a peaceful settlement ; representations may, however, have been made to the King of Portugal ; but if, as stated by D'Ongressill, he had pocketed a tithe of the spoil, one can imagine that there might be some difficulty in the matter ; the possession of one-tenth would naturally appear, in the eyes of his Majesty of Portugal, to constitute nine points of the law !

The application of the term letter of marque to vessels which were in reality privateers has caused a good deal of confusion ; some naval historians of great repute have fallen into error over it, one of them, for instance, alluding to the commissions granted by Henry III., in 1243, as the " first recorded instance of the issue of letters of marque " ; rather an inexcusable mistake, from which the present reader is happily exempt.

While guarding, in this explanation, against such confusion of terms, we must, notwithstanding, accept the ultimate adoption of it ; and so we shall find included among our privateers and their commander some who were quite improperly described as letters of marque, and one, at least, who may correctly be thus designated, but who, as an interesting example of a sort of privateering at an early period, appears to deserve mention.

The bearer of a letter of marque—or "mart," as it was constantly termed by writers and others of that class of persons who never will take the trouble to pronounce an unusual word properly—came to be adopted as the type of a sort of swashbuckler—a reckless, bullying individual, armed with doubtful credentials in the pursuit of some more or less discreditable object: allusion of this nature is made more than once by Beaumont and Fletcher in their plays, as well as by other writers.

The immense value of a fleet of privateers, more especially to a country opposed to another possessing a large mercantile marine, is obvious, and their use developed very rapidly.

By the middle of the sixteenth century the fitting out of vessels by corporations and individuals, for their own protection and the "annoying of the king's enemies" with the further advantage of substantial gains by plunder, was clearly recognised, for we find King Henry VIII., in the year 1544, remonstrating with the Mayor and burgesses of Newcastle, Scarborough, and Hull for their remissness in this respect. He points out what has been done elsewhere, especially in the west parts, "where there are twelve or sixteen ships of war abroad, who have gotten among them not so little as £10,000"; and adds: "It were overburdensome that the king should set ships to defend all parts of the realm, and keep the narrow seas withal."

In the American and French wars of the eighteenth and early part of the nineteenth centuries there were literally thousands of privateers engaged. It would appear as though almost every skipper and ship-owner incontinently applied, upon declaration of war, for a commission, or warrant, or letter of marque—no matter what it was called; the main thing was to get afloat, and have a share in what was going.

Valuable as have been the services of privateers, at various periods, as auxiliaries to the Navy, there is an obvious danger in letting loose upon the seas a vast number of men who have never had any disciplinary training, and whose principal motive is the acquisition of wealth—is, in fact, officially recognised as such ; and although there existed pretty stringent regulations, amended at various times as occasion demanded, covering the mode of procedure to be adopted before the prize-money could be paid, these laws were constantly evaded in the most flagrant manner. Even the most honourable and well-disposed privateer captain was liable at any moment to find himself confronted by the alternatives of yielding to the demands of his rapacious crew for immediate and unlawful division of the spoil, or yet more lawless capture of an ineligible vessel, and personal violence, perhaps death, to himself ; and the ease with which an unarmed vessel, overhauled within the silent circle of the horizon, unbroken by the sails of a solitary witness, could be compelled, whatever her nationality, upon some flimsy excuse to pay toll, frequently proved too strong a temptation to be resisted.

There is abundant evidence of the notoriety of such unlawful doings; Sir Leoline Jenkins, Judge of the High Court of Admiralty in the reign of Charles II., says, in a letter to Secretary Williamson: "I see that your embarrass hath been much greater about our Scotch privateers. The truth is, I am much scandalised at them in a time of war; they are, in my poor judgment, great instruments to irritate the king's friends, to undo his subjects, and none at all to profit upon the enemy; but it will not be remedied. The privateers in our wars are like the *mathematici* in old Rome: a sort of people that will always be found fault with, but still made use of."

Von Martens, a great authority upon maritime law, is equally plain-spoken: "Pirates have always been considered the enemies of mankind, and proscribed and punished accordingly. On the contrary, privateers are encouraged to this day (1801), notwithstanding all the complaints of neutral Powers, of which they are the scourge; and notwithstanding all their excesses, which it has been in vain attempted to suppress by ill-observed laws."

Admiral Vernon, in 1745, while acknowledging the services of privateers in distressing the enemy's trade and bringing an addition of wealth into the country, deprecates their employment on the ground of the general tendency to debauch the morals of our sea-

men, by substituting greed of gain for patriotism [1];
and Lord Nelson, in 1804, says : " The conduct of
all privateers is, as far as I have seen, so near piracy
that I only wonder any civilised nation can allow
them."

This is a sorry story of the privateer, and tends to
discount sadly the romantic element so commonly
associated with him.   This is not a romance, however,
and, having thus cleared the ground, we must be con-
tent to take the privateer, like Kipling's " Absent-
minded Beggar," as we find him ; and, by way of
consolation and reward for our ingenuousness, we shall
come across privateersmen whose skill, gallantry,
and absolute integrity of conduct would do credit to
many a hero of the Royal Navy.

The almost universal practice which prevailed in
former times, of arming merchant vessels, particularly
in certain trades, as a protection against pirates and
privateers, has led to a considerable amount of mis-
understanding.   There are many instances upon record
of spirited and successful defence, even against a very
superior force, on the part of these armed traders,
which have frequently been cited as privateer actions.
These vessels, however, carried no warlike commission, and must not therefore be included in this category. Captain Hugh Crow, of Liverpool, who was
engaged for many years in the West African slave
trade, is a case in point. He fought some severe
actions, upon one occasion with two British sloops-of-

---

[1] In an original letter formerly in the possession of the late
Sir William Laird Clowes, quoted by him in "The Royal Navy."

war, which he mistook in the dark for French privateers ; the error being reciprocal, they pounded away
at each other in the darkness, and it was not until
Crow, after a desperate and most creditable resistance,
was compelled at length to surrender, that victors and
vanquished discovered their error : a very remarkable
incident. Captain Crow was a shining light, in those
unhappy slaving times, by reason of his humanity and
integrity, and was beloved by the negroes from Bonny
to Jamaica, where he landed so many cargoes.

Some celebrities of the sea have also been erro-
neously styled privateers ; among others, the notori-
ous Paul Jones, and Captain Semmes, of *Alabama*
fame. Jones was a renegade, being a Scotsman by
birth, and his proper name John Paul ; but he
fought under a regular commission from the United
States, and was subsequently accorded the rank
of Rear-Admiral in the Russian service. It must
be admitted, however, that his conduct afforded some
grounds for the appellation of " Paul Jones the Pirate,"
by which he was sometimes known ; but he was a consummate seaman, and a man of infinite courage and
resource.

Semmes was also employed as a commissioned naval
officer by the Confederate States, in the Civil War of
1860 ; and though he was classed at first as a " rebel "
by the Northerners, and threatened with a pirate's fate
if captured, the recognition of the Confederates as a
belligerent State by foreign Powers had already rendered such views untenable.

It appears desirable to allude to these instances,

in order to anticipate a possible question as to the exclusion of such famous seamen from these pages.

There is also considerable confusion among authors as to the distinction between a pirate and a privateer, some of them being apparently under the impression that the terms are synonymous, while others, through imperfect knowledge of the details and ignorance of international law, have classed as pirates men who did not merit that opprobrious title, and, on the other hand, have placed the " buccaneers "—who were sheer pirates—in the same category as legitimate privateers.

For instance, Captain Woodes Rogers, of whom we shall have a good deal to say later on, is alluded to by one writer as " little more than a pious pirate," and by another simply as a pirate, bent upon " undisguised robbery " ; whereas he was, in fact, more than once in serious conflict with his crew, upon the occasion of their demanding the capture and plunder of a ship which he was not entitled to seize—and, moreover, he had his own way.

There have been, no doubt, and with equal certainty there will be, incidents in warfare which afford very unpleasant reading, and in which the aggressors appear to have been unduly harsh and exacting, not to say cruel, towards defenceless or vanquished people ; but that does not prove that they were not within their rights, and to impugn the conduct of an individual from a hastily and perhaps ignorantly adopted moral standpoint, at the expense of the legal aspect of the matter, must obviously involve the risk of gross injustice. War is a very terrible thing, and is full of terrible incidents which are quite inevitable, and the rough must be taken with the smooth—if you can find any smooth !

It is an axiom of international law that, when two nations are at war, every subject of each is at war with every subject of the other ; and, in view of this fact, it appears extremely doubtful whether any merchant vessel is not at liberty to capture one of the other side, if she be strong enough. It is, in fact, laid down by Sir Travers Twiss, a high authority, that if a merchant vessel, attacked by one of the enemy's men-of-war, should be strong enough to turn the tables, she would be entitled to make a prize of her : an unlikely incident, of course.

It is unnecessary, however, to enter upon further discussion of this subject, which would involve us in very knotty problems, upon some of which the most accomplished authorities are still at variance, and which would afford very indifferent entertainment for the reader, who will now turn over the page and follow the fortunes of our privateers—which will be found by no means devoid of interest, in spite of strict adherence to the plain unvarnished truth.

TWO EARLY INCIDENTS

CHAPTER II

ANDREW BARTON

THERE was living at the commencement of the sixteenth century a Scotsman, named Andrew Barton, who acquired considerable notoriety by reason of his exploits at sea ; and indeed, he was instrumental in bringing to a definite issue the condition of high tension existing between England and Scotland at that time, which culminated in the battle of Flodden Field.

It appears, from certain State Papers, that one John Barton, the father of Andrew, somewhere about the year 1476, in the reign of James III. of Scotland, got into trouble with the Portuguese, who captured his vessel and goods and otherwise ill-treated him ; upon representation of which injuries he obtained letters of marque against the Portuguese, in the usual terms.

Apparently, however, John did not succeed in obtaining substantial restitution by this means, for we learn, in a letter from James IV. to Maximilian, Emperor of Germany, dated December 8th, 1508, that the letters of marque had been repeatedly suspended, in the hope of obtaining redress ; but had been renewed during the previous year, in favour of

the late John Barton's three sons, one of whom—Robert
—was the occasion of the writing of this letter ; the
Portuguese having taken him prisoner, and proposing
to hang him as a pirate, which, says King James,
he is not, having authority to act against the Portuguese, by virtue of my letters of marque.

All this argues a considerable amount of favour
towards the Bartons on the Scottish monarch's part ;
for it must be admitted that the renewal of letters of
marque, after they had run intermittently for thirty
years in respect of one incident, was a straining of the
elasticity of conventions.

The Bartons had, in fact, been high in favour both
with James III. and his successor, and were constantly
employed by them in maritime affairs, being frequently entrusted, as we learn from the accounts of
the Lord Treasurer of Scotland, with the handling of
large sums of money.

They were formidable fellows, these Bartons ; hardy
and daring, skilled in all the strategy of the sea, and,
when occasion arose, perfect gluttons at fighting.
Andrew appears to have been the most formidable,
and added to his other attributes that of being a born
leader of men.

We are told by Bishop John Leslie, in his " History
of Scotland," that in the year 1506 King James caused
a great ship to be built, in the design and rigging of
which Andrew Barton played a prominent part, and
was afterwards placed in command of her to harry
the Flemish pirates then infesting the narrow seas:
a task which he set about with characteristic energy

and ferocity, with the result that he captured some and completely scattered and demoralised the remainder. By way of demonstrating his success in graphic and convincing fashion, he presently despatched to his august master sundry pipes, or casks, containing Flemish heads! He little guessed, however, that his own head was destined—according to some authorities—to make, before many years had elapsed, a similar journey, unaccompanied by his body.

Having disposed of the Flemish pirates, Andrew Barton resumed his operations, under letters of marque, against the Portuguese, and captured, during following years, a good many vessels under that flag; nor were his brothers idle. One cannot help wondering whether the Barton family had not by this time exacted more than adequate restitution of their losses of five-and-thirty years previously; and, as we know, it was of the essence of such authorised reprisals that they should cease when this end was attained. Very probably some contemporary persons, more or less interested in their doings, began asking this same question; at any rate, there prevailed in the year 1511 a very strong feeling in England against Andrew Barton; he was constantly alluded to as the " Scottish pirate," and accused of many outrages against vessels other than Portuguese; and, as there existed just then very strained relations with Scotland, these stories met with ready credence. The general dislike of Andrew Barton and his doings was embodied in a representation by Portuguese ambassadors to King Henry VIII., who does not appear to have complained to the Scots King, or taken any steps in the matter.

The public feeling was voiced, however, by Thomas Howard, Earl of Surrey—afterwards victor of Flodden, and second Duke of Norfolk—who exclaimed that " The King of England should not be imprisoned in his kingdom, while either he had an estate to set up a ship, or a son to command it."

This somewhat theatrical attitude is indicative of the exaggerated stories in circulation as to Andrew Barton's terrorism of the narrow seas ; the immediate sequel, however, was the fitting out of two vessels, commanded respectively by Surrey's sons, Lord Thomas and Lord Edward Howard, with the express object of capturing Barton. It is said by some writers that the Howards provided these ships at their own cost, and, in view of Surrey's enthusiastic outbreak, it appears not improbable that this was the case. However this may be, the two brothers put forth from the Thames one day in June 1511 in quest of Andrew, who was then returning from Flanders, by way of the Downs, in his ship, the *Lion*, accompanied by a smaller vessel, or pinnace, the *Jenny Pirwin*.

The Howards had to wait for more than a month, however, and then, being separated by bad weather, Lord Thomas sighted the *Lion*, which had also parted from her consort.

Barton appears to have endeavoured, in the first instance, to escape ; according to Leslie, he made friendly advances to Howard, insisting that the English and Scotch were not at war ; this would have been a sound and logical attitude for Barton to assume, and it may be that he acted so; but in the end Howard chased him, and, finding himself outsailed, the Scot faced the foe with his usual boldness, and a desperate encounter ensued.

Howard's force was probably superior to that of his antagonist, but Andrew Barton and his ship's company were not to be intimidated by odds against them, when once they entered upon an engagement, and Lord Thomas soon realised that the task he had undertaken was no child's play.

Reeling alongside each other, at the closest quarters, the two vessels exchanged shots from their cannon as rapidly as they could be loaded and fired, while the crossbowmen and arquebusiers discharged a perfect hail of arrows, "quarrells," and bolts; Howard placed his ship again and again alongside, in the attempt to board, only to be beaten off by the valiant Scots, the decks of both vessels plentifully strewn with the wounded and dying.

At length Howard, as courageous and persistent a fighter as Barton, gained a footing on the *Lion's* deck, with a few of his men; others speedily followed, and a hand-to-hand fight ensued.

Barton was by this time mortally wounded; his leg was shattered by a cannon-shot, and his body pierced in several places; but he sat up against the bulwarks, blowing his whistle and beating a drum to rally his men, as long as the breath remained in him; and it was not until they saw the fighting flame quenched in the eye of their intrepid and yet unconquered leader, and his chin drop upon his breast, that the sturdy Scots were fain at length to yield to Howard and his men.

Lord Edward Howard, meanwhile, had captured the *Jenny Pirwin*, not without some stubborn opposition, in spite of the odds in his favour, the smaller vessel having suffered heavily in killed and wounded before capitulating.

Both vessels were immediately added to the English Navy, the nucleus of which was then in process of formation ; the prisoners were conveyed to London, and confined in the palace of the Bishop of York, awaiting the king's pleasure.

As might be expected, the Scottish historians, Leslie and Buchanan, give a somewhat different account from that of Edward Hall, in whose chronicle the most nearly contemporary narrative is to be found. Leslie's allegation as to the friendly overtures of Barton finds no corroboration in Hall's Chronicle ; and indeed, it is difficult to believe that Andrew Barton did not thoroughly comprehend the situation from the first.

King Henry VIII. appears to have been willing to give the prisoners every chance, for he sent some members of his Council, with the Bishop of Winchester, to parley with them. The bishop, according to Hall, " rehearsed to them, whereas peace was yet between England and Scotland, that they, contrary to that, as thieves and pirates, had robbed the king's subjects within his streams, therefore they had deserved to die by the law, and to be hanged at the low-water mark. Then said the Scots, we knowledge our offence, and ask mercy, and not the law. Then a priest which was also a prisoner, said, My lords, we appeal from the king's justice to his mercy. Then the bishop asked him, if he was authorised by them to say so, and they cried all, Yea, yea; then said he, You shall find the king's mercy above his justice; for where you were dead by law, yet by his mercy he will revive you; wherefore you shall depart out of this realm within twenty days, upon pain of death, if you be found after the twenty days; and pray for the king; and so they passed into their country."

Thus far Edward Hall; Buchanan says: "They who were not killed in the fight were thrown into prison at London; from whence they were brought to the king, and, humbly begging their lives of him, as they were instructed to do by the English, he, in a proud ostentation of his great clemency, dismissed, and sent the poor innocent souls away."

When James remonstrated, demanding redress for the death of Andrew Barton and his comrades, and the capture of their ships, Henry replied that the doing of justice upon a pirate was no occasion for a breach of friendly relations between two princes. "This answer," says Buchanan, "showed the spite of one that was willing to excuse a plain murder, and seemed as if he had sought an occasion of war."

This incident was celebrated in verse, not immediately afterwards, but in the reign of Elizabeth.

The " Ballad of Sir Andrew Barton " gives a most circumstantial account of the fight, introducing many

details which are probably fictitious, and confusing
the identity of the Howards who took part in it.
According to the writer, Lord *Charles* Howard was
the hero of the occasion ; but there does not happen
to have been any such person to the fore at that
time, the conqueror of the Spanish Armada—Charles
Howard, Lord Effingham, afterwards created Earl
of Nottingham—not having been born until five-and-
twenty years later.

Probably the ballad was written after 1588—the
Armada year—by way of glorifying the Howards,
who were very high in royal and popular favour at
that time ; such anachronisms were very common in
popular ballads of this and later times.

The writer represents that Barton's smaller vessel
was sunk ; and he it is who tells us about that alleged
journey of Andrew's head :

> My Lord Howard tooke a sword in his hand,
>   And smote of Sir Andrew's head ;
> The Scotts stood by did weepe and mourne,
>   But never a word durst speake or say.

> He caused his body to be taken downe,
>   And over the hatch-bord cast into the sea,
> And about his middle three hundred crownes :
>   " Whersoever thou lands, itt will bury thee."

> With his head they sayled into England againe,
>   With right good will, and fforce and main,
> And the day before new Yeereseven
>   Into Thames mouth they came againe.

   .   .   .   .   .

Then King Henerye shiffted his roome ;
  In came the Queene and ladyes bright ;
Other arrand they had none
  But to see Sir Andrew Bartton, Knight.

But when they see his deadly face,
  His eyes were hollow in his head ;
" I wold give a hundred pound," sais King Henerye,
  " The man were alive as hee is dead."

A gruesome sight, indeed, for the Queen—the courageous but gentle Katharine of Aragon—and her ladies !

There is a disposition in some quarters to regard the whole incident as fictitious, but this does not appear to be at all justifiable. Edward Hall, the Chronicler, was a lad of thirteen or fourteen at the time, and so may be regarded as, practically, a contemporary writer ; while Bishop Leslie (1527–96) and George Buchanan (1506–82) must certainly have known many persons who remembered the fight. Moreover, it appears to be certain that the *Lion* and *Jenny Pirwin* were at that time added to the infant Navy, while the official correspondence of the King of Scotland tells of the grant and renewal of the letters of marque.

Barton was not entitled to the " handle " which the Elizabethan rhymester prefixes to his name : he was not a knight, though he might very possibly have become one, had he lived.

Whether or not he was, strictly speaking, a pirate is very doubtful ; he was probably no worse in this respect than many, both in prior and later times, who have escaped the odium and the consequences of piracy. He was certainly empowered by his sovereign to overhaul and plunder Portuguese ships and appropriate the goods of Portuguese subjects ; and if he permitted himself some latitude in the matter of Portuguese cargoes carried in English or other bottoms —well, there are some naval commanders of the twentieth century who would scarcely find themselves in a position to cast the first stone at him ; there were some curious doings in the Russo-Japanese War, some of which still await the final decision of the courts.

Andrew Barton, as has already been hinted, was not, strictly speaking, a privateer ; but he occupies an exceptional position, by reason of his intimate association with the two Scottish kings, which places him somewhat outside of the sphere of the ordinary letter of marque ; while as an intrepid sea-fighter, in command of a private ship, he is second to none.

THE "AMITY" AND THE SPANIARDS

In the year 1592 the privateer *Amity*, of London, commanded by Thomas Whyte, captured two armed Spanish vessels, the *St. Francisco* and *St. Peter*, respectively of 130 and 150 tons. The crew of the *Amity* numbered forty-three, but we are not told her armament. The *St. Francisco* carried three iron guns, two copper pieces of twenty quintals each, and one of fourteen quintals—that is, two pretty nearly one ton in weight, and one about two-thirds of a ton ; but it is not quite clear what weight of shot they fired. She had also twenty muskets on board, and carried a crew of twenty-eight men and two boys ; she was licensed to carry twenty passengers. The force of the *St. Peter* is not given, but was probably slightly in excess of that of the *St. Francisco*. They were bound for the West Indies, with cargoes in which were included 112 tons of quicksilver—a pretty valuable freight— 28 tons of papal Bulls,[1] and some wine.

The description of the action, by someone on board the *Amity*, is given in the Lansdowne MSS., and transcribed by Mr. M. Oppenheim, in his " History of the Administration of the Royal Navy," as below, except that the spelling is here modernised, to render the account more readily intelligible to the reader :

" The order and manner of the taking of the two ships laden with quicksilver and the Pope's Bulls, bound for the West Indies, by the *Amity* of London, Master Thomas Whyte.

" The 26th of July,1592, being in 36 degrees, or thereabouts [somewhere off the Strait of Gibraltar], we had sight of the said ships, being distant from us about three or four leagues ; by 7 of the clock we fetched them up and were within gun-shot, whose boldness (having the King's arms displayed) did make us conceive them

---

[1] This traffic in " Bulls " from the Pope was, of course, a gross abuse of papal prerogative, which was probably engineered by some of his underlings for their own enriching. A packet of nearly one million and a half of such documents obviously could not have been signed by the Pope himself.

rather to be ships of war than laden with merchandise.
And, as it doth appear by some of their own speeches,
they made full account to have taken us, and was
question among them whether they should carry us to
St. Lucar [just north of Cadiz] or Lisbon. We waved
each other amain [i.e. called upon each other to strike
or lower the sails], they having placed themselves
in warlike order, the one a cable's length before the
other ; we begun the fight, in the which we continued
so fast as we were able to charge and discharge the
space of five hours, being never a cable's length distant
either of us the one from the other, in which time we
received divers shots both in the hull of our ship,
masts, and sails, to the number of 32 great shot which
we told after the fight, besides five hundred musket-
shot and harquebus à croc [a large musket, fired from
a stand] at the least. And for that we perceived they
were stout, we thought good to board the Biscayan
[i.e. the St. Francisco], which was ahead the other,
where lying aboard about an hour plying our ordnance and small shot, with the which we stowed all
his men [i.e. drove them from the deck] ; now they in
the fly-boat [1]—the St. Peter—making account that we
had entered our men, bare room with us [i.e. ran down
upon us], meaning to have laid us aboard, and so to
have entrapped us between them both, which we
perceiving, made ready ordnance and fitted us so as

---

[1] The fly-boat was a flat-bottomed Dutch vessel, with a
high stern ; probably the term is used loosely here, to dis-
tinguish between the two vessels ; the St. Peter more
nearly resembling a fly-boat.

we quitted ourselves of him, and he boarded his fellow, by which means they both fell from us [a very neat manœuvre]. Then presently we kept our luff [hauled to the wind], hoisted our topsails, and weathered them, and came hard aboard the fly-boat with our ordnance prepared, and gave her our whole broadside, with the which we slew divers of their men, so as we might perceive the blood to run out at the scuppers; after that we cast about, and now charged all our ordnance, and came upon them again, and willed them amain, or else we would sink them, whereupon the one would have yielded, which was shot between wind and water, but the other called him traitor; unto whom we made answer that if he would not yield presently also we would sink him first. And thereupon he, understanding our determination, presently put out a white flag and yielded; howbeit they refused to strike their own sails, for that they were sworn never to strike to any Englishman. We then commanded the captains and masters to come aboard of us, which they did, and after examination and stowing them, we sent aboard them, struck their sails and manned their ships, finding in them both one hundred and twenty and six souls living, and eight dead, besides those which they themselves had cast overboard; so it pleased God to give us the victory, being but 42 men and a boy, of the which there were two killed and three wounded, for which good success we give the only praise to Almighty God."

The number found on board the two vessels—one hundred and thirty-four, including the dead—and the implication that some corpses had been thrown overboard, making up the total to, say, one hundred and forty, points to the conclusion that there must have been a large number of passengers. The *St. Francisco* was only entitled to have fifty souls on board, all told, and her consort probably not above sixty at the outside ; so there is a surplus of thirty or so between the two to be accounted for. No doubt the skippers, in the absence of any strict inquisition, carried more passengers than they were licensed for. The captains of ferry-boats and coasting steamers do so to this day, in spite of the very stringent regulations of the Board of Trade—and they do not very often get found out, except by the supervention of some dire catastrophe, due to overloading and panic.

The futile Spanish bravado, in refusing to lower their sails to any Englishman, after having displayed the white flag in token of surrender, is decidedly amusing ; one cannot help wondering whether any one of them really persuaded himself that he had " saved his face " by such a piece of tomfoolery.

PRIVATEERING IN THE SOUTH SEAS

CHAPTER III

WILLIAM DAMPIER

THE title of this section requires, perhaps, some explanation ; and first as to the phrase " South Seas." In the sixteenth and two following centuries this term was applied to that portion of the Pacific Ocean which borders the west coast of South America, from Cape Horn to the Gulf of Panama. It had been first exploited by the Spaniards, and became a great treasure-hunting ground for them, until France and England stepped in to obtain a share in the spoils, and the Spanish treasure-ships were tracked and waylaid by English privateers and men-of-war ; which also attacked Spanish ports and towns.

To this end there were several privateering expeditions sent out, at the end of the seventeenth and during the eighteenth century : and it is of some of these that it is proposed to treat in this chapter.

In this connection, it is impossible to omit the name of William Dampier ; for he was, for a time, a privateer captain, duly supplied with a commission to fight against the enemies of his sovereign. He had served, in his youth, in the Royal Navy, but had subsequently been in very bad company, sailing with the famous buccaneers, who were practically pirates, in the South Seas. This did not prevent him, however, from eventually obtaining, after many vicissitudes, the command of a man-of-war, the *Roebuck* : he lost his ship, and was tried by court-martial for cruelty to Lieutenant Fisher ; and this was the end of his connection with the Navy, for the court found the charge proved against him, sentenced him to forfeit his pay, and pronounced him to be an unfit person to command a king's ship.

Dampier was not, indeed, fit for any post of command, though he was a very distinguished man, by reason of his skill as a navigator, and the immense pains he took in noting and recording the characteristics, natural history, winds, currents, and every imaginable detail of those portions of the world which he visited. The results of his observations were treated with the greatest deference for generations afterwards, and in many respects hold good to the present day. His praises have been sung in all the languages of Europe, and one at least of his admirers alludes to him as " a man of exquisite refinement of mind." The word " refinement " must be taken as signifying, in this instance, the faculty of recognising and distinguishing between cause and effect in what came under his notice, a kind of natural intuition with regard to matters of scientific interest, a love of science for its own sake ; for of refinement, in the commonly accepted sense of the word, Dampier certainly displayed a grievous lack, at least in his capacity as captain of a ship, even in those rough days.

From a photograph by Emery Walker after the painting by
Thomas Murray in the National Portrait Gallery.

WILLIAM DAMPIER, THE FAMOUS CIRCUMNAVIGATOR : BUCCANEER,
NAVAL OFFICER, PRIVATEERSMAN ; B. 1652, D. 1715.

p. 36]

However, after his trouble in the *Roebuck*, he was placed in command of a privateer, the *St. George*, of twenty-six guns, for a voyage to the South Seas, having for a consort a smaller vessel, the *Cinque Ports*, commanded by one Pickering, and they sailed from Kinsale—a favourite port of call and place of departure in those days—on September 11th, 1703.

The voyage was almost entirely a failure; the crews were more or less insubordinate from the first, neither Dampier nor Pickering knowing how to manage them. Pickering died when on the coast of Brazil, and Stradling, his mate, succeeded him.

When they had got round Cape Horn, and made the island of Juan Fernandez, the crews mutinied openly; some of them went on shore, and declared their intention of deserting altogether. When this was patched up, there still remained an utter lack of confidence between Dampier and his subordinates. The two ships engaged a French cruiser, against Dampier's wish, and the action was futile and ill-fought, so that the Frenchman got away. Nothing prospered with them.

Dampier was for ever making plans which held out the prospect of wealth, but had not the courage to follow them up. Alarmed at the sight of two French ships as they returned to Juan Fernandez, he sheered off, leaving a quantity of stores, and six men who had secreted themselves on the island. When at length they were in great straits for food, they captured a large Spanish ship laden with provisions; over this capture there was a final rupture between Dampier and Stradling, and they parted for good. They took two or three small vessels also, of no value, which only facilitated the defection of Dampier's followers. One of them Stradling had appropriated ; in the other two, first John Clipperton, Dampier's mate, and then William Funnell, his steward, decamped, each with a party of men. The *St. George* was too rotten to venture in any longer, and eventually, after plundering a small Spanish town, Dampier seized a brigantine, and sailed for the East Indies, only to be taken and imprisoned in a Dutch factory for some months. At last he arrived in England, towards the end of 1707, to find that William Funnell—who represented himself as Dampier's mate—had published an account of the cruise, in which Dampier was belittled and held up to ridicule.

Dampier immediately set to work and wrote a vindication of his conduct during the cruise—an angry and incoherent tirade, which probably convinced no one, and was answered shortly afterwards by one George Welbe, one of his former officers, in a pamphlet which was also a wordy and violent assault ; but the impression finally left upon the mind of the reader is that Dampier was a very fine navigator and amateur scientist, but a very bad commander. We shall hear of him again very shortly, in a more subordinate capacity.

In connection with this luckless cruise, there is one incident of considerable interest, which should not be overlooked. The *Cinque Ports* carried as sailing master one Alexander Selkirk, of Scotch extraction.

Obviously, he must have been a seaman of considerable
experience and capacity, to have been selected for
this post ; and presumably he would have knowledge
of the navigation of the South Seas. He had, in fact,
quitted his home in Scotland at the age of eighteen,
and been absent for six years, during part of which
time he is believed to have been with the buccaneers.

When Captain Pickering died Selkirk viewed with
great dissatisfaction the prospect of sailing under his
successor, Stradling, whom he hated ; and on the
return of the *Cinque Ports* to Juan Fernandez, after
parting from Dampier, he took occasion of a violent
quarrel with Stradling to carry out a mad project
which he had formed some time previously—to desert
the vessel and fend for himself on this or some other
island.

Stradling took him at his word, and, when on the
point of sailing, conveyed Selkirk, with all his traps,
on shore and " dumped " him on the beach.

The Scotchman shook hands with his shipmates
very cheerfully, wishing them luck, while Stradling,
apprehensive of more desertions, kept calling to them
to return to the boat, which they did.

As the boat pulled away, and Selkirk realised that he
was to be left there, absolutely severed from all inter-
course with mankind, probably for years, possibly until
death, a sudden terrible revulsion of feeling rushed
upon him, and he ran down the beach, wading into
the sea, with outstretched hands imploring them to
return and take him on board.

Stradling only mocked him ; told him his conduct

in asking to be landed was rank mutiny, and that his present situation was a very suitable one for such a fellow, as he would at least not be able to affect others by his bad example; and so rowed away and left him : and it was nearly four and a half years later that he was rescued, by the crew of another English privateer, as we shall see.

The special interest attached to this incident lies, of couse, in the fact that, had Stradling not hardened his heart and rowed away, that wonderful book " Robinson Crusoe," the delight of our early years, would in all probability never have been written— or at least the principal portion, dealing with his life on the island, would not have been written; for it was undoubtedly the story of Alexander Selkirk's long, solitary sojourn on Juan Fernandez which gave Daniel Defoe the idea, though there is no reason to suppose that he obtained any details from Selkirk himself; indeed, the story of Robinson Crusoe and his adventures is, without doubt, pure romance. So there we may leave Alexander Selkirk for the present : a miserable man enough at first, we may well imagine.

CHAPTER IV

WOODES ROGERS

Captain Woodes Rogers was a very different stamp of man from Dampier, and far better adapted by nature for the command of a privateering expedition.

His father was a Bristol man, a sea-captain, and subsequently resided at Poole ; Woodes Rogers the younger was probably born at Bristol, about the year 1678. Of his early life we know nothing in detail, but he was evidently brought up as a seaman and attained a good position, for in the year 1708 he proposed to some merchants of Bristol that they should fit out a couple of privateers for a voyage to the South Seas. Whether he put any money in the venture we do not know, but he held strong views as to the folly of permitting the French and Spaniards to have it all their own way in that part of the world, and put his case to such good purpose that the necessary funds were speedily forthcoming. We are told, in Seyer's "Memoirs of Bristol," that among the gentlemen who financed the business, and to the survivors of whom, sixteen in number, Rogers dedicates his account of the cruise, there were several Quakers : a remarkable statement which, if true, would appear to indicate that the privateering fever, with huge gains in prospect, was too much for the principles even of the Society of Friends.

Like many another sailor who has sat down to write an account of his doings, Rogers commences by disclaiming any pretensions to literary skill: " I had not time, were it my talent, to polish the stile ; nor do I think it necessary for a mariner's journal." Nevertheless, the account is written in pleasing fashion, occasionally very quaint in phraseology, and has the merit also—which is decidedly lacking in some writings whereof great parade is made of " polishing the stile " —of being very lucid.

The two vessels, named the *Duke*, of 320 tons, 30 guns, and 117 men, and the *Duchess*, of 260 tons, 26 guns, and 108 men, sailed from King Road, near Bristol, on August 2nd, 1708, for Cork, where Rogers hoped to complete his crews, or exchange some of the very mixed company for more efficient seamen, having not more than twenty such on board, while the *Duchess* was very little better off ; so they were fortunate in not meeting with an enemy of any force on the way to Ireland ; indeed, they appear to have sailed from Bristol in the greatest disorder—the rigging slack, ships out of trim, decks lumbered up, stores badly stowed, and so on, which must have gone greatly against the grain with a good seaman like Rogers. It is not difficult to imagine, however, the causes which led to such hurried departure : merchants who had been putting their hands in their pockets pretty freely for some months would be anxious to see the two ships at sea, commencing to rake in the spoil. Even the Quakers, perhaps, were impatient over the matter; and Rogers was probably told that it was time he was off.

However, he made good use of the time at Cork, and reconstituted his crews, if not entirely to his liking, at least with considerable improvement.

The owners, with, as we may conclude, the assistance of Rogers, had drawn up the constitution of a council, by which the progress of the voyage was to be determined, and all questions and disputes were to be settled. This is a very sensible document, providing for all probable contingencies; and, in the event of an equality of votes upon any matter, the casting vote was to be given by Thomas Dover, Rogers's second in command, who was appointed president of the council; this brings us to the subject of the officers of the two ships, and we find some very improbable persons included among them.

In the first place, Thomas Dover, second captain, president of the council, and captain of the Marines, appears to have been neither a sailor nor soldier, but a doctor.[1] There were three lieutenants and three

---

[1] The reader may be interested to learn that this Thomas Dover was the inventor of the well-known preparation, "Dover's Powder." After his adventures with Woodes Rogers he settled down as a regular practitioner, and in the year 1733 he published a book entitled, "The Ancient Physician's Legacy to his Country," in which the recipe for Dover's Powder appeared; it was afterwards altered, but retained the name. Dover died in 1742.

mates, but John Ballet, third mate, was "designed surgeon if occasion arose; he had been Captain Dampier's doctor, in his last unfortunate voyage round the world." Samuel Hopkins, a kinsman of Dover's, and an apothecary, was to act as Dover's lieutenant in case of landing a party. Then there was John Vigor, a "Reformado," to act as Dover's ensign if landed; while George Underwood and John Parker, *two young lawyers*, were designed to act as midshipmen. The whole arrangement has a savour of Gilbert and Sullivan, or Lewis Carroll, about it; one is irresistibly reminded of the "Hunting of the Snark," where the captain was a bellman, and had for his crew a butcher, a billiard-marker, and a beaver!

However, Rogers and his merry men were not for hunting any such shadowy affair as a "Snark"; they meant business, and the list of sub-officers includes further two midshipmen, coxswain of the pinnace, surgeon, surgeon's mate, and assistant—they were well off in the medical branch—gunner, carpenter, with mate and three assistants; boatswain and mate; cooper, four quarter-masters, ship's steward, sailmaker, armourer, ship's corporal (who was also cook to the officers), and ship's cook.

Also, as sailing-master and pilot for the South Seas, William Dampier sailed under Rogers in the *Duke*, probably the best man who could have been found for the post; he was a member of the council, and was no doubt a very valuable addition to the staff.

The *Duchess*, commanded by Captain Stephen

Courtney, was similarly officered, the second lieutenant being John Rogers, a brother of Woodes Rogers, some ten years his junior.

"Most of us," says Rogers, "the chief officers, embraced this trip of privateering round the world, to retrieve the losses we had sustained by the enemy. Our complement of sailors in both ships was 333, of which alone one-third were foreigners from most nations; several of her Majesty's subjects on board were tinkers, tailors, haymakers, pedlars, fiddlers, etc., one negro, and about ten boys. With this mixed gang we hoped to be well manned, as soon as they had learnt the use of arms, and got their sea-legs, which we doubted not soon to teach them, and bring them to discipline." Very hopeful!

One curious characteristic common to this mixed crew was that, as Rogers puts it, they "were continually marrying whilst we staid at Cork, though they expected to sail immediately. Among others there was a Dane coupled by a Romish priest to an Irish woman, without understanding a word of each other's language, so that they were forced to use an interpreter; yet I perceived this pair seemed more afflicted at separation than any of the rest. The fellow continued melancholy for several days after we were at sea. The rest, understanding each other, drank their cans of flip till the last minute, concluded with a health to our good voyage and their happy meeting, and then parted unconcerned."

This "continual marrying" constitutes, in truth, a tribute to the character of Irish women; had it been at Wapping there would have been, it is to be feared, but little question of marrying.

Even when they had restowed their holds and set up the rigging, Rogers is somewhat disheartened over the condition of the two ships : " Our holds are full of provisions ; our cables, a great deal of bread, and water-casks between decks : and 183 men aboard the *Duke*, with 151 aboard the *Duchess* : so that we are very much crowded and pestered ships, not fit to engage an enemy without throwing provision and store overboard."

However, they sailed on September 1st, in company with the *Hastings* man-of-war and some other vessels, from whom they parted on the 6th, bound for Madeira ; and a few days later there was trouble with the undisciplined crew, who had as yet found neither their sea-legs nor their manners.

Rogers had overhauled a vessel, sailing under Swedish colours ; some of her crew, who were more or less drunk, had declared that she carried gunpowder and cables, so she was detained, in spite of the captain's remonstrances. However, no sign of any contraband goods could be discovered, so Rogers very properly let her go ; upon which his men, who had no notion of going a-privateering without the joys of plunder, assumed a mutinous attitude, the boatswain at their head—all the mutineers were Englishmen. One man was flogged, ten were put in irons, and with the remainder Rogers reasoned, admitting, however, that he was forced to wink at the conduct of some. Next day a seaman came aft, " with near half the ship's company of sailors following him, and demanded the boatswain out of irons. I desired him to speak with me by himself on the quarter-deck, which he did, where the officers assisted me, seized him [*i.e* tied him up], and made one of his chief comrades whip him. This method I thought best for breaking any unlawful friendship among themselves ; which, with different correction to other offenders, allayed the tumult, so that now they begin to submit quietly, and those in irons beg pardon and promise amendment."

An excellent method of " breaking friendship," unlawful or otherwise !

On September 18th, in sight of Teneriffe, a small Spanish vessel was captured, belonging to Orotava, a port of Teneriffe.

" Amongst the prisoners were four friars, and one of them the Padre Guardian for the island Forteventura, a good, honest old fellow. We made him heartily merry, drinking King Charles III.'s health ; but the rest were of the wrong sort."

The quarrels and intrigues of other nations brought a good deal of profit to privateersmen ; the War of the Spanish Succession was then still in progress, the Grand Alliance striving to place the Archduke Charles of Austria on the Spanish throne, while others—" the wrong sort " from Rogers's point of view—upheld the cause of Philip, grandson of Louis XIV. of France ; later on, as we shall see, the Austrian Succession was the occasion of some more profitable privateering.

Rogers and his colleagues now found themselves involved, to their surprise, in a dispute with their own countrymen over their capture, the Vice-Consul and three merchants sending off a letter to say that it had been agreed between Queen Anne and the Kings of Spain and France, that vessels trading to the Canaries were to be exempt from interference, and that unless the prize were released, Mr. Vanbrugh, owners' agent on board the *Duke*, who had gone on shore, would be detained.

Rogers was not to be so easily hoodwinked; he immediately detected the self-interest which prompted a disingenuous representation, and insisted that the prize should be ransomed; the cargo of wine and brandy he designed for his own ships; and he finished his letter as follows: " We are apprehensive you are obliged to give us this advice to gratify the Spaniards ": which hit the nail very fairly on the head. Still pressed by the Spaniards, the Consul and his friends persisted; upon which Rogers told them that, had it not been for their agent being on shore, they would not have remained a moment to discuss the matter; but that now they would remain longer among the islands, in order to make reprisals, and that the Consul and his English and Spanish friends might expect a visit from their guns at eight o'clock the next morning.

Accordingly, at that hour the two English privateers stood close in shore; but the guns were not needed, for a boat put off immediately with one of the merchants and Mr. Vanbrugh, bringing the ransom " in kind "—wine, grapes, hogs, and other accessories.

And so they proceeded on their voyage; and a few days later they crossed the tropic of Cancer, which appears to have been made the occasion, in this instance, of some fun with those who had not come so far south before. Usually it is the crossing of the Equator which is selected as the occasion of these delights.

Rogers's tinkers, tailors, pedlars, fiddlers, etc., had a lively time of it. " The manner of doing it was by a rope through a block from the mainyard, to hoist 'em above half-way up to the yard, and let 'em fall at once into the water; having a stick across through their legs, and well fastened to the rope, that they might not be surprised and let go their hold. This proved of great use to our fresh-water sailors, to recover the colour of their skins, which were grown very black and nasty."

Exemption could be purchased at the cost of half-a-crown, the whole amount to be expended on an entertainment for all hands on their return to England. Some of the crew—especially the Dutchmen—begged that they might be ducked ten or twelve times—on the principle that, if immunity could be paid for, an excess of dipping should logically entitle them to a larger share of the pool! Sailors are queer creatures.

After the capture of the small Spanish craft, Rogers found it advisable to lay down some rules, admitting the principle of plunder; he foresaw incessant trouble and probable mutiny in the future, if the right of the crew to the immediate distribution of a certain amount of spoil was not recognised. It was quite irregular, and had not been contemplated by the owners. However, the decision as to what should constitute plunder was, with the consent of the men, left to the senior officers and agents, so there was a certain safeguard against abuse.

The next place of call was the Cape Verde Islands, where they anchored in the harbour of St. Vincent; here they watered with some difficulty, on account of the sea; and they lost one of their crew, one Joseph Alexander, who, by reason of his being a good linguist, was sent in a boat to the Governor at St. Antonio, with a letter, and was left behind to negotiate for supplies. However, he appears to have found the prospect of life in the Cape Verde Islands more promising than privateering. On October 5th " our boat went to St. Antonio to see for our linguist, according to appointment "; on the 6th " our boat returned with nothing but limes and tobacco, and no news of our linguist "; again on the 7th the boat was sent in quest of " our linguist "—and by this time they must have been getting pretty tired of his antics; on the 8th " no news of our linguist "; so, as the Trade-wind blew fresh, they concluded to leave him to practise his linguistic and other accomplishments on shore, and made sail for the coast of Brazil, Captain Rogers summing up the situation in a marginal note : " Our linguist deserts."

The captains frequently exchanged visits, and even had little dinner-parties on board each other's ships, in mid-ocean, when it was held to be necessary to call a council; Rogers was very scrupulous about having everything done in order, and properly recorded. It may appear strange that there should be such frequent communication, especially when a council or dinner-party is recorded together with the remark, " fresh breeze, with heavy sea," and so on ; but such boating exploits were the fashion in those days, and very much later. When Nelson was bound for the Baltic, as second in command under Sir Hyde Parker, with whom he was never upon cordial terms, he set his men fishing for turbot on the Doggerbank, and, having caught one, despatched it in a boat to his chief, in spite of a heavy sea and approaching darkness, with a polite note ; the mission was accomplished without mishap, and the turbot is said to have brought about a better under-standing between the Admirals. Such measures of policy were not, however, very much in Nelson's line. The point is that the seamen of those times must have been very masterly boatmen, for the lowering and hoisting of a boat in a heavy sea is a very ticklish process, in which a small blunder may mean disaster ; yet it was constantly done, just for a friendly visit, and we hear of no fatalities arising therefrom.

On October 22nd we hear of more trouble from insubordination. Mr. Page, second mate of the *Duchess*, refusing to accompany Cook, who was Courtney's second in command, on board the *Duke*, " occasioned Captain Cook, being the superior officer on board, to strike him, whereupon Page struck him again, and several blows passed ; but at last Page was forced into the boat, and brought on board of us. And Captain Cook and others telling us what mutiny had passed, we ordered Page on the forecastle into the bilboes " (leg-irons sliding upon a long iron bar).

Page, however, evaded his captors by a ruse and jumped overboard to swim back to his own ship—a dangerous business, somewhere near the Equator, for there is always the chance of a shark.   But this foolish attempt availed him little : he was brought back, flogged, and put in irons ; and he found a week of this kind of thing sufficient, submitting himself humbly and promising amendment.   Captain Rogers was already beginning to realise that the lot of a privateer commander, unless he is willing, as so many were, to degenerate into a mere filibuster, is not a happy one.

Possibly it was this conviction—or maybe that he found the Southern Hemisphere a more devotional environment than the Northern—which occasioned the following entry : " At five last night we were on the Equinoctial [the Equator]. . . . This day we began to read prayers in both ships mornings or evenings, as opportunity would permit, according to the Church of England, designing to continue it the term of the voyage."

Passing by the small island of Trinidad, on the night of November 13th, the two ships lay to, Rogers believing they were near land : and sure enough, at daybreak they sighted the coast of Brazil, and a few days later anchored at Isle Grande, just to the southward of Rio Janeiro.

Here they were very busy—heeling both vessels to clean the bottoms, and executing sundry repairs aloft —all of which was done under a broiling sun, besides getting in a plentiful supply of wood and water, in so short a space of time that we must conclude that

Captain Rogers and Captain Courtney had under them both well-disciplined and willing crews; no man-of-war's men could have done better.

Here also Mr. Carleton Vanbrugh, owner's agent on board the *Duke*, got into trouble for assuming executive command. A boat being manned to overhaul a passing canoe, he shoved off, without any orders, pursued and fired into the canoe, killing an Indian. This officiousness and presumption obtained for him a wigging from Captain Rogers, who also brought the matter before the council: " I thought it a fit time now to resent ignorant and wilful actions publicly, and to show the vanity and mischief of 'em, rather than to delay or excuse such proceedings; which would have made the distemper too prevalent, and brought all to remediless confusion, had we indulged conceited persons with a liberty of hazarding the fairest opportunities of success."

Mr. Vanbrugh was accordingly " logged " as being censured by the council, and was subsequently transferred to the *Duchess*, his opposite number there, William Bath, taking his place.

On December 3rd they sailed from Isle Grande and made their way down the coast of South America towards Cape Horn, chasing but losing a large French ship on the 26th. On New Year's Day there was a large tub of hot punch on the quarter-deck, of which every man had over a pint to drink the health of the owners and absent friends, a happy New Year, a good voyage, and a safe return. The *Duke* bore down close to her consort, and there, rolling and lurching at close quarters in the big seas, they exchanged cheers and good wishes.

On January 5th it came on to blow hard, with a heavy sea, and while the mainyard was being lowered on board the *Duchess* the sail got aback, and a great portion of it bagged in the water on the lee side, the " lift " on that side having given way. This was rather a serious business, in so heavy a sea ; they were obliged to put the ship before the wind for a time, and the sea " broke in the cabin windows, and over their stern, filling their steerage and waist, and had like to have spoiled several men ; but, God be thanked, all was otherwise indifferent well with 'em, only they were intolerably cold, and everything wet." Next day Rogers found them " in a very orderly pickle, with all their clothes drying, the ship and rigging covered with them from the deck to the maintop."

Though it was high summer in these southern latitudes, they experienced no genial warmth, only gales of wind, with an immense sea ; they attained the latitude of 61.53 South, which, as Rogers remarks, was probably the furthest south reached at that time ; and so they fought round the Horn, and before the end of January we find the entry : " This is an excellent climate."

This was in latitude 36.36 South, and they were looking forward anxiously to sighting the island of Juan Fernandez. Many of the men had suffered greatly from cold and exposure, some were down with scurvy, and a rest in port, with fresh vegetables and sweet water, was very necessary.

Juan Fernandez was not in those days accurately placed on the chart, and all eyes no doubt were turned to William Dampier to bring them there ; which he did on January 31st, though they appear to have had a narrow escape of missing it, for when they sighted land it bore W.S.W., so that they had already somewhat overshot it. When we consider the very inadequate means which these men possessed for navigating thousands of leagues of trackless ocean, and making land which was very inefficiently charted, we can only marvel at their success. The quadrant of those days was a very rough affair, the compass was not perfect in construction, neither were its vagaries understood as they are at the present day—for the compass, emblem of faithfulness and constancy, is, alas ! a most capricious and inconstant friend ; only we understand it nowadays, and realise that it never—or hardly ever—points due north. Then chronometers, sufficiently reliable to give correct longitude, were not constructed until some sixty years later, when the earliest maker contrived to turn out, to his credit, a marvellously good one. This was John Harrison, and very scurvily he was treated by the authorities, only receiving the full reward which was offered upon the intervention of King George III. on his behalf.

Well, here was Juan Fernandez, and very welcome was the sight of the high land, some five-and-twenty miles distant ; but they were becalmed, and got but little nearer for twenty-four hours. Next day, in the afternoon, Rogers consented, rather against his better judgment, to Dover taking a boat in, the land being then at least twelve miles distant. At dark, a bright light was observed on shore, and the boat returned at 2 a.m., Dover having been afraid to land, not knowing what the light could mean.

The general idea was that there were French ships at anchor, and all was prepared for action : " We must either fight 'em or want water, etc."

These desperate measures were not, however, necessary ; sailing along the land the following day, the two bays, which afford good anchorage, were found to be empty. The yawl was sent in at noon, and after some hours the pinnace was despatched to see what had become of her ; for it was feared that the Spaniards might be in possession.

Presently, however, the pinnace arrived, and, as she approached, it was seen that she carried a passenger—a most fantastic and picturesque person, attired in obviously home-made garments of goatskin.

This, of course, was Alexander Selkirk. On the afternoon of January 31st, sweeping the horizon, as he did so constantly, from his look-out, he had seen the two sails in the offing. As they gradually rose, his experienced eye told him that they were English ; dusk was settling down, and they were still a long way off—would they pass by ?

Reasonably contented as he had latterly been in his solitude—broken in upon twice by Spaniards, who upon one occasion saw and chased him, forcing him to take refuge in a tree—the sight of these two English ships filled him with a frantic longing to grasp the hand of a countryman, to hear and speak once more his native language. Mad with apprehension lest this joy should be torn, as it were, from his very grasp, he hastily collected materials, and, as darkness set in, lit a huge bonfire. He spent a couple of sleepless nights, keeping up his fire, and preparing some goat's-meat for guests who, he fondly hoped, would appear on the following day.

He saw the boat approaching, and, taking a stick with a rude flag attached, ran down to the beach—they saw him—they shouted to him to point out a good landing place. In a transport of joy at the sound of their voices, he ran round with incredible swiftness, waving them with his flag to follow him.

When they landed he could only embrace them; his emotion was too deep, his speech too rusty—no words could he find; while they, on their part, were mute with surprise at his wild and uncouth appearance.

Recovering themselves at length, Selkirk entertained them as best he could with some of the goat's-flesh which he had prepared, and while they ate he gave them some account of his sojourn and adventures on the island.

There is but little in common with De Foe's description of Robinson Crusoe's doings, excepting, of course, the expedients adopted for obtaining food, which could scarcely have been different.

There was no " man Friday," no mysterious footprint in the sand, no encounter with savages. There was, however, a narrow escape, already alluded to, of capture by Spanish sailors; a fate to which Selkirk decided that he preferred his solitary existence, for the Spaniards would either have ruthlessly murdered him or sold him as a slave to work in their mines. So when he found that he had incautiously exposed himself while reconnoitring, he ran for the woods, the Spaniards in chase; but he had acquired such fleetness of foot in catching the goats that they had no chance, and, sitting aloft in a large tree, he saw them below, completely at fault. They helped themselves to some of the goats, and retired.

In describing his adventures and emotions, Selkirk attributed his eventual contentment in his solitude to his religious training. He appears to have possessed in full measure the deep, emotional religious temperament of the Scots, and this in all probability saved his reason, and certainly deterred him from suicide, which at one time presented itself as the only possible release from acute mental suffering. He used to recite his prayers and sing familiar hymns aloud, and it is easy to understand what an immense solace such exercises were to him.

Learning from Dover and his companions that William Dampier was with the expedition, Selkirk demurred at once to going on board. Not that he had any personal quarrel with Dampier, but he had a most vivid recollection of the hopeless mismanagement of that cruise under his command; of the futile delays, half-fought actions, hastily abandoned plans which promised some measure of success; and he declined to enlist again under such an incompetent chief. This extreme reluctance on Selkirk's part to sail again under the famous navigator constitutes a very strong indictment against Dampier as commander of a privateer ; nothing, indeed, could well be stronger. When a man says practically, " I prefer to remain alone on an island to sailing under him," there appears to be little more to be said.

Understanding, however, that Dampier occupied a subordinate position as pilot, he was ready enough to accompany his rescuers ; and so presented himself to the " admiring " gaze—using the term as it was frequently used in those days—of the crew of the *Duke*.

Whatever Selkirk may have thought of Dampier, the latter, recognising him as the former sailing-master of the *Cinque Ports*, gave him the highest character, declaring that he was the best man on board Stradling's ship ; upon which Rogers at once engaged him as a mate on the *Duke*, in which capacity he was, we are told, greatly respected, " as well on account of his singular adventure as of his skill and good conduct ; for, having had his books with him, he had improved himself much in navigation during his solitude."

Such application appears, under the circumstances, almost heroic ; there are probably few men so situated who would have had recourse to it.

It was long before Selkirk began to throw off the reserve which was the natural outcome of his solitude, and it is said that the expression of his face was fixed and sedate even after his return to England ; nothing, indeed, could ever efface the recollection of those years of absolute loneliness, the grim lessons of self-restraint, endurance, and resignation, so hardly learned.

CHAPTER V

WOODES ROGERS—*continued*

ROGERS and his companions made no long stay at
Juan Fernandez. Having now arrived upon their
cruising ground, all were eager to be at work, and
on February 14th they were once more under way,
the banished Vanbrugh being received on board the
Duke again. " I hope for the best," says Captain
Rogers doubtfully.

On the 17th a committee-meeting was held at sea,
in order to appoint responsible persons for the custody
of " plunder." There was evidently considerable
anxiety among the superior officers on this head.
Rogers and Courtney, and probably most of the
officers, were perfectly straight and aboveboard ;
but no certainty could be felt about any one else, so
the following plan was adopted : Four persons were
selected by the officers and men of the *Duke*, two of
whom were to act on board the *Duchess* ; similarly,
four were selected on board the latter, two of whom
were to go on board the *Duke* ; thus the interests of
each ship's company were equally safeguarded ; and
to these " plunder guardians " the council addressed
a letter containing detailed instructions for their

guidance. Every probable contingency was provided for, and the letter concluded : " You are by no means to be rude in your office, but to do everything as quiet and easy as possible ; and to demean yourselves so towards those employed by Captain Courtney (or Captain Rogers) that we may have no manner of disturbance or complaint ; still observing that you be not over-awed, nor deceived of what is your due, in the behalf of the officers and men."

A difficult and thankless office, one would say ; nor did this device avail to prevent discord later on.

They were now bound for the small island of Lobos, off the coast of Peru, which was to be their starting-point for the conquest of Guayaquil ; and on March 16th they captured a small Spanish vessel, which they took with them into Lobos on the following day. From the crew of this vessel they heard some news about Captain Stradling, who, it appears, lost the *Cinque Ports* on the Peruvian coast, and with half a dozen men, the only survivors, had been for upwards of four years in prison at Lima, " where they lived much worse than our Governor Selkirk, whom they left on the island Juan Fernandez."

This little bark Rogers resolved to convert into a privateer, as she seemed to be a fast sailer ; and the business was accomplished with remarkable celerity. On March 18th she was hauled up dry, cleaned, launched, and named the *Beginning*, Captain Edward Cooke being appointed to command her. A spare topmast of the *Duke* was fitted as a mast, and a spare mizzen-topsail altered as a sail for her. By the even-

ing of the 19th she was rigged, had four swivel-guns
mounted, and a deck nearly completed ; on the 20th
she was manned and victualled, and sailed out of the
harbour, exchanging cheers with the *Duke*, to join
the *Duchess* cruising outside : a very smart piece of
work.

Another small prize was renamed the *Increase*,
and converted into a hospital-ship, all the sick, with
a doctor from each ship, being sent on board her;
Alexander Selkirk in command.

Rogers makes merry over the exploit of one of his
officers who, mistaking turkey buzzards—the " John
Crow " bird of the West Indies—for turkeys, landed
in great haste with his gun, jumping into the water
before the boat touched ground in his eagerness, and
let drive, " browning " a group of them ; but he was
grievously disappointed when he came to pick up his
" bag "—the " John Crow " is not a sweet-smelling bird.

This impetuous sportsman was, perhaps, that
difficult person Mr. Carleton Vanbrugh : for we learn
later that, having threatened to shoot one of the men
for refusing to carry some carrion crows he had shot,
and having abused Captain Dover, his name was
struck off the committee.

The Spanish prisoners had some attractive stories
to tell of possible prizes—it appears somewhat unsportsmanlike on their part, and one is disposed to
wonder whether Rogers or his men put any pressure
on them—particularly of a stout ship from Lima,
and a French-built ship from Panama, richly laden,
with a bishop on board.

These two vessels were captured, also a smaller one ; but the Panama ship was not taken without some misadventure, for the two ships' pinnaces attacking her insufficiently armed—despising the foe, a common British failing, for which we have often paid dearly—were repulsed with loss ; and John Rogers, a fine young fellow of one-and-twenty, was killed. He had no business there, as a matter of fact ; but, happening to be on board his brother's ship to assist in preparations for the land expedition, he jumped into the boat—and so perished.[1]

However, the ship was taken next day, without resistance ; but the bishop had been put ashore : a disappointment, no doubt, as he would probably represent a round sum for his ransom—the only use a privateer could find for a prelate !

And now for Guayaquil, from the capture and ransom of which great gains were expected ; but further disappointment was in store for Captain Rogers and his companions.

In the first place, upon landing at Puna, a small town upon an island at the entrance of the Gulf of Guayaquil, an Indian contrived to elude them and give the alarm, so that the surprise was not complete. They captured the Lieutenant-Governor, however,

[1] Why this young man is alluded to in the " Dictionary of National Biography " and elsewhere as Thomas Rogers, I am at a loss to understand. Woodes Rogers alludes to him as "my brother John," and a manuscript note in one edition of Rogers's cruise tells us that " John, son of Woodes Rogers and Frances his wife, was baptized Nov. 28th, 1688 ; vide Register of Poole, Coun. Dorset."

who cunningly assured them that, having caught him, there would be nobody who could give the alarm at Guayaquil : surely an obviously futile deduction. They destroyed all the canoes, etc., which they could find ; but, by the time they had made their prisoners, we may be sure that one or two had already made good their escape to the mainland ; and later developments proved that this must have occurred.

Moreover, they discovered among the papers of the Lieutenant-Governor a disquieting document : no less than a warning against a squadron which was said to be coming, under the pilotage of Captain Dampier—who, it will be recollected, had plundered Puna some years previously. The force of the squadron was greatly exaggerated ; but there was the warning, a copy of which had been sent from Lima to all the ports.

However, it was impossible to relinquish the attack, and accordingly, after some delays, the boats, with 110 men, arrived off the town of Guayaquil about midnight on April 22nd. As they approached they saw a bonfire on an adjoining eminence, and lights in the town, and, rowing up abreast of it, there was a sudden eruption of lights, and every indication that the townspeople, instead of being quietly a-bed, were very wide awake. The Indian pilot negatived the notion that this was some saint's-day celebration, and thought that " it must be an alarm " ; very possibly the wily pilot had something to do with it ! While they lay off they heard a Spaniard shouting that Puna was taken, and the enemy was coming up the river. Then the bells commenced clanging, muskets and guns were fired off, and it became obvious that, if they were to attack, it must be in the face of the fullest resistance. What was to be done ?

Rogers, not easily daunted, gave it as his opinion that the alarm was only just given, and preparations would not be complete. He was all for going on, but the others were not ; and Captain Dampier being asked what the buccaneers would do under such circumstances, replied at once that " they never attacked any large place after it was alarmed." The buccaneers were not such fire-eaters as their own accounts and boys' books of adventure would have us believe : there was a strong spice of prudence in their temperament.

Cautious counsels prevailing, the boats dropped down-stream again, about three miles below the town, where the two small barks, prizes attached to the *Duke* and *Duchess*, arrived during the day, having apparently been safely piloted up by Indians—with pistols at their heads possibly.

When the flood-tide made in the afternoon, Captain Rogers once more ordered an advance on the town, but Dover again dissuaded him, and they held a council of war in a boat made fast astern of one of the barks, so as to avoid eavesdroppers.

Dover advised sending a trumpeter with a flag of truce, and certain proposals as to trading, to be enforced by hostages. These half-hearted measures found no favour with the majority, but Rogers gave way and eventually they sent two of their prisoners—

the lieutenant from Puna, and the captain of the French-built ship—who presently came back, and were followed by the Corregidor, to treat for the ransom of the town.

However, all the talk came to nothing. The Spaniards evidently imagined that the English were a little bit shy about attacking, and so kept shilly-shallying about the terms, perhaps hoping for reinforcements ; until at length Rogers lost patience, landed his men and guns, and drove the enemy from the near houses, the barks firing over their heads. It was a very spirited attack, and deserved success.

Opening up the streets, they found four guns facing them in front of the church ; but the supporting cavalry fled at sight of the English sailors, and Rogers, calling upon his men, immediately took the guns, and turned them on the retreating foe.

In little more than half an hour the town was their own ; and, had it not been for the cautious advice of Dover and others, they would have achieved the same result on the first night, before the treasure was carried away. As it was, though they broke open every church and store-house, etc., they found but little of any value ; jars of wine and brandy were, however, very plentiful.

Two of the officers, Mr. Connely, and Mr. Selkirk, " the late Governor of Juan Fernandez," with a party of men, paid a profitable visit to some houses up the river, where they found " above a dozen handsome, genteel young women, well dressed, where our men got several gold chains and earrings, but were otherwise so civil to them that the ladies offered to dress them victuals, and brought them a cask of good liquor." The seamen, however, quickly suspected that the ladies had chains and other trinkets disposed under their clothing, " and by their linguist modestly desired the gentlewomen to take 'em off and surrender 'em. This I mention as a proof of our sailors' modesty." Well, well; their " modesty " was rewarded by plunder to the tune of about £1,000; but no doubt their method of commandeering it was more polite than the frightened Spanish ladies anticipated.

In the church Rogers himself picked up the Corregidor's gold-headed cane, and also a captain's with a silver head; from which he concludes that these gentlemen quitted the church in a hurry.

It would have been well if Rogers and his men had seen a little less of the church, for buried under it, and immediately outside, were the putrefying corpses of hundreds of the victims of a recent malignant epidemic.

An agreement was drawn up by which the town was to be ransomed by the payment of 30,000 pieces of eight within six days—equivalent to £6,750, reckoning the piece of eight at four shillings and sixpence [1]—Rogers holding two hostages meanwhile; but the Spaniards' *mañana* proved too much for them, and the amount paid fell far short of this.

[1] The piece of eight was of equal value to a dollar, and was probably worth more than this; forty years later it was valued at 6s. Rogers, however, in distributing plunder, placed it at 4s. 6d., so the ransom money was probably reckoned upon that basis.

On April 27th they marched down to the boats with colours flying. Captain Rogers, bringing up the rear with a few men, " picked up pistols, cutlasses, and pole-axes, which showed that our men were grown very careless, weak, and weary of being soldiers, and that it was time to be gone from hence."

John Gabriel, a Dutchman, was missing, but he returned on the following day ; it transpired that he had lain asleep, drunk, in a house, and the " honest man," who was probably his involuntary host, called in some neighbours, who removed the Dutchman's weapons before cautiously arousing him ; and, when he was sufficiently wide awake to comprehend the situation, restored his arms and advised him to go on board his ship : really, a very honest man, this Spanish American. Rogers declares that this was the only case of drunkenness among his men after they took possession : a fact which speaks volumes for the discipline.

And so, on the 28th, they weighed anchor and dropped down to Puna ; " and at parting made what noise we could with our drums, trumpets, and guns, and thus took our leave of the Spaniards very cheer-fully, but not half so well pleased as we should have been had we taken 'em by surprise ; for I was well assured, from all hands, that at least we should then have got above 200,000 pieces of eight in money (£45,000), wrought and unwrought gold and silver, besides jewels, etc."

And now they were to experience some hard times. Sailing for the Galapagos Islands, off the coast of Peru, they had not been many days out when deadly sickness broke out among the men who had been on shore at Guayaquil. On the two ships, near one hundred and fifty were down at one time ; there were a good many deaths, and the medicine-chests were not adequate to this unexpected demand. Worse than all, when they reached the Galapagos Islands they could find no water there. Again and again they sent their boats in, for it was said that upon one island, at least, there was abundance of excellent water—upon the authority of one Davis, a buccaneer, who frequented it twenty years previously : which induces Captain Rogers to discourse upon the unreliability of such adventurers' reports; but that did not help the thirsty, fever-stricken men.

Then one of the barks, in command of Mr. Hatley, was missing, which was another source of anxiety. They were compelled at length to give him up as lost, and sailed over to the island of Gorgona, where there was abundance of water.

Here they refitted the *Havre de Grace*—the French-built prize, which should have contained a bishop—and renamed her the *Marquis* ; and here also they careened and cleaned the ships, and sent away their prisoners, landing them on the coast of Peru.

The crew were getting impatient about the plunder obtained at Guayaquil, and on July 29th it was resolved to overhaul and value it for distribution, sending all that was adjudged to be eligible on board the prize galleon. And there was, of course, trouble over this business : a plot was discovered, a number of the men having signed a paper to the effect that they would not accept any booty, nor move from the upper deck, until they obtained justice. Their notions of "justice" not tallying with those of their superiors, pistols and handcuffs came again to the front, and the ringleaders were seized; but Rogers found himself compelled to compromise, for there were too many men involved, and he did not know what the crews of the other ships might do; so he made a conciliatory speech, and conceded a demand that the civilians, who were not seamen, should have their shares cut down—by which Mr. Carleton Vanbrugh and two others suffered. "So that we hoped," says Captain Rogers, "this difficult work would, with less danger than we dreaded, be brought to a good conclusion. . . . Sailors usually exceed all measures when left to themselves, and account it a privilege in privateers to do themselves justice on these occasions, though in everything else I must own they have been more obedient than any ships' crews engaged in the like undertaking that ever I heard of. Yet we have not wanted sufficient trial of our patience and industry in other things; so that, if any sea-officer thinks himself endowed with these two virtues, let him command in a privateer, and discharge his office well in a distant voyage, and I'll engage he shall not want opportunities to improve, if not to exhaust all his stock."

Two or three small prizes had been taken during these few weeks; but after waiting about a long while for a rich Manila ship, it was at length decided that they must give her up, and sail for Guam, in the Ladrone Islands, and thence for the East Indies.

The day after this decision was recorded the Manila ship hove in sight ; two boats kept in touch with her all night, and at daybreak, it being still calm, they " got out eight of our ship's oars, and rowed above an hour ; then there sprung up a small breeze. I ordered a large kettle of chocolate to be made for our ship's company (having no spirituous liquor to give them) ; then we went to prayers, and before we had concluded, were disturbed by the enemy's firing at us."

They got up off their knees, and fought to some purpose by the space of an hour and a half, when, the *Duchess* coming up, the Spaniard hauled down his colours.

This was a splendid haul : and they speedily learned that there was a second ship, of even greater value, in the vicinity. In due course they encountered her, but she proved too strong for them, being a brand-new vessel, very well built, with 40 guns and 450 men.

Captain Rogers, who had hitherto come off unscathed from all their adventures, was very roughly handled in these two engagements, getting a ball through his jaw in the first and a splinter in his left foot in the second, both very serious wounds.

While he was laid on his back, unable to speak or walk, he had to suffer a further trial of patience in a dispute which arose about the command of their valuable prize on the voyage to the East Indies and homeward, a majority of the council electing Dover to the post. Now Dover, as we have seen, was a doctor, not a seaman, and was absolutely incapable of commanding and navigating a ship upon such a voyage ; but, having a large stake in the original venture, he claimed and obtained more consideration than was his due. Probably it was on this account that the gentlemen in Bristol had made him president of the council.

Poor Captain Rogers, chafing on his sick-bed, could only protest vigorously in writing against this proposed arrangement, which was obviously fraught with peril, and his officers supported him ; the thing was, in fact, a job, the majority truckling to Dover as a part-owner. The utmost concession Rogers could gain was that two capable officers—Stretton and Frye—should be appointed to act under Dover as navigators and practical seamen, and that he should not interfere with them in their duties as such ; and under these conditions the prize—her name conveniently abbreviated from *Nostra Seniora de la Incarnacion Disenganio*, to *Batchelor*—was safely conveyed to the East Indies, and thence to England, the cruise terminating on October 14th, 1711.

Captain Rogers recovered from his wounds, and made a good thing out of his cruise. He was subsequently Governor of the Bahamas, where he displayed great moral courage and resource under difficult circumstances ; and there he died, on July 16th, 1732.

In a volume entitled " Life aboard a British Privateer in the Reign of Queen Ann "—a sort of running commentary upon Woodes Rogers's account of his cruise —the author, Mr. R. C. Leslie, remarks, after the capture of Guayaquil : " Though Woodes Rogers himself would now rank little above a pious sort of pirate, it is curious to note from what he says here [about the buccaneers] and again after visiting the Galapagos Islands, one of the chief haunts of buccaneers, that he looked upon them as much below him socially."

This is not fair to Rogers ; he was entirely within his rights in sacking and ransoming Guayaquil, as a subject of a Power at war with Spain, and armed with a commission from his sovereign. It may not appear to be a very high-class sort of business, but it was conducted in this instance with great humanity, though not probably without some of the " regrettable incidents " which are inseparable from warfare—to adapt the saying of the French general at Balaclava, " Ce n'est pas magnifique, mais c'est la guerre." Rogers does not deserve to be dubbed " pirate," or classed with a gang of cut-throat ruffians like the buccaneers.

William Dampier apparently had no more sea-adventures ; he died in London in March 1715.

Alexander Selkirk, returning to Scotland early in 1712, was received by his people with affectionate enthusiasm ; but, after a time, he took to living entirely alone, and sometimes broke out in a passion of regret over his island home : " Oh, my beloved island ! I wish I had never left thee ! I never was before the man I was on thee ! I have not been such since I left thee ! and, I fear, never can be again ! "

One day, in his solitary wanderings, he came across a young girl, seated alone, tending a single cow ; their meetings became frequent, and eventually he persuaded her—Sophia Bruce was her name—to elope with him to London.   In 1718 he made a will in her favour, under her maiden name, and it is said that, after his death, Sophia Selcraig (for this was the original form of Selkirk's name), represented herself as his widow, but could produce no evidence of marriage ; so it is to be feared that she remained Sophia Bruce to the end, while Selkirk married a widow named Candis, to whom he left everything by another will.

He died, a mate on board the *Weymouth* man-of-war, in 1721.   A monument was erected to his memory on Juan Fernandez, in 1868, by Commodore Powell and the officers of the *Topaze*.

Thus, by a pure accident, he becomes a well-known character and a sort of hero ; certainly, he displayed some heroic attributes during his sojourn on Juan Fernandez.

CHAPTER VI

GEORGE SHELVOCKE AND JOHN CLIPPERTON

ABOUT seven years after Captain Woodes Rogers returned from his cruise another privateering expedition to the South Seas was started by some London merchants ; but, as England was not then at war with Spain, it was to sail under commission from the Emperor Charles VI.—which was quite a legitimate proceeding.

The owners selected, as commanders of the two ships—named *Success* and *Speedwell*—George Shelvocke, who had formerly served in the Navy as purser, and also probably as a lieutenant, and John Clipperton, who, it will be remembered, was with William Dampier on his disastrous voyage, and left his chief, with a number of men, to pursue his own fortunes. It was deemed politic and complimentary to give the vessels other names, and accordingly they were re-christened respectively *Prince Eugene* and *Staremberg*.

Shelvocke, who was to command the expedition, went over to Ostend in the *Staremberg* to receive the commission ; but scarcely had it been drawn up and signed, when war was declared by England against

Spain, and the owners then resolved to send the ships out under a commission from their own sovereign ; and, being greatly dissatisfied with Shelvocke's dilatory and extravagant conduct while he was in Ostend, they gave Clipperton the chief command, with Shelvocke under him, in the other ship, the vessels now reverting to their English names.

Shelvocke, a jealous, passionate, and somewhat unscrupulous man, was from the first at loggerheads with Clipperton and with several of his own officers, who all appear to have hated him ; he was not, in fact, fitted for command, and all went wrong from the first. As his second captain, Shelvocke had Simon Hatley, who was with Rogers, and had some rough experiences, being captured and kept in prison at Lima for a considerable time ; and as Captain of the Marines one William Betagh, of whom more anon.

After sailing from Plymouth on February 13th, 1719, the two ships got into bad weather ; all the liquor for both ships had, by some stupid arrangement, been put on board Shelvocke's vessel, the *Speedwell*, and Shelvocke says that when they were two days out he hailed Clipperton, desiring him to send for his share, in order that the *Speedwell* might be better trimmed ; however, nothing was done in the matter, and on the night of the 19th they encountered a terrific storm, during which they separated ; but this should have made no difference, as they had agreed to meet at the Canary Islands.

Shelvocke had, however, apparently determined from the first that he would not sail under Clipperton—at least, that is the only conclusion that can be arrived at, from the different accounts—and he took advantage of this storm to carry out his design. In his account of the voyage, he tries to make out that Clipperton deserted him ; but, seeing that he himself records the fact that he steered next morning to the north-west, which certainly was not the course for the Canary Islands, while Clipperton steered south by east, which was, approximately, there would appear to be no question about the matter ; in fact, Shelvocke deliberately wasted time, while Clipperton, waiting for him in vain at various rendezvous, proceeded on his voyage alone, and was in the South Seas before Shelvocke had got anywhere near Cape Horn.

The owners had stipulated that the expedition should proceed upon the lines of Rogers, and had provided each captain with a copy of his journal ; but there was no attempt made to carry out these instructions. We find no regular journal kept, no council meetings, no proper command over the crew ; and, so far from emulating Rogers's scrupulous observation of the law, which brought him into conflict with his crew, Shelvocke did not refrain from acts of piracy when it suited him.

His first exploit was overhauling a Portuguese vessel off Cape Frio, in Brazil ; and there is a very marked difference between his account and that of William Betagh, who published his own experiences some two years after Shelvocke's book came out. Shelvocke says : " On Friday, June 5th, in the afternoon, we saw a ship stemming with us, whom we spake with.

I ordered the five-oared boat to be hoisted out and sent Captain Hatley in her to inquire what news on the coast, and gave him money to buy some tobacco ; for the *Success* had got our stock on board of that (as well as other things), which created a West-country famine amongst us. When Hatley returned he told me she was a Portuguese from Rio Janeiro, and bound to Pernambuco, that he could get no tobacco, and had therefore laid out my money in unnecessary trifles, viz. *china cups and plates, a little hand-nest of drawers, four or five pieces of china silk, sweetmeats, bananas, plantains, and pumpkins*, etc. I gave him to understand that I was not at all pleased with him for squandering away my money in so silly a manner. He answered that he thought what he did was for the best, that he had laid out his own money as well as mine, and in his opinion to a good advantage, and that, to his knowledge, the things he bought would sell for double the money they cost at the next port we were going to. However, I assured him I did not like his proceedings by any means."

Betagh's version of the incident is somewhat otherwise : " On June 5th, 1719, we met a Portuguese merchantman near Cape Frio. Our captain ordered the Emperor's colours to be hoisted, which, without any reflection, look the most thief-like of any worn by honest men ; those of his Imperial Majesty are a black spread-eagle in a yellow field, and those of the pirates a yellow field and black human skeleton ; which at a small distance are not easily distinguished, especially in light gales of wind. So he brings her to, by firing

a musket thwart her forefoot, sends aboard her the
best busker (as he himself called Hatley), with a boat's
crew ; each man armed with a cutlass and a case of
pistols. The Portuguese not only imagines his ship
made prize, but thinks also how he shall undergo that
piece of discipline used by the merry blades in the West
Indies, called blooding and sweating. . . . So Don
Pedro, to save his bacon, took care to be very officious
or yare-handed (as we say), with his present. For no
sooner was Hatley on his quarter-deck but the Portuguese seamen began to hand into the boat the fruits
and refreshments they had on board, as plantains,
bananas, lemons, oranges, pomegranates, etc., three or
four dozen boxes of marmalade and other sweetmeats,
some Dutch cheeses, and a large quantity of sugars.
If they had stopped here it was well enough, and
might pass as a present ; but after this there came
above a dozen pieces of silk, several of which were
flowered with gold and silver, worth at least three
pounds a yard, by retail ; several dozen of china
plates and basins, a small Japan cabinet, not to
mention what the men took. . . . Among other things,
Hatley brought the last and handsomest present of
all, a purse of 300 moidores. This convinced Shelvocke he was not deceived in calling Hatley the best
busker ; that is, an impudent sharp fellow, who, perhaps
to reingratiate himself, did the devil's work, by
whose laudable example our boat's crew robbed the
man of more than I can pretend to say ; but I remember the boat was pretty well laden with one trade
or another, and none of the officers dared so much

as peep into her till all was out. While these things were handing into the ship a sham kind of quarrel ensues between our chieftains."

Betagh's view is corroborated by the fact that, when Shelvocke returned to England, he was arraigned on a charge of piracy for this very incident.

Dawdling down the coast, they spent nearly two months at St. Catherine's Island, Brazil, where there was a great deal of trouble with the crew, who drew up new articles for the regulation of the distribution of spoil, which Shelvocke found himself eventually compelled to sign, having previously, according to his own account, quelled a mutiny with the assistance of M. de la Jonquière, the captain of a French-manned ship which had been employed under Spanish colours —the whole of which is a most improbable, nay, incredible story, and is ridiculed by Betagh.

On rounding Cape Horn, Shelvocke got very nearly as far south as Rogers had done, and here there is mention of an incident which has a certain interest. Says Shelvocke: " We all observed that we had not had the sight of one fish of any kind, since we were come to the southward of the Straits of Le Mair, nor one sea-bird, except a disconsolate black albatross, who accompanied us for several days, hovering about us as if he had lost himself; till Hatley, observing, in one of his melancholy fits, that this bird was always hovering near us, imagined, from his colour, that it might be some ill omen. That which, I suppose, induced him the more to encourage his superstition, was the continued series of contrary tempestuous winds which had oppressed us ever since we had got into this sea. But be that as it would, he, after some fruitless attempts, at length shot the albatross, not doubting, perhaps, that we should have a fair wind after it."

Many years afterwards, in 1797, one English poet—Wordsworth—mentioned to another—Coleridge—that he had been reading Shelvocke's account of his voyage and related the albatross incident, which Coleridge introduced into " The Ancient Mariner " in the following year. It does not appear, however, that the crew of the *Speedwell* expressed any indignation at Hatley's act, or proceeded to any such extreme measure as hanging the dead albatross—which was probably not recovered—round his neck ; and, whatever may have been the superstitious significance attached to the continual hovering of the solitary bird about the ship—not at all an unusual incident in that latitude—no change resulted from its death, the boisterous winds and huge mile-long seas continuing to buffet the ship without reprieve ; and it was six weeks before they got fairly round the Horn and sighted the coast of Chili.

Shelvocke, still bent, apparently, upon killing time, put into Chiloe and Concepcion on trivial pretexts, and at the latter place captured one or two prizes of trifling value ; but, a party being sent in a small prize which they had renamed *Mercury* to capture a vessel laden with wine, etc., in a bay about six miles distant, were cleverly ambushed by the natives. They found the vessel, but she was hauled up on shore, and empty ; seeing a small house near by, they imagined her cargo was stored there, and, running up to it, helter-skelter, out came the enemy, mounted, each man lying along his horse and driving before them a double rank of unbacked horses, linked together. The Englishmen were quite powerless to resist, so they fled for their ship, which had grounded, the horsemen pursuing with guns and lassos. James Daniel, one of Shelvocke's foremast men, was lassoed just as he was wading out, and was dragged on shore, as he described it, " at the rate of ten knots." However, he appears to have escaped after all ; but five of the party were overtaken and captured, three being killed and the others severely wounded. Another ship named *St. Fermin*, which they captured, Shelvocke eventually burned, after the Spaniards had repeatedly failed to send the money which had been agreed upon for her ransom.

And so they sailed for Juan Fernandez, " to see," as Shelvocke says, " if we could find by any marks that the *Success* was arrived in these seas," and arrived off the island on January 12th, 1720. Shelvocke, however, would not go in and anchor at first ; he appears to have been unwilling to seek any evidence of Clipperton's visit, and kept standing off and on, fishing and filling the water-casks ; until one day, " some of my men accidentally saw the word ' Magee,' which was the name of Clipperton's surgeon, and ' Captain John,' cut out under it upon a tree, but no directions left, as was agreed on by him in his instructions to me."

Betagh says that Brook, the first lieutenant, " being the first officer that landed, immediately saw ' Captain John —— ' and ' W. Magee ' cut in the tree-bark ; upon the news of which everybody seemed to rejoice but our worthy captain, who would have it an invention of Brook's, for which he used him scurvily before all the company, telling him 'twas a lie. . . . Brook had hitherto been a great favourite with Shelvocke, but for this unwelcome discovery he is now put upon the black list."

It appears, however, from two different accounts, that the Viceroy at Lima had obtained from some of Clipperton's men, who became prisoners through the recapture of a prize, an account of the bottle hidden under the tree at Juan Fernandez, and of two men who had deserted there, and had despatched a vessel to bring both the men and the bottle; and Shelvocke, though he was not aware of this at the time, must have known it very well when he wrote his book; so his abuse of Clipperton is very disingenuous.

Even then, he went where he knew that Clipperton was not likely to be, sailing across to Arica, where he took a couple of small prizes, one of them "laden with cormorant's dung, which the Spaniards call *guano*, and is brought from the island of Iquique to cultivate the agi, or cod-pepper, in the Vale of Arica."

It was not until more than one hundred years later that we began regularly to ship guano to England as manure; Richard Dana describes a voyage for that purpose, in "Two Years before the Mast," published in 1840; this was probably one of the earliest ventures, though the existence of these huge deposits had been known for many years previously.

Then followed a plan for capturing the town of

Payta—a matter which, Shelvocke says, had been considered in the scheme of the voyage as one of great importance. He landed there with forty-six men, to find the town almost deserted; but presently saw great bodies of men on the surrounding hills, who however, retreated before his forty-six. He demanded 10,000 pieces of eight as ransom for the town, and a small prize he had taken; the Spaniards temporised, because they could see from their look-outs that a Spanish Admiral's ship, carrying fifty guns, was just round the high bluff, and thought they had a nice rod in pickle for the English. Shelvocke threatened, failing immediate ransom, to burn the town; the Spaniards replied that he might do what he liked, as long as he spared the churches—an absurd stipulation, for fire, once started, is not discriminating as to sacred edifices—and eventually the town was set on fire in three places.

No sooner, however, was Payta fairly in a blaze, than Shelvocke became aware that urgent signals for his return were being made from the *Speedwell*, whose guns were blazing away towards the harbour mouth. Ordering his crew on board, the captain preceded them in a canoe with three men, and, as he opened the point, became speedily aware of the significance of these doings; for there was a large ship, with the Spanish flag flying—a very much larger ship than the *Speedwell*.

"At this prospect," he says, "two of my three people were ready to sink, and had it not been for my boatswain, I should not have been able to fetch the ship.   When I looked back on the town, I could not forbear wishing that I had not been so hasty."

The Spaniard did not, however, avail himself of his opportunities, being deterred by the bold tactics of Mr. Coldsea, master of the *Speedwell*, who, with only a dozen men on board, opened a hot fire.

It is an extraordinary story.   The *Speedwell's* men, delayed by embarking a gun which had been landed, did not get on board until the Spanish ship was within less than pistol-shot ; then Shelvocke cut his cable, and, the ship not falling off the right way, " I had but just room enough to clear him."   The men were so dismayed at the appearance of the enemy's ship that some of them had proposed to jump overboard on the way off, and swim ashore—one actually did so.

The Spaniard at length attacked in earnest, and, according to Shelvocke's account, handled his ship cleverly, keeping the *Speedwell* in a disadvantageous position, and battering her with his broadsides, Shelvocke making what return he could.   Suddenly the Spaniards crowded on deck, shouting, and it was realised that the *Speedwell's* colours had been shot away, giving the appearance of a surrender.   Shelvocke immediately displayed his colours afresh ; upon which, " designing to do our business at once, they clapped their helm well a-starboard, to bring the whole broadside to point at us ; but their fire had little or no effect, all stood fast with us, and they muzzled themselves [*i.e.* got the ship stuck head to wind, or " in irons "], by which I had time to get ahead and to windward of him before he could fill again."   And so the *Speedwell* got off, their assailant being the *Peregrine*, of 56 guns and 450 men ; and Shelvocke tells us that he had not a single man killed or wounded !

The *Speedwell* was hulled repeatedly, and severely damaged aloft—but no casualties ! There are, it must be admitted, too many tales of immunity in privateer accounts, in spite of the " tremendous fire," or " shattering broadsides " of the enemy ; and, as a skipper cannot well manufacture casualties while all his crew are alive and well, one can only suppose that the terrible fire of the enemy is exaggerated.

Mr. Betagh—who had been detached with Hatley in a small prize, the *Mercury*, which was captured by the *Brilliant*, the *Peregrine's* consort—gives another version of this fight, from details obtained from the Spaniards. The ship, he says, mounted only 40 guns, and out of her crew of 350 men there were not above a dozen Europeans, the remainder being negroes, Indians, and half-castes, with no training, who were so terrified by the first discharge from the *Speedwell* that they ran below : " The commander and his officers did what they could to bring them to their duty : they beat them, swore at them, and pricked them in the buttocks ; but all would not do, for the poor devils were resolved to be frighted. Most of them ran quite down into the hold, while others were upon their knees praying the saints for deliverance. The *Speedwell* did not fire above eight or nine guns, and, as they were found sufficient, Shelvocke had no reason to waste his powder. However, this panic of theirs gave Shelvocke a fair opportunity to get his men aboard, cut his cable, and go away right afore the wind. This is the plain truth of the matter, which everybody was agreed in, for I heard it at several places ; though Shelvocke has cooked up a formal story of a desperate engagement to deceive those who knew him not into a wondrous opinion of his conduct."

The reader can take his choice between these two versions ; probably the truth lies somewhere midway, for, while Shelvocke was undoubtedly addicted at times to "drawing a long bow," Betagh was certainly a very bitter enemy of his, and all his statements are more or less coloured, no doubt, by animosity.

The *Speedwell's* days were numbered ; on May 11th, 1720, she arrived once more at Juan Fernandez, Shelvocke designing to remain there for a time and refit, giving the Spaniards to believe that he had quitted the cruising-ground. He had only been there a fortnight, however, when in a hard onshore gale with a heavy sea, the cable—a new one—parted, and the vessel drove on shore ; the masts went by the board, and though only one life was lost, the *Speedwell* was done for—a hopeless wreck.

Clipperton, meanwhile, having given up all hope of rejoining Shelvocke, had crossed the Atlantic and made his way, with much labour, through the Straits of Magellan, to the South Seas—it took them two months and a half to get through, and in September 1719 they visited Juan Fernandez, Clipperton being resolved to carry out his part of the bargain, and this being one of their appointed meeting-places. There the name of Magee, the doctor, was cut on the tree, and the instructions for Shelvocke buried in a bottle. Clipperton's name, we are told, was not cut in full, because he was well known out there, had been a prisoner for some time, and did not wish to advertise his return; but the precaution was futile, as we have seen.

Clipperton had great trouble with his crew, who declared that there would be no chance of much booty with a single ship, which might easily have the odds against her; and they cursed Shelvocke freely for running away with their liquor.

After leaving Juan Fernandez they took several prizes, one of them being the *Trinity*, of 400 tons, which had been taken by Woodes Rogers at Guayaquil, ten years before, and ransomed; one of the captains, however, being a sharp and intrepid fellow, got the better of Clipperton. His ship, the *Rosario*, being taken, he saw at once that, from the number of prizes the English privateer had in company, her crew must be already very much reduced, so he kept his eye open for an opportunity. He had about a dozen passengers, whom he took into his confidence, hiding them in the hold. Clipperton sent a lieutenant and eight men to take possession, and all the crew they could find were confined in the cabin, with a sentry at the door. The ship was presently got under sail by the Englishmen, to join the *Success*, and the prize crew went down to see what plunder they could discover in the hold; upon which the concealed passengers fell upon them and secured them, while those in the cabin, taking the sounds of the scuffle below as their signal, knocked the sentry on the head and broke out, the boatswain meanwhile flooring the lieutenant by a blow from behind. The captain then ran the vessel on shore, and, in spite of a heavy surf, both crews landed safely, the Englishmen being sent to Lima as prisoners ; and it was one of these who was unsportsmanlike enough to let out about the bottle buried on Juan Fernandez.

The Viceroy of Peru, we are told, immediately ordered a new ship to be built for the plucky and resourceful captain of the *Rosario*, and imposed a tax on all the traders to pay for her.

While watering at the island of Lobos de la Mar, a plot was discovered among the crew to seize the ship, but was suppressed ; later on another misfortune befell them, for, capturing a good prize, laden with tobacco, sugar, and cloth off Coquimbo, they discovered, on entering that port, three Spanish men-of-war, which were on the station for the express purpose of looking after the English privateers. These, of course, immediately cut their cables and made sail in chase, the *Success* and her prize hauling their wind to escape ; the latter, however, was soon recaptured, with a lieutenant and twelve men of the *Success*, which contrived to escape.

This was a great blow to the already discontented and half mutinous crew. To make matters worse, Clipperton began to solace himself with liquor, and was frequently more or less drunk. Provisions began to run short, so that they were glad to land all their Spanish prisoners.

At the island of Cocoas—one of the Galapagos

Islands—they built a place for their sick and rested a little ; when they prepared to sail, on January 21st, 1721, eleven of the crew—three whites and eight negroes—hid themselves and deserted, preferring to live as they could on a fertile island to braving the privations and disappointments of the sea again.

On January 25th, having arrived at the island of Quibo, off the coast of Mexico, a great surprise was in store. The pinnace being sent in chase of a sail, came up with her about eleven o'clock at night, and found her to be a Spanish vessel, the *Jesu Maria* ; but not in Spanish hands, for she was manned by Shelvocke and what remained of the *Speedwell's* crew. They had contrived to build some crazy sort of craft out of the wreck of their ship at Juan Fernandez, and had eventually taken this vessel, a very good and sound one, of two hundred tons.

Thus they met, after two years ; and it was not a pleasant nor cordial meeting. Clipperton called Shelvocke to account for the plunder which he had taken, and the portion set aside for the owners ; but no account was forthcoming, of course, for Shelvocke and his crew were by that time on a sort of piratical footing, with no attempt at discipline or regularity of proceedings. They met several times, and Clipperton supplied the other with some articles ; eventually, Clipperton sent a sort of ultimatum to Shelvocke, that if he and his crew would refund all the money shared among themselves, contrary to the original articles with the owners, and put it into a common stock, the past should be forgiven, and they would cruise together for the rich ship from Acapulco.   This proposal was not, of course, entertained by Shelvocke and his men; and so they parted.

Clipperton eventually sailed for China, and, after many difficulties, came home to Ireland in a Dutch East Indiaman.   He did not long survive his return; his ill-success, and probably his intemperate habits, broke down his health, and he died a few weeks later.

Shelvocke, meanwhile, had captured, at Sansonate, a vessel named the *Santa Familia*; and, finding her a better ship than the *Jesu Maria*, he exchanged.

When he was on the point of sailing, however, he received a letter from the Governor notifying the conclusion of peace between Spain and England, and demanding the return of the ship.   He demanded a copy of the articles of peace, which the Governor promised to obtain for him; but there was evidently a strong conviction on shore that Shelvocke was not ingenuous in the matter.   A lieutenant and five men whom he sent on shore were seized, and eventually he sailed with his capture, leaving behind a protest, signed by all the crew.

They were, however, getting very sick of the cruise, and contemplated surrendering themselves at Panama; but meanwhile they took another vessel, the *Conception*—the doubt which existed as to the establishment of peace not troubling them very much—and eventually, abandoning the idea of surrender, they sailed for China.

Shelvocke had some queer and suspicious dealings with the Chinese authorities at Whampoa, disposing of his ship for £700, after having, as he alleges, paid more than £2,000 for port dues. Betagh says he cleared some £7,000 out of the cruise, and he gives figures which go far towards proving his assertion; the owners did not make much out of the venture, though Clipperton endeavoured to act honestly towards them; and when Shelvocke, returning in an East Indiaman, presented himself before them, he was immediately arrested—Betagh says on the strength of a letter which he had written while a prisoner at Lima—and put in prison.

He was charged with two acts of piracy—to wit, the affair off Cape Frio, and the capture of the *Santa Familia*; but there was not adequate legal proof against him. On the further charge of defrauding his owners he was detained, but contrived to escape, and left England.

This was in 1722. Four years later he published his book, " A Voyage Round the World," which was followed in two years by that of his late officer, William Betagh.

Making every allowance for Betagh's animosity, it is impossible to believe that Shelvocke was a favourable specimen of a privateer commander; his own admissions are in several instances against him, and there can be little doubt that he and his crew degenerated into unscrupulous pirates. Clipperton, though very rough and eventually a drunkard, was a better type of man; and, had Shelvocke been loyal, and stuck to him from the first, the story of the cruise might have been a very different one.

SOME ODD YARNS

CHAPTER VII

CAPTAIN PHILLIPS OF THE "ALEXANDER"

In the year 1744 a British 20-gun ship, the *Solebay*, was captured, together with two others, by a French squadron under Admiral de Rochambeau.

Less than two years later the Lords Commissioners of the Admiralty called before them a certain Captain Phillips, master mariner, commanding the *Alexander* privateer; and the following is the "minute" of the interview, officially recorded:

"29 April, 1746. Captain Phillips, of the *Alexander* privateer, attending, was called in, and told the Lords that he chased the *Solebay* and a small ship, laden with naval stores, that she had under her convoy, into St. Martin's Road[1] on the 10th instant; that he came up with the *Solebay* just at the entrance of the Road, where he believed there were 100 sail of ships at anchor, and boarded her athwart the bowsprit, sword in hand, and cut her out about three o'clock p.m. Said the wind was at S.S.W., which was fair for his running in and coming out. The Lords asked him how many men she had on board. He answered she had 230, and

---

[1] Inside Isle de Rhé, off the coast of France, close to La Rochelle.

he had but 140 ; that they kept a very bad look-out, but as soon as he boarded her they were forced to fly from their quarters ; that they killed 15 of her men, and he had lost but three ; that she is still called the *Solebay*, and that the French have made no other alteration in her than lengthening her quarter-deck. The Lords asked him what he thought the two Martinico ships he had taken were worth ; he answered about £8,000 or £9,000. He told the Lords that at the Isle of Rhé there were two ships of 64 guns each, and four East India ships outward bound ; said he was to be heard of at Lloyd's Coffee House, and then withdrew."

Thus an English man-of-war was restored to the Royal Navy by the boldness and enterprise of this privateer captain, who was another specimen of a good man lost to the Service. He would willingly have entered the Navy, but, like George Walker, he was deterred by the stringent regulations, which compelled him at first to take a subordinate post as lieutenant. He was presented, however, with five hundred guineas and a gold medal, in recognition of his excellent services ; and his name will not be overlooked in the roll of honour by naval historians.

THE CASE OF THE "ANTIGALLICAN"

In the year 1755 there appears to have existed a certain body which had adopted the title of " The Society of Antigallicans," having for its object the promotion of British manufactures, the extension of the commerce of England, the discouragement of French *modes*, and of the importation of French commodities.

War being regarded as inevitable, and the king having already issued a proclamation licensing the granting of commissions to privateers, the Antigallicans, always busy "concerting some good for the sake of the public," discussed the propriety of fitting out a vessel of this nature—an undertaking which, if successful, might obviously bring them a rich reward for their public spirit.

The scheme, proposed by one William Smith, Esq., was relished by the whole company, and the motion carried by acclamation. When the applause had subsided there rose Mr. Torrington, who informed the company present that he happened to possess at that moment a ship most admirably adapted for the purpose : being the *Flamborough*, formerly a man-of-war, but then in the Jamaica trade, and known as the *Flying Flamborough* on account of her great speed ; Mr. Torrington, in his naturally enthusiastic eulogy of the ship he wished to sell, declaring that, with a fair wind and crowded canvas, she had frequently run fourteen knots—which was certainly very unusual with the short, bluff-bowed vessels of that period.

It was immediately agreed to purchase her, and she was appropriately renamed the *Antigallican*. She was a formidable vessel, of 440 tons, mounting 28 guns and 16 swivels, with a crew of 208 men, commanded by William Foster—a man apparently of humble birth, for he is said to have been a " cockswain " on board H.M.S. *Defiance*, and to have attracted notice by his brave conduct during the action between Anson and De la Jonquière on May 3rd, 1747.[1]

On July 17th, 1756, the *Antigallican* was ready for sea, and the owners brought down their wives and daughters and numerous friends, who were handsomely entertained on board ; she had on board, we are told, " six months' provision, all of the product of Middlesex and Kent, generally supplied from the estates of the proprietors. There was not the least thing in or about her but what was entirely English "— which, of course, was only right and consistent with the principles of the Society.

Sailing on September 17th, she fell in, about a month later, with an armed French vessel, about 300 miles west of Lisbon. This ship fell an easy prey, surrendering after delivering one broadside and receiving a raking fire from the Englishman. She had on board, we are told, four English prisoners, " part of the crew taken on board the *Warwick* man-of-war." This ship had been captured by a French squadron on March 11th preceding. Why these four men were on board this armed merchantman does not appear, but

---

[1] Perhaps Mr. William Foster is responsible for the story here told by the Antigallican narrator, that Anson " had no hand in the matter. That morning he desired a council of war, but Sir Peter Warren told him, ' There are French colours flying ! which is a sufficient council of war ' ; and so bore down upon them, while his lordship lay at a distance." Anson, however, received his peerage for this very action— he was not " his lordship " when he fought it ; Warren was knighted at the same time.

the French captain, who was a cheerful soul, not readily cast down by adversity, had always treated them well, and, when the *Antigallican* hove in sight, served out a complete outfit of clothes to them. They remained on deck at work until the first shot was fired, when they were put under hatches, and the captain himself was the first to inform them of their release. Smiling upon them through the open hatchway, he said: "Come out, gentlemen; *it be vel wit you, but ill wit me!*"

This vessel was the *Maria Theresa*, 14 guns and 30 men. She was valued, with her cargo, at £23,000: so the *Antigallican* made a promising commencement of her cruise. The prize was sent to Portsmouth. Another, valued at £15,000, was taken into Madeira, in company with the privateer.

This was all very pleasant, and the Antigallican Society could congratulate itself upon the success of its scheme for the good of the public—and, incidentally, for the pockets of its members; and one day in December 1756 a Dutch vessel gave news of a very rich prize, the *Duc de Penthièvre*, a French Indiaman. "The news was communicated to the crew, who heard it joyfully and behaved with a true Antigallican spirit."

The privateer was off Corunna on the morning of December 26th, and at 6 a.m. a sail was observed standing inshore. It being almost calm, the sweeps were got out, and by noon the *Antigallican* was within gunshot, under Spanish colours. Upon receiving a shot she ran up English colours, and the French ship

then delivered a broadside; the English captain,
however, reserved his fire until he was close aboard.
They fought for nearly three hours; then the Frenchman struck, and the vessel proved to be the one they
were in search of, her value being placed at something
like £300,000! Here was a fine haul. They made
haste to get into port with her, aiming at Lisbon; but
they had some characteristically rough winter weather
on that coast, and, after bucketing about for over a
fortnight, they ran for Cadiz, where they arrived
on January 23rd, 1757. That gale proved very
disastrous for the Antigallicans, for the Spaniards,
green with envy over such gains, immediately set to
work to show that the _Duc de Penthièvre_ was captured
in Spanish waters, _i.e._ within three miles of the
coast.

The French officers, in the first instance, deposed
quite ingenuously, before the consular authorities,
upon their oath, that their ship was captured two or
three leagues—six or eight miles—off the coast; that
they did not see any fort, nor hear any guns fired;
in fact, they accepted the position that they were fairly
made prisoners, and their vessel, with all her rich cargo,
was now English property. The depositions of the
English and French officers were sent to the Admiralty
Court at Gibraltar, and the ship was condemned as
" good prize " without hesitation.

Meanwhile, the Spanish naval authorities had
politely given permission for the English privateer to
be taken over to the Government yard for refitting,
and all her movable gear, of every description, was

landed and placed in the warehouse, in order that the ship might be "careened," or "hove down," to examine and clean her bottom.

On February 19th came the first attack from the Spaniards. The Governor of Cadiz sent for the English Consul, Mr. Goldsworthy, and told him that he was obliged to send troops on board the prize, having received orders to detain her. In spite of the Consul's vigorous protest, the threat was confirmed with every warlike accompaniment—guns manned in the fort, artillerymen standing by with lighted matches, and so on. Both vessels were seized, but before dark the Governor, having apparently some misgivings as to the legality of the business, ordered the troops to be withdrawn, "after having broken open several chests, and carried away everything they could find of the officers and crew, and the very beef that was dressing for dinner."

On February 26th the Governor informed the Consul that he had orders to deliver the prize to the French Consul. Captain Foster offered to place the ship in the Governor's hands until the case should be decided, which was a very proper and businesslike proposal; but it was refused, and the captain declaring that the English colours flying on the prize should never come down with his consent, matters came to a climax, and, in spite of the unwillingness of the Spanish Admiral, who probably realised the injustice of the proceedings, the Governor insisted that two men-of-war should be sent to enforce his orders; a 60-gun ship and a 36-gun frigate took up their positions quite close to the prize, and upon Foster refusing to lower his colours, they opened fire, killing six men and wounding two. The flag halyards were shot away almost immediately; but, in spite of the colours coming down, they would not desist. The prize made no attempt at resistance, and on the following day— March 3rd—the captain and crew were imprisoned.

On the 5th came an order from Madrid to stop all proceedings against the prize and consult with the English captain alone; to allow the prize to remain in our possession, but not to leave the port until further orders.

The Spanish Governor, however, having evidently some very amenable perjurers up his sleeve, disregarded the injunction, refusing to return the ship to the English Consul; and on the following day there arrived from Gibraltar the formal decision of the Admiralty Court, condemning the *Duc de Penthièvre* as " good prize," on the evidence of the French officers, delivered two days before she was forcibly seized.

However, the French Ambassador at Madrid, inspired and instructed by the Consul at Cadiz, was very urgent in the matter, and the Spaniards succeeded in finding some unscrupulous persons who swore that the action took place within gunshot, while other independent witnesses were very certain that it did not; and the King of Spain, being somewhat uneasy in his mind, intimated to our Ambassador at Madrid that the prize was only to be detained until strict inquiry could be made into the merits of the case.

This appears to have been hailed, by the Antigallican Society, as equivalent to victory ; the narrator of the story expresses his great joy over the restitution of the prize, and gives a copy of a letter from his Society to Pitt, whose good offices with the Spanish Government had been enlisted, thanking him enthusiastically for his successful intervention.

They were counting their chickens before they were hatched ; the Spanish half-concession was merely an elaboration of their favourite word, *mañana*—and this " to-morrow," upon which the English were to have the ship which they had fairly captured, never dawned ! There was an immense amount of correspondence on the subject, but in 1758, two years later, the matter was not settled—or rather, it was settled against the English ; and they never got their £300,000, or their ship. It appears almost incredible, but this appears to be the truth about the *Antigallican* and her rich prize. We have no more reports of any privateering business by the Antigallican Society ; so we must conclude that the members had had enough of such ventures.

The following is a translation of the deposition of the first lieutenant of the *Duc de Penthièvre*, made before the British Consul at Cadiz :

" M. François de Querangal, first lieutenant of the ship *Duc de Penthièvre*, belonging to the French East India Company, commanded by M. Ettoupan de Villeneuve, since dead of his wounds after the engagement, deposes that the said ship sailed from the Island of St. Mary, on the coast of Madagascar, on

the 12th of September, 1756, bound for the port of
L'Orient, in France; that the said ship was compelled,
by contrary winds and other stress, to run for the
harbour of Corunna, on the coast of Spain; that on the
26th December last, being about one league from
land, the *Antigallican*, displaying Spanish colours and
coming within gunshot, they fired a gun across her
bows. The vessel immediately hoisted English colours,
and we commenced the action.

"The Iron Tower was then about two and a half or
three leagues distant. Asked whether he had seen
any flags or batteries on shore, he declares that he had
seen neither.

"That the said ship, *Duc de Penthièvre*, was armed
with 20 guns at the time of the action, and carried
a crew of 150 men; that he had no knowledge of the
papers contained in the boxes thrown overboard
before the colours were hauled down.

"The said gentleman declares before me, having
taken his oath according to the French custom, that
the above statement is true."

This is signed by the deponent and duly attested
by the Consul, the depositions of the other French
officers being in precisely similar terms.

It was on these depositions, together with those of
Captain Foster and his assistants, that the Admiralty
Court at Gibraltar condemned the ship as "good
prize," and with perfect justice; had any ground
existed for protest, it should then have been put
forward; so the flagrant injustice and iniquity of the
Spanish authorities is very apparent. There had been

other complaints previously, and the British Ambassador at Madrid had very strongly protested against the favour shown by the Spaniards to French privateers, and had also induced Pitt, the Prime Minister, to support him in a strong letter. But it was all of no avail: there were wheels within wheels, and, rather than make it an occasion of war, the just claims of the Antigallicans were suffered to go by the board.

CHAPTER VIII

CAPTAIN DEATH, OF THE "TERRIBLE"

ONE of the bloodiest privateer actions on record was that between the *Terrible*, owned in London, and the *Vengeance*, of St. Malo.

The *Terrible* carried 26 guns, with a crew of 200 men, and was commanded by Captain Death. She was cruising off the mouth of the Channel at the end of the year 1756, and had had some success, capturing an armed French cargo ship, the *Alexandre le Grand*, (the narrator very simply translates this "Grand Alexander"!), which she was escorting into Plymouth, with a prize crew of an officer—the first lieutenant—and fifteen men, when on December 27th, at daylight, two sails were sighted to the southward, about twelve miles distant. Some communication was observed to take place between the two vessels, and then the larger one steered for the *Terrible* and her prize, which was far astern, so that the *Terrible* was obliged to back her mizzen-topsail and wait for her.

Meanwhile, every preparation was made for action; but, from the absence of the prize crew and other causes, no more than 116 men out of 200 were able to stand to the guns; indeed, the narrator, who was third lieutenant of the *Terrible*, tells rather a sad story of her crew—" the rest being either dead or sick below with a distemper called the spotted fever, that raged among the ship's company." This may have been malignant typhus, or the plague, terribly infectious ; and there would be great reluctance to handle the dead bodies—hence some of these were left below.

The enemy approached, as was usually the practice, under English colours until within close range, when she shortened sail and hoisted French colours. The *Terrible* was ready for her, with her starboard guns manned, and the prize had by this time come up; but she was a clumsy sailer, deep-laden, and fell off from the wind; so the Frenchman got in between them, gave the prize a broadside, and then, ranging close up on the *Terrible's* port quarter, delivered a most destructive fire, diagonally across her deck, killing and wounding a great number. So close were the two ships, that the yardarms almost touched, and the *Terrible's* people, in spite of the awful battering they had just received, returned a broadside of round and grape, which was equally destructive. For five or six minutes they surged along side by side, while each disposed his dead and wounded, and a touch of the helm would have run either vessel aboard her opponent. The Frenchmen, more numerous in spite of their losses, might have boarded, and the " Terribles " were in momentary expectation of it— but they held off, and the English did not find themselves strong enough to attempt it. Separating again, they exchanged a murderous fire at close range, the casualties being very heavy on both sides.

The French ship had, however, one great advantage at such close quarters ; in each " top " she had eight or ten small-arm men, who were able to fire down upon the *Terrible's* deck, and pick off whom they would— the latter was too short-handed to spare any men for this purpose.

This slaughter, to which they were unable to reply, really decided the action. Every man in sight was either killed or miserably wounded—the captain and the third lieutenant escaped for some time, but the latter was grazed on his cheek, and the captain, he states, was shot through the body after he had struck his flag. This is a very common accusation, and no doubt it has often been true, though probably only through a misapprehension ; men who are blazing away and being shot at in a hot action do not always know or realise at the moment that the enemy has struck, and so some poor fellow loses his life un-necessarily.

It was too hot to last. The enemy was a ship of considerably superior force, and probably had three times the number of the *Terrible's* available crew at the commencement of the action. On board the English vessel nearly one hundred men were dead or wounded, the decks were cumbered with their bodies, and only one officer was left untouched ; they had not a score of men left to fight the ship, and the enemy continued to pour in a pitiless fire, which at length brought the mainmast by the board.

Captain Death, a brave man, could then see no course but to surrender, having put up a very gallant fight; and so he ordered down the colours, and was then, as is said, fatally wounded by a musket-ball.

Then follows a dismal story of the treatment of the English prisoners, which we may hope, for the sake of French humanity and generosity, is somewhat exaggerated—as we know that such things can be, under the smart of defeat and surrender: " They turned our first lieutenant and all our people down in a close, confined place forward the first night that we came on board, where twenty-seven men of them were stifled before morning; and several were hauled out for dead, but the air brought them to life again; and a great many of them died of their wounds on board the *Terrible* for want of care being taken of them, which was out of our doctor's power to do, the enemy having taken his instruments and medicine from him. Several that were wounded they heaved overboard alive."

If this is a true account one shudders to think what may have been the fate of those unhappy, plague-stricken men below—probably brought up and hove overboard in a ferocious panic!

The French ship was named the *Vengeance*, of 36 guns and about 400 men; so there was no discredit to Captain Death in yielding, after such a plucky resistance. The merchants of London opened a subscription at Lloyd's Coffee House for his widow and the widows of the crew, and for the survivors, who had suffered the loss of all their possessions.

This desperate fight was much talked about at the time, and inspired some rhymester, whose name has not come down to us, to compose the following :

CAPTAIN DEATH

The muse and the hero together are fir'd,
The same noble views has their bosom inspir'd ;
As freedom they love, and for glory contend,
The muse o'er the hero still mourns as a friend ;
So here let the muse her poor tribute bequeath,
To one British hero—'tis brave Captain Death.

The ship was the *Terrible*—dreadful to see !
His crew was as brave and as valiant as he.
Two hundred or more was their full complement,
And sure braver fellows to sea never went.
Each man was determined to spend his last breath
In fighting for Britain and brave Captain Death.

A prize they had taken diminish'd their force,
And soon the brave ship was lost in her course.
The French privateer and the *Terrible* met,
The battle began with all horror beset.
No heart was dismayed, each bold as Macbeth ;
The sailors rejoiced, so did brave Captain Death.

Fire, thunder, balls, bullets were soon heard and felt,
A sight that the heart of Bellona would melt.
The shrouds were all torn and the decks fill'd with blood,
And scores of dead bodies were thrown in the flood.
The flood, from the time of old Noah and Seth,
Ne'er saw such a man as our brave Captain Death.

At last the dread bullet came wing'd with his fate ;
Our brave captain dropped, and soon after his mate.
Each officer fell, and a carnage was seen,

That soon dy'd the waves to a crimson from green ;
Then Neptune rose up, and he took off his wreath,
And gave it a triton to crown Captain Death.

Thus fell the strong *Terrible*, bravely and bold,
But sixteen survivors the tale can unfold.
The French were the victors, tho' much to their cost,
For many brave French were with Englishmen lost.
For thus says old Time, " Since Queen Elizabeth,
I ne'er saw the fellow of brave Captain Death."

There is another poetic effusion on the subject, under the title " The Terrible Privateer " ; but it is such halting doggrel that the reader shall be spared the transcription ; with the exception of the last verse, which breathes such a blunt British spirit that it would be a pity to omit it :

Here's a health unto our British fleet.
Grant they with these privateers may meet,
And have better luck than the *Terrible*,
And sink those Mounsiers all to hell.

The *Vengeance* was, in fact, captured about twelve months later by the *Hussar*, a man-of-war, after a stout resistance, in which she lost heavily ; it is impossible, however, to say how far the devout aspiration of the poet was fulfilled !

MR. PETER BAKER AND THE "MENTOR"

In the Reading-room of the Free Library in Liverpool there hangs an oil-painting, of which a reproduction is here given, illustrating an incident which occurred during the American War of Secession, in 1778.

Liverpool merchants and shipowners were very active at that time in the fitting out of privateers ; and some, or one of them, entered into a contract with one Peter Baker to build a vessel for this purpose. Now, Baker does not appear to have had the necessary training and experience to qualify him as a designer and builder of ships. He had served a short apprenticeship with some employer in the neighbourhood of Garston, near Liverpool, and had then worked as a carpenter in Liverpool, eventually becoming a master. However, he set to work to fulfil his contract ; but he turned out of hand such a sorry specimen of a ship —clumsy, ill-built, lopsided, and with sailing qualities more suited to a haystack than a smart privateer— that the prospective owner refused her, throwing her back on his hands—a very serious matter for Peter Baker, who was heavily in debt over the venture.

Strangely enough, this apparent calamity proved to be the making of him.

Despairing of paying his debts, he resolved upon the somewhat desperate course of fitting out the ship as a venture of his own, and contrived to obtain sufficient credit for this purpose. Probably his creditors agreed to give him this chance, as the privateers not infrequently made considerable sums of money.

Baker did not, however, aspire to the post of privateer captain ; he appointed to the command his son-in-law, John Dawson, who had made several voyages to the coast of Africa, and knew enough about navigation to get along somehow. The vessel measured 400 tons, carried 28 guns, and shipped a crew of 102 men; but they were a very queer lot: loafers picked up on the docks, landsmen in search of adventure, and so on. With this unpromising outfit—a lopsided, heavy-sailing vessel, an inexperienced commander, and a crew of incapable desperadoes—Peter Baker entered upon his privateering venture, and in due course the *Mentor*, provided, no doubt, with a king's commission, proceeded down the Irish Sea, hanging about in the chops of the Channel for homeward bound French merchantmen. Dawson was not very persistent or enterprising, for we are told that in something under a week he was on the point of returning, not having as yet come across anything worthy of his powder and shot. Falling in with another privateer, homeward bound, he made the usual inquiry as to whether she had seen anything, either in the way of a likely prize or a formidable enemy; and was informed that a large vessel, either a Spanish 74-gun ship, or Spanish East Indiaman, had been seen just previously in a given latitude.

Dawson thereupon resolved to put his fortune to the test—"For," said he, "I might as well be in a Spanish prison as an English one, and if I return empty I shall most likely be imprisoned for debt." So he made sail after the assumed Spaniard, and found her readily enough; as he closed, he made out through his glass that she was pierced for 74 guns, and was, of course, in every respect a far more formidable craft than the lopsided *Mentor*. Handing the

8

glass to his carpenter, John Baxter, evidently an observant and intelligent man, the latter exclaimed that the stranger's guns were all dummies !

Thereupon John Dawson bore down to the attack, boarded the enemy, and carried her, with his harum-scarum crew, almost unopposed.

She proved to be a French East Indiaman, the *Carnatic*, with a most valuable cargo—said to be worth pretty nearly half a million sterling. One box of diamonds alone was valued at £135,000.

The crew had been three years in the vessel, trading in gold and diamonds, and did not even know that war had broken out.

Here was a piece of luck for Peter Baker ! When the rich prize was brought into the Mersey, in charge of the proud and happy Dawson and his crew, bells were set ringing, guns were fired, and both captors and victors were entertained in sumptuous fashion by the delighted townspeople. Baker became, of course, immediately a person of importance: he was jocosely alluded to as " Lord Baker," and was later elected Mayor of Liverpool and made a county magistrate.

He proceeded to build himself a large house at Mossley Hill, outside Liverpool, which either he or some facetious friend dubbed " Carnatic Hall " ; it was partially destroyed by fire later on, and rebuilt by the present owners, Holland by name.

Baker and Dawson entered into partnership as shipbuilders, and the uncouth but lucky *Mentor* continued her cruising, capturing two or three more

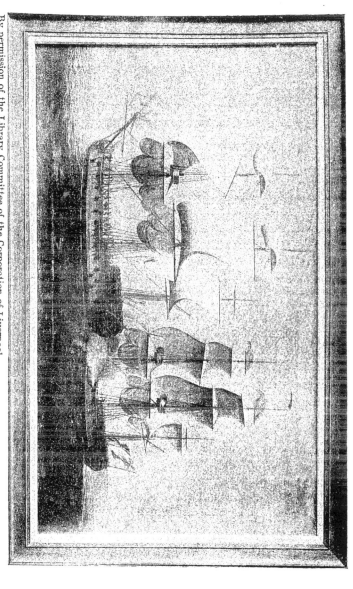

By permission of the Library Committee of the Corporation of Liverpool.

CAPTURE OF THE FRENCH EAST INDIAMAN "CARNATIC" BY THE "MENTOR" PRIVATEER, BUILT AND OWNED BY MR. PETER BAKER, OF LIVERPOOL, AND COMMANDED BY CAPTAIN JOHN DAWSON; IN THE YEAR 1778.

[p. 114]

prizes of trifling value. In 1782, however, while on her passage home from Jamaica, she foundered off the Banks of Newfoundland, thirty-one of her crew perishing.

Such is the story of Peter Baker's sudden rise of fortune, illustrating the extraordinary uncertainty of those privateering times. Baker had, so to speak, no business to succeed; one cannot help regarding him, in the first instance, as something of an impostor in undertaking to build a ship under the circumstances—for we may be sure that she was not rejected without good reason; but she caused all this to be forgotten by one piece of good luck. Her fortunate builder and owner died in 1796.

CAPTAIN EDWARD MOOR, OF THE "FAME"

A privateer commander of the best type was Captain Edward Moor, of the *Fame*, hailing from Dublin. His vessel carried 20 six-pounders and some smaller pieces, and a crew of 108 men. It was in August 1780, when he was cruising off the coast of Spain and the northern coast of Africa, that he received news of the departure of five ships from Marseilles, bound for the West Indies: all armed vessels, and provided with fighting commissions of some kind—letters of marque, as they are styled.

Being a man of good courage, and not afraid of such trifling odds as five to one, Moor went in search of these Frenchmen; and on August 25th he was lucky

enough to sight them, off the coast of Spain. As
dusk was approaching he refrained from any demon-
stration of hostility, but took care, during the night,
to get inshore of the enemy.

At daybreak they were about six miles distant,
and, upon seeing the *Fame* approach in a businesslike manner, they formed in line to receive her.

Adopting similiar tactics to those of George Walker
in attacking eight vessels—perhaps purposely following the example of a man who had such a great name,
and whose exploits were sure to be known among
privateersmen [1]—Moor bade his men lie down at their
guns, and not fire until he gave the word.

At half-past six they were within gunshot, and
the Frenchmen opened fire ; but the *Fame* swept on
in silence until she was close to the largest ship ;
then they blazed away, and in three quarters of an
hour she surrendered. Without a moment's delay
Moor tackled the next in size, which also shortly
succumbed. Putting an officer and seven men on
board, with orders to look after *both* ships—what
glorious confidence in his men !—he went after the
others, which were now endeavouring to escape ;
only one succeeded, however, though one would have
imagined that, by scattering widely, they might have
saved another. These two fugitives made no further
resistance, and Captain Moor thus got four ships, to
wit—*Deux Frères*, 14 guns, 50 men ; *Univers*, 12 guns,
40 men ; *Zephyr* (formerly a British sloop-of-war,
according to Beatson's " Memoirs "), 10 guns, 32 men ;

[1] The account of George Walker's exploits comes later on.

and *Nancy*, 4 guns, 18 men—a total of 40 guns and 140 men, against his 26 guns and 108 men. The Frenchmen certainly ought to have made it hotter for him ; but probably their crews were not trained, and Moor evidently had his men well in hand, just as Walker had.

He took his prizes into Algiers, where he landed the prisoners, who gave such a good account of the kind and generous treatment they had received from their captors that the French Consul-General at Algiers wrote a very handsome letter to Moor, expressing in the strongest terms his appreciation of his conduct.

This Edward Moor was evidently one of those commanders like Walker and Wright ; a gentleman by birth and instinct, combining the highest courage with refinement of mind and humanity ; he would have been well employed in the Royal Navy.

CAPTAIN JAMES BORROWDALE, OF THE "ELLEN"

Earlier in this same year, 1780, a Bristol ship made a very brilliant capture. This was the *Ellen*, an armed merchantman, provided with a letter of marque. She carried 18 six-pounders and a crew of 64, half of them boys and landsmen on their first voyage. She was commanded by James Borrowdale, a careful man, who, while fully aware that he was expected to make as good a passage as possible, and refrain from engaging in combat unless it was forced upon him, took some pains to ensure that, in such event, the foe should not have a walk-over.

He had as passenger one Captain Blundell, of the 79th—Liverpool—Regiment, going out to join his regiment in Jamaica ; and this gentleman, in order, no doubt, to beguile the tedium of the voyage, undertook to train sixteen of the crew to act as marines— hoping, probably, for an opportunity of proving their metal ; and he was not disappointed.

A month out, on April 16th, a ship was sighted to windward, apparently of much the same size and force as the *Ellen*. Captain Borrowdale, with all his canvas set to catch the Trade-wind, stood on, apparently unheeding the approach of the stranger ; but his men had the guns cast loose and loaded, and Blundell, with his little band of amateur marines, was very much on the alert.

Arriving within gunshot, the stranger fired a gun, hoisting Spanish colours ; upon which Borrowdale shortened sail, seeing that it was impossible to avoid a fight, and hoisted American colours, to gain time ; for his idea was to commence the action at very close quarters.

He then addressed his crew, bidding them ram down a bag of grape-shot into every gun—on top of the round shot, of course—to keep cool, and reserve their fire for close quarters, keeping the guns trained on the enemy meanwhile ; to fire as quickly as possible, and to fight the ship to the last extremity.

When the other was within hailing distance down came the American colours, up went the English, and a deadly broadside was delivered, accompanied by a well-directed volley from Blundell's contingent. So effective, in fact, was the sudden and vigorous attack, that it quite staggered the Spaniards, who fell into confusion, neglecting the proper handling of their vessel, so that she fell off from the wind and got under the *Ellen's* lee ; upon which the other broadside was poured into her. The Spanish captain, imagining that he had only an ordinary armed trader to deal with—and many of them were very poor fighters— had perhaps not made full preparation for action ; at any rate, he and his men were so demoralised by these two broadsides that he put his helm up and ran for it. The English captain, having successfully defended his ship, might now have pursued his voyage, without any loss of credit, that being his business ; but no such idea entered his head. The crew gave three hearty cheers as they trimmed and cracked on sail, and the Spaniard, having sustained some damage aloft, was unable to escape. Running alongside, the *Ellen* attacked again, and the action was maintained for an hour and a half, the two vessels running yard-arm to yardarm ; and then, the *Ellen's* fire having completely disabled the foe aloft, the Spanish colours came down, and Captain Borrowdale found himself in possession of the *Santa Anna Gratia*, a Spanish sloop-of-war, mounting 16 heavy six-pounders and a number of swivels, with a crew of 104 men, of whom seven were killed and eight wounded ; the *Ellen* had only one killed and three wounded ; but these small losses were doubtless owing to the two vessels mutually aiming at the spars and rigging, each endeavouring to cripple her opponent aloft.

This was a very brilliant little affair, and Borrowdale and his merry men must have felt very well pleased with themselves as they sailed into Port Royal, Jamaica, the prize in company, with the English colours surmounting the Spanish.

TWO GREAT ENGLISHMEN

CHAPTER IX

FORTUNATUS WRIGHT

Surely the fairies must have been busy with suggestions at the birth and naming of this fighting seaman—great seaman and determined fighter, and withal a smack of romantic heroism about him, which is suggested at once by his Christian name—Fortunatus. No man with such a name, one is disposed to assume, could be an ordinary and commonplace sort of person, muddling along in the well-worn grooves of every-day life. This, of course, would be an absurd assumption ; men have been named after all kinds of heroes, naval and military, statesmen, masters of the pen, and so on, and have fallen very far short—to put it mildly— of the aspirations of their fond and admiring parents.

Wright's father was a master-mariner of Liverpool, of whom we are told that he had upon one occasion defended his ship most gallantly for several hours against two vessels of superior force—an exploit which is recorded upon his tombstone in St. Peter's churchyard, Liverpool, and from which we gather that he was either a privateer commander, or that his vessel, an ordinary trader, was armed for the purpose of defence. We do not know, however, why he named his son Fortunatus—we can only fall back upon the fairies ; but a supplementary inscription upon the tombstone tells us that " Fortunatus Wright, his son, was always victorious, and humane to the vanquished. He was a constant terror to the enemies of his king and country " ; and that is a very good sort of epitaph ; moreover—unlike many such effusions, recording amiable or heroic characteristics of the dead which few had been able to recognise in the living—it is a true one. If not always victorious —and a probably true story, presently to be narrated, appears to point to one instance, at least, in which he and his antagonist parted indecisively—he was, at any rate, never beaten ; and his conduct and character obtained for him, from a brave seaman and fighter of his own stamp, who sailed under him, the epithet, " that great hero, Fortunatus Wright " ; the actual words, by the way, are " that great but unfortunate hero," and herein is an allusion, no doubt, to some very ungenerous treatment meted out to Wright by foreign authorities, and also to his unknown, and probably tragic, fate.

We have but little information concerning his early manhood ; there is not, indeed, any evidence to hand of even the approximate date of his birth. Smollett, in his " History of England," alludes to Wright's exploits, and describes him as " a stranger to a sea-life," until he took to privateering in the Mediterranean ; but it is not easy to see upon what grounds the historian bases such an assumption.

Fortunatus Wright was, as we have seen, the son of a sea-captain of no ordinary stamp, and the probability is that he would be brought up in his father's calling—a probability which becomes, practically, a certainty when we reflect that, immediately upon assuming the position of privateer commander, he displayed a consummate skill in seamanship, combined with remarkable tactical powers in sea-fighting, which elicited the enthusiastic admiration of his subordinates ; and these qualifications are not acquired on land.

No ; Fortunatus Wright was undoubtedly trained as a seaman, and very possibly a privateersman ; but it appears that, somewhere about the year 1741, having previously retired from the sea, and settled in Liverpool as a shipowner, he realised his business, and went to reside abroad ; and in 1742 we come across news of him in Italy.

Mr. (afterwards Sir) Horace Mann, at that time British Resident at the Court of Florence, in a letter to his friend Horace Walpole—with whom he kept up an enormous correspondence—relates how he had had complaints concerning the violent conduct of Mr. Wright at Lucca. It appears that our friend, travelling in that part of Italy, with introductions to some of the nobility, presented himself one day at the gates of Lucca, never doubting but that, as a respectable and peaceably disposed person, he would immediately be admitted. He had not reckoned, however, with the particular form of " red tape " which prevailed there. He had upon him a pair of pistols ; and, upon being informed that the surrender

of these weapons was the condition of being permitted
to pass the gates, his English choler immediately
rose against what appeared to him to be a tyrannical
and unnecessary proceeding ; and his natural instinct
being—as it always is in fighting men of his stamp—
rather to beat down and override opposition than to
yield to it, disregarding the serious odds against him
—twenty soldiers and a corporal *versus* Fortunatus
Wright—he presented one of the offending pistols
at the guard, and clearly indicated that the first man
who endeavoured to arrest him would do so at the
cost of his life. This was very awkward ; no one
cared to be the first victim of the " mad Englishman,"
who was evidently a man of his word, and how it
might have ended nobody knows, had there not
appeared upon the scene a superior officer—a colonel
—with thirty more soldiers. Mr. Wright was thereupon persuaded that the odds were too heavy even
for a " mad Englishman," and was escorted to his
hotel by this imposing bodyguard, being there made
a prisoner while representations were made to the
English Ambassador.

Fortunately, one of the Luccese noblemen to whom
he had an introduction intervened, undertaking that
no harm should result ; and on the morning of the
fourth day, at the early hour of four, the irate Englishman was informed that since he had been so
daring as to endeavour to enter the town by force of
arms, it was therefore ordered that he should forthwith leave the State, and never presume to enter it
again without leave from the Republic ; and that

post-horses, with a guard to see him over the border, were waiting at the door.

"He answered a great deal," says Sir Horace Mann, "not much to the purpose"; and so was seen safely out of Lucca, with his pistols in his pocket, we may presume, swearing at the unreasonableness of Italians and their laws. He continued, however, to reside in Italy, and was living at Leghorn when, in 1744, war was declared with France; and then there came to Fortunatus Wright the imperative call to return to a seafaring life.

The war had not been long in progress before the English merchants in Leghorn began to suffer immense annoyance and loss from the depredations of the French privateers which swarmed upon the coast of Italy. Their trade was stifled, their ships compelled to remain in port, or almost inevitably captured if they ventured out; apparently there were not men-of-war available for escort, and the situation became unbearable.

When men have come to the conclusion that things are past bearing they look about for some drastic remedy, and in this instance Mr. Wright was the remedy; Mr. Wright, living quietly in Leghorn, with his wife and family, but with his sea-lore available at the back of his mind, and, for all we know, the love of the salt water tugging at his heart-strings—sailors are made that way. Why not fit out a privateer, and place Mr. Wright in command? The suggestion may, indeed, have come from him in the first instance; at any rate, no time was lost. There was a vessel available, to wit the *Fame*, a staunch brigantine. We have no precise details of her tonnage and force, but she was undoubtedly an efficient craft for the purpose, and Wright speedily demonstrated that he was an entirely fit and proper person to be placed in charge.

Carefully studying the winds of the Mediterranean, and the probable track of the enemy's privateers and merchant vessels, he had his plan of action matured by the time the ship was ready ; and this is how it is set forth by William Hutchinson, one of his officers, writing thirty years later :

" Cruising the war before last, in the employ of that great but unfortunate hero, Fortunatus Wright, in the Mediterranean Sea, where the wind blows generally either easterly or westerly—that is, either up or down the Straits—it was planned, with either of these winds that blew, to steer up or down the channels the common course, large or before the wind in the daytime without any sail set, that the enemy's trading ships astern, crowding sail with this fair wind, might come up in sight, or we come in sight of those ships ahead that might be turning to windward ; and at sunset, if nothing appeared to the officer at the masthead, we continued to run five or six leagues, so far as could then be seen, before we laid the ship to for the night, to prevent the ships astern coming up and passing out of sight before the morning, or our passing those ships that might be turning to windward ; and if nothing appeared to an officer at the masthead at sunrise, we bore away and steered as before. And when the wind blew across the channel, that ships could sail their course either up or down, then to keep the ship in a fair way ; in the daytime to steer the common course, under the courses and lower staysails, and in the night under topsails with the courses in the brails, with all things as ready as possible for action, and to take or leave what we might fall in with."

Before many months had elapsed the soundness of these tactics, and the sagacity with which Wright determined what to take and what to leave, were very conspicuous.

In the months of November and December, 1746, the *Fame* had to her credit no fewer than eighteen prizes, one of which was a privateer, of 200 tons, with 20 guns and 150 men, fitted out by the French factories on the coast of Caramania, with the express object of putting a stop to the inconveniently successful cruising of Fortunatus Wright, who, however, turned the tables upon her, sending her as a prize into Messina. The Frenchmen, to avoid being taken prisoners, had run her on shore and decamped ; but the English captain was not going to be deprived of the prize-money which he and his men had justly earned, so they set to work and got the vessel afloat again, in order that she might be produced and duly condemned as " good prize."

Wright's success, both in fighting and in the pursuit of traders, infuriated the French, and particularly the Knights of St. John, in Malta, where there was very hot antagonism between the two factions—the

9

French and Spaniards on one side, and the Austrians
and English on the other.

When Wright kept on sending in his prizes the
Austrians would " chaff " the French. " Here's another
of your ships coming in, under the care of Captain
Wright," we can imagine them saying. Some
duels were fought by angry officers, and eventually the French sent urgent representations to Marseilles, and a vessel was fitted out and manned with
the express object of humiliating the English by
capturing the *Fame* and putting a stop to Wright's
victorious career.

In due course the privateer put in an appearance
at Malta. She was of considerably superior force to
the *Fame*, the captain was a man of repute as a seaman
and fighter, and was entertained by the French, who
patted him on the back and sent him forth to conquer.

But it is never safe to pat a man on the back for
prospective triumphs.

As the days passed excitement and expectation
became intense ; the points of vantage, whence a
good view of incoming vessels could be obtained, were
thronged with anxious spectators of both factions ; and
we may suppose that there was a considerable amount
of mutual banter, not in the best of good-humour.

At length two vessels were sighted ; as they approached it was seen that one was towing the other.
Then the French privateer was recognised, and it
was noticed that the other vessel, in tow, was very
much knocked about. While conjecture was ripening
into triumphant conviction up went the colours—

French colours! That decided the question—the career of the obnoxious Wright—" ce cher Wright," sarcastically—was at an end, and the enthusiastic Frenchmen shook hands and embraced, and waved hats and handkerchiefs to the victor.

There was one delightful characteristic of " ce cher Wright," however, which they had failed to realise—he was possessed of a very keen sense of humour. In spite of the shattered condition of the staunch little *Fame*, she had come off victorious, and Wright had very naturally placed her in tow of the larger vessel, which he himself was navigating, her crew his prisoners of war ; and seeing the crowded ramparts from afar, this agreeable but unsuspected little trait of his had displayed itself in the hoisting of French colours.

Then, when the cheering and embracing was at its climax, as the vessels rounded the fort, the English colours sailed up to the peak, with the French below !

And then—well, then we may imagine that there was the making of some more duels !

Fortunatus Wright was no mere filibustering swashbuckler, like so many other privateer commanders who, as we have seen, brought their calling into sad disrepute ; nor was he a man to be intimidated by his crew into committing any unlawful act for the sake of plunder ; but he was very tenacious of his rights, and on more than one occasion came to serious loggerheads with high authorities ; very much, eventually, to his cost.

In December 1746, while reports were going home of his numerous captures, he overhauled and seized a French vessel, on a voyage from Marseilles to Naples, having on board the servants and all the luggage and belongings of the Prince of Campo Florida. The French skipper produced a pass, from no less a person than King George II. of England, by which these persons and goods should be exempt from molestation by English cruisers ; but there was a flaw in this document, for the name of the ship was not entered upon it. " All very well," said Wright, " but how am I to know that King George intended this ship to go free ? She is not named on the safe-conduct " ; and into Leghorn she went as a prize, prince's servants, baggage, and all, to the horror of the British Consul, and to the great disgust of the Prince of Campo Florida ; nor would Wright listen to the remonstrances of the Consul, maintaining that he was technically justified in his action ; and there was undoubtedly some ground for this contention. However, the British Minister persuaded him to refer the matter to the Admiral commanding on the station, by whose adverse decision Wright loyally abided, and the vessel was released accordingly.

It was a much more serious affair when, in 1747, he fell out with the Turkey Company—officially known as " The Company of English Merchants trading to the Levant Sea "—a very wealthy and powerful organisation, jealous of its rights, and somewhat perturbed, moreover, at this particular period, by the falling off in its returns ; so that it was exceedingly annoying to find Turkish goods being seized by Captain Wright on board French ships.

There were two vessels in question, and the English Consul at Leghorn received orders from home to investigate the business. With his previous experience of the privateer captain's stiffness and command of technical knowledge of prize law, the Consul, we may be sure, did not anticipate an easy acquiescence in any suggestions he might make ; and, in fact, Wright's reply was a very decided refusal to admit that he was in fault. He said that both ships had a French pass, hailed from Marseilles, and hoisted French colours ; and one of them offered a stout resistance before she struck. " For these reasons I brought them to Leghorn, and have had them legally condemned in the Admiralty Court, by virtue of which sentence I have disposed of them and distributed the money."

Quite an unassailable position, one would imagine ; but the irate Governors of the Turkey Company were able to procure, by some means or other, an order from the English Government that Turkish cargoes in French vessels were to be exempt from capture. Upon this order being communicated to the privateer captains and Admiralty Courts in the Mediterranean, it was expected that Wright would refund the prize-money ; but he, very properly, as it appears, refused to admit that such an order could be retrospective— he had the money, and meant to keep it ; and then there was trouble. Orders were sent from England to have him arrested and sent home ; the Italian authorities obligingly caught him and locked him up, refusing, with singular and gratuitous crookedness, to yield him up to consular jurisdiction—and there he remained in prison at Leghorn for six months, when he was at length handed over to the Consul. Wright had, however, had enough of prison, and, upon giving bail to answer the action in the High Court of Admiralty, he was set at liberty.

The action appears to have dragged on for two or three years, without result—at any rate, Captain Wright never refunded the money, and one cannot help feeling gratified at his success. He wrote, in June 1749, a long letter to the Consul in vindication of his right, which concludes as follows : " They attacked me at law ; to that law I must appeal ; if I have acted contrary to it, to it I must be responsible ; for I do not apprehend I am so to any agent of the Grand Signior, to the Grand Signior himself, or to any other Power, seeing I am an Englishman and acted under a commission from my prince " ; surely a most logical, and certainly a most dignified attitude.

Peace restored, Wright engaged in commerce, in partnership, apparently, with William Hutchinson. They fitted out as a trader an old 20-gun vessel— the *Lowestoft*—which made several voyages to the West Indies—Wright continuing to reside at Leghorn.

CHAPTER X

FORTUNATUS WRIGHT—*continued*

IN 1755 it became apparent that a renewal of hostilities between France and England could not be long delayed ; and the staunch little *Fame* not being again available, Wright had a vessel built for him at Leghorn—quite a small vessel, which he named the *St. George*.

The Tuscan authorities were, however, in spite of declared neutrality, very strongly in sympathy with France, and they did not regard Captain Wright's little ship-building venture with any favour ; in fact, they instituted a minute supervision over all English vessels in the port, and naturally, knowing his reputation, they paid particular attention to Wright's little craft ; and thereby they stimulated that sense of humour which he had previously exhibited at Malta.

Humbly begging for precise information as to the force he was permitted, as a merchant vessel, to take on board, he was informed, after some deliberation, that he must limit himself to four small guns and a crew of five-and-twenty, and the authorities kept a very sharp eye upon him to see that he complied. Not in the least disconcerted, Wright displayed the greatest anxiety not to exceed the limit, and even suggested that guard-boats should be kept rowing round his ship, as a precautionary measure ; one would imagine that these Tuscan magnates could have had but little sense of humour ! Finally, before sailing, Wright obtained from the Governor a certificate to the effect that he had complied with all requirements.

Armed with this, he put to sea on July 28th, 1756, in company with four merchant vessels, with valuable cargoes, bound for England. In their anxiety to prevent any irregularities on board the *St. George*, the port authorities had overlooked the lading of these vessels, which carried a proper armament and a large accession of men for the former !

In spite of his astuteness, Wright nearly got into a mess ; for the authorities had apparently given timely notice to the French that Wright's little squadron would be worth attention, and that he could offer but a feeble resistance, and a vessel had been fitted out with the express purpose of waylaying the *St. George* : those little incidents at Malta had not been forgotten, we may be sure. This vessel, a large zebeque—that is to say, a vessel with three masts, each carrying a huge three-cornered sail, probably a fast sailer, and very efficient at beating to windward —carried, according to *The Gentleman's Magazine* of August 1756, sixteen guns of considerable size, besides swivels and a full supply of small arms, with a crew of 280 men. She had been waiting off the port for some time, and her captain had been heard to ask in Leghorn, " When is Captain Wright coming out ? He has kept me waiting a long time already." No wonder he was impatient, for it is said that the French king had promised knighthood and a handsome pension for life to the man who should bring Wright into France, *alive or dead* ; while the merchants of Marseilles had posted up " on 'Change " the offer of double the value of Wright's vessel to her captor. Here were nice pickings, indeed ! And these offers afford in themselves a pretty good indication of the Englishman's personality ; he was, indeed, a terror to the enemies of his country.

Sailing out from Leghorn in the hot summer weather, Wright had to make what seamen term an offing, before he could set about transhipping his guns and men ; and before he had got half-way through with it, the zebeque, bristling with cannon and crowded with men, was sighted, bearing down with the confidence assured by vast superiority of force.

Fortunatus Wright saw her coming, and measured the decreasing distance, calculating the time which remained for him to prepare with a cool and critical eye, while his men worked like giants ; and, when all was done, he could mount but twelve guns, including the four pop-guns which he had been permitted to ship in port : while his crew—a medley of half a dozen nationalities, who had never worked together —numbered seventy-five all told.

Hastily telling off his men to their stations, and

leaving his four traders lying to in a cluster, Wright made sail for the Frenchman; the wind, we may conclude, must have been light or the latter would have been down upon him before. And now the royal favour and comfortable pension, the handsome donation from the Marseillaise merchants, must have loomed very large in the eyes of the French skipper. Even supposing, as would seem probable, that he was not altogether unaware of the operations of the Englishman, his vastly superior force, with his practised crew, should have placed the betting at three to one in his favour; but the layer of such odds would have failed to reckon with the forceful personality of Fortunatus Wright, which inspired his men with the conviction that, odds or no, they must win. When men go into action with that sort of spirit they invariably do win; nothing will stand against them.

Handling his ship with his customary skill, Wright manœuvred repeatedly to the disadvantage of his antagonist, while his rag-tag-and-bob-tail crew, standing to their guns with the utmost intrepidity, poured in such a hot fire that the French captain speedily realised that his only chance was to board and overwhelm the English by superior numbers; but when he got alongside he found them quite as handy with pikes and cutlasses as with guns, and a desperate minority, which is not going to acknowledge itself beaten, soon daunts the hearts of a superior force. The French were repulsed with great slaughter, and, after some further attention from the guns of the gallant little *St. George*, the enemy hauled off, and

ran, having suffered such serious damage as rendered
their vessel almost unseaworthy. Wright followed,
but, seeing another Frenchman threatening his convoy,
he returned to their protection, sent them back into
Leghorn, and anchored there himself on the following
day. According to the account in *The Gentleman's
Magazine*, the French ship lost her captain, lieutenant, lieutenant of Marines, and 88 men killed and
70 men wounded.

No sooner had the gallant Wright cast anchor in
Leghorn, than he realised that he had landed in a
nest of hornets. The authorities were furious at the
failure of their schemes, and the clever fashion in
which Wright had hoodwinked them. He was ordered
to bring his vessel to the inner harbour, or she would
be brought in by force. He refused, and two vessels
of vastly superior force were placed alongside his.
He appealed to Sir Horace Mann, and there was a fine
battle of words between him and the Tuscans, the
latter alleging that Wright had deceived them as to
his force, and had fought in their waters ; and they
were very angry also that he should have dared to
refuse to take his vessel inside the mole. To all of
which Sir Horace very properly replied that—well,
that it was a parcel of lies, though he put it in the
language of diplomacy ; and he flourished the Governor's certificate in their faces, which made them feel
very sick indeed—having no sense of humour.

A couple of months elapsed without either side
giving way ; and then the problem was solved by
the appearance of two powerful English men-of-war ;

to wit, the *Jersey*, of 60 guns, commanded by Sir William Burnaby, and the *Isis*, of 50 guns. Sir William explained politely to the authorities that he was under orders from the Admiral (Sir Edward Hawke) to convoy any English vessels which might be there, and also to release the *St. George*. To the Governor's protest the English captain replied that he had his orders, and intended to carry them out, if necessary, by force ; and so the little fleet of English vessels took their departure in a few days, and Wright was free to resume his operations.

In a little while, having taken some more prizes, he put into Malta, only to find that French influence was there as potent as at Leghorn. He was not permitted to buy necessary stores for his crew, and when he took on board a number of English seamen, who had been landed there from ships taken by French privateers, he was compelled to send them on shore again ; and so he went to sea again, on October 22nd, 1756.

Twenty-four hours later a big French privateer, of 38 guns, sailed with the intention of eating him up ; but, according to the account of one Captain Miller, of the English vessel *Lark*, " When the great beast of a French privateer came out Wright played with him, by sailing round him and viewing him, just to aggravate him, as Wright sailed twice as fast as him."

Of the further exploits of Fortunatus Wright there is but little definite account. Early in 1757 the Italian authorities, realising that they had, by their duplicity and anti-English rancour, done their trade an infinity of harm, undertook, on the representation of Sir Horace Mann, to observe a strict neutrality in future; and thereupon Sir Horace wrote to Wright that he might bring his prizes into Leghorn. But he was compelled to rescind this permission; whatever else they might be prepared to yield, they could not stomach Wright!

In July 1757, after lamenting the injury to trade caused by French privateers, etc., Sir Horace Mann continues: " A few stout privateers, as in the last war, would totally prevent this. . . . Captain Wright, of the *St. George* privateer, did great service of this kind in the beginning of the war; but it is feared by some circumstances, and by his not having been heard of for some months, that he foundered at sea. Several prizes made by him have lain some months at Cagliari in Sardinia, waiting for an opportunity to get with safety to Leghorn."

And so this great man disappears; his father's tombstone holds the sentence already recorded, inscribed, no doubt, at the instigation of his children; but neither filial piety nor national esteem could avail to place the legend, " Here lies Fortunatus Wright." His place of rest remains, " unmarked but holy." Mr. Smithers, in his " History of the Commerce of Liverpool," says: " Tradition tells that he became a victim to political interests." This is possible, for he was well hated, as is usual, by those who had injured him; but it appears more probable that he was lost at sea.

In connection with the career of this fine Englishman, it is impossible to omit some reference to a romantic tale which appears in *The Gentleman's Magazine* for August 1757. The story is told, without preface or explanation, as it is alleged to have been narrated by the hero of the adventure, and evidently refers to a period ten or eleven years previously to its publication, when the *Fame* was afloat. It is, as has been stated, a most romantic tale, but by no means an incredible one : and the specific allusion to Fortunatus Wright, which renders it of interest in this volume, also constitutes a certain guarantee of genuineness.

Selim, the son of a Turkish grandee, on a voyage to Genoa, was captured by a Spanish corsair, and eventually sold as a slave to a young Moor at Oran, in Barbary. Here he suffered many cruel hardships, but after a time there appeared upon the scene a beautiful girl, cousin to Selim's master, and destined, according to family arrangements, to be his wife. The lovely Zaida had, however, like other young women of all ages, her own ideas about the sort of man she favoured. Being kind and pitiful by nature, she exerted herself to mitigate the sorrows of her cousin's slaves, discovered that Selim was of superior birth, and fell in love with him. All this is told at great length ; the upshot was that the lovers escaped together, and got on board a French privateer, together with a Swede, also a captive. Then they were informed that the privateer " had orders to cruise near Malta, in order to take a bold Englishman called Fortunatus Wright, and, if the winds would permit, we should be landed in that island. . . . Ten days were passed before we obtained a sight of Malta, . . . when a signal was made for standing out to sea in pursuit of a ship which, upon a nearer view, was found to be the very privateer which the French captain had orders to take."

Then ensued a hot engagement, during which Selim remained below for some time, consoling and encouraging his lady-love until the issue became doubtful, when he felt impelled to take the Frenchman's part.

" Pretending to Zaida we were victorious, I sprang upon the deck, and, observing that the English endeavoured to board us ahead, I slew the first who attempted our deck, and, beckoning to the French to follow me, leapt on board the enemy's ship, unseconded by any excepting my Swedish fellow-captive, who, seeing me overpowered, leapt back and regained his ship. Thus was I made a prisoner, and my fair Moor left a prey to all the wretchedness of despair. After several vain attempts to board each other, the two ships parted ; the French steered towards France, and I was carried into Malta. The good captain, whose prisoner I was, observing my despondence, ordered me to be set free, though I had killed one of his men ; and when I informed him of my unhappy story, and my resolutions to go in quest of Zaida, he gave me 100 guineas, and advised me to sail for England ; ' where, though I am unhappily exiled from it,' said he, ' you will be generously treated, and will hear the fate of the French privateer.' "

Selim took this sound advice, backed by such a generous donation, and, after a two months' voyage, arrived in England, where the first thing he saw was the identical vessel in which his Zaida had been borne away from him : she had been captured and sent home.

The officer in charge lent a sympathetic ear to Selim's tale of woe, and, after some fruitless inquiries, " We landed at a fair town, on the banks of a small river called Avon ; and the captain, who had not drowned his humanity in the rough element on which he traded, conveyed me to the prison, where, after searching various apartments, at last I found my fair, afflicted Zaida lying on the ground, with her head on the lap of her women, and the Swede sitting near to guard her. As soon as she saw me her voice failed her ; I had almost lost her by an agony of astonishment and joy as soon as I had recovered her. Hours were counted ere she would believe her senses, and even days passed over us in which she sat with a silent admiration, and even still doubts whether all is real."

The reader is, of course, at liberty to share the doubts of the fair Zaida ; but it appears probable that the story is true with regard to the main incidents.

The remark attributed to Wright—which it is scarcely possible to imagine could have been invented by the narrator—that he was " unhappily exiled " from England appears to point to some complications at home to which there is no clue.

And so we must bid farewell to Fortunatus Wright, who, had he been an officer in the Royal Navy, might certainly have rivalled some of our most illustrious seamen in his exploits, and, in place of an unknown and nameless grave, have found his last resting-place in Westminster Abbey.

William Hutchinson, already alluded to as Wright's subordinate and subsequent partner, is justly entitled to some further notice. He was born at Newcastle-on-Tyne, in 1715, and commenced his sea-career at an early age as "cook, cabin-boy, and beer-drawer for the men" on board a collier. From this humble beginning he worked his way up, with varied fortune and a full share of the hardships which were so frequently the lot of seamen in those days. He was always apparently a strenuous, conscientious, and courageous man, and attained immense skill as a seaman. His first privateering experience was, as far as can be gathered, under Wright in the *Fame*, when he conceived that profound respect and admiration of his captain which is exhibited in his remarks, already quoted. It was probably during this time that an incident occurred which called for ready wit and pluck in order to avert disaster, not to say disgrace. Hutchinson may have been in command of a privateer at the time—1747—but it is more likely that he was with Wright, and in charge of the deck; and there were a number of French prisoners on board, the crews of three prizes, who were, perhaps somewhat rashly, permitted to be on deck, with full liberty, all at one time. Hutchinson had occasion—no doubt in connection with the scheme of cruising already described—to take all the canvas off the ship,

and, having clewed up everything, he sent all his men
aloft to furl sails. While they were so employed he
detected a movement among the prisoners which
appeared suspicious : one of the French captains was
going about among them, evidently inciting them to
some concerted action ; which, with all the English
crew aloft, might well have been entirely successful.
But they had not reckoned with the officer in charge.
With his hand in his pocket, clutching his pistol, but
not exhibiting it so as to precipitate violence, he
approached the French captain, and quietly told him
that instant death was his portion on the smallest
evidence of any attempt to capture the ship ; then,
hailing his own men, he bade them look sharp down
from aloft, and the danger was averted in a few minutes.
Nothing save undaunted courage, combined with
absolute outward calm, could have saved the situation ;
had Hutchinson appeared alarmed or flustered he
would have been lost ; and this incident, briefly and
modestly related by himself, affords a sure indication
of his character.

In 1757, after the war with France was renewed,
Hutchinson was in command of a fine privateer, the
Liverpool, named after the port from which she hailed,
in which he made several successful cruises. We are
told that " he would not permit the least article to
be taken from any of the French prisoners," from
which we may conclude that, as we should expect of
a man of his stamp, he was an honourable and strict
privateer commander, who was emphatically captain
of his ship, and insisted upon a high standard of duty.

One night he made a lamentable mistake. Continuing, after dark, the chase of a vessel which had been previously sighted, and was believed to be a French privateer, he came up with her and hailed her in *French*. The only reply was a tremendous and well-directed broadside, which did serious damage aloft, pierced the hull close to the waterline, and wounded no fewer than twenty-eight of the crew. Captain Hutchinson devoutly wished that he had stuck to his native tongue, instead of airing his French, for the vessel turned out to be his Majesty's ship *Antelope* !

Hutchinson did no more in the way of privateering after the year 1758. In the following year he was appointed principal water-bailiff and dockmaster of Liverpool, and held this post for nearly forty years. In 1777 he published a book entitled " A Practical Treatise on Seamanship," and justified—if it needed justification—this act by a verse under the frontispiece (a vessel under full sail), whether original or a quotation does not appear :

> Britannia's glory first from ships arose ;
> To shipping still her power and wealth she owes.
> Let each experienced Briton then impart
> His naval skill to perfect naval art.

He was certainly well qualified for the task, and the work is very full and complete, containing incidentally some yarns concerning his own experiences, and practical hints upon sundry subjects, as, for instance, the brewing of tea when at sea, without the

common adjuncts of teapot, cups and saucers, etc. :
put the tea-leaves into a quart bottle, filled with
fresh water, and well corked up, and boil it in the ship's
copper, along with the salt beef! Whether the salt
beef added to the virtue of the " brew " we do not
know ; probably the gallant and hardy skipper was
" tannin-proof " inside !

Hutchinson was a religious man apparently, in a
true sense, always seeking to discharge his duties in
accordance with the high standard thus derived. It
is related of him that, when his ship had foundered—
the date is not mentioned—upon one occasion, and he
and some of his shipmates were in danger of perishing
through hunger and thirst, they adopted the terrible
device of drawing lots as to which of them should die
and furnish the remainder with this ghastly means
of prolonging life. The lot fell upon Hutchinson ;
but, before the horrible act could be consummated, a
sail appeared, and they were rescued. Hutchinson, it
is said, observed the anniversary of this day with
strict devotions of thanksgiving for the remainder of
his life. Such recognition was certainly due ; but
how many sailors would so faithfully have rendered it ?

CHAPTER XI

GEORGE WALKER

IN the year 1745 some merchants of London fitted out three privateers—the *Prince Frederick*, 28 guns, 244 men, commanded by Captain James Talbot, who was in chief command ; the *Duke*, of 20 guns, 150 men, Captain Morecock ; and the *Prince George*, 20 guns, 134 men. This little squadron sailed from Cowes on June 2nd, and on the 7th a frightful disaster befell them, the *Prince George*, under circumstances not explained, capsizing and going down. These vessels were very heavily masted, and, if the weights were not carefully bestowed, a sudden squall when under full sail, with, perhaps, the lee gun-ports open, might easily be fatal. The unfortunate *Eurydice*, though of somewhat later construction, was of this type of vessel, and, as will be remembered, capsized off the Isle of Wight one Sunday afternoon, only two being saved out of the whole crew.

The Commodore contrived to save some twenty men from his unhappy consort ; and then proceeded, with the *Prince Frederick*, to cruise between the Azores and the banks of Newfoundland.

This cruise is remarkable for two things : its brevity and the richness of the prizes captured.

On July 10th three sails were seen, bearing west, and the two privateers immediately gave chase. These were the *Marquis d'Antin*, 450 tons, 24 guns, and 68 men, commanded by Magon Serpere ; the *Louis Erasmé*, 500 tons, 28 guns, and 66 men, commanded by Pedro Lavigne Quenell ; and the *Notre Dame de Deliverance*, 300 tons, 22 guns, and 60 men, commanded by Pedro Litant ; all three hailing from St. Malo. They were now returning from Lima ; and little did Talbot and his men suspect the riches they carried.

However, they chased, and the others kept their wind, paying little heed. At seven o'clock Talbot fired a shot at them, upon which they hoisted their colours and formed line. The *Duke*, to windward, attacked first ; Talbot afterwards engaged the *Marquis d'Antin* for three hours, when she struck, though the *Prince Frederick* was for a while between two fires, the *Louis Erasmé* getting on her bow. When the *Marquis d'Antin* surrendered the other attempted to flee, but was caught and captured. Meanwhile, Captain Morecock had been hotly engaged with the *Notre Dame de Deliverance*, which, however, realising that her consorts had struck, crowded sail and contrived to escape—the *Duke* being probably hampered by damage aloft.

The casualties were not heavy on either side, but the two French ships were dismasted.

Reaching Kinsale on July 30th, the news of the immense value of the prizes caused special care to be used ; they were escorted to Bristol by three men-

From an engraving by Ravenet after a painting by Brooking.

CAPTURE OF THE FRENCH ARMED SHIPS "MARQUIS D'ANTIN" AND "LOUIS ERASMÉ" BY THE "DUKE" AND "PRINCE FREDERICK" PRIVATEERS, UNDER CAPTAIN JAMES TALBOT, JULY 10, 1745.

P. 150]

of-war, and thence the treasure was conveyed to London in forty-five waggons. This tremendous cavalcade made its way through the city to the Tower, colours flying, bands playing, and a strong guard of bluejackets marching with it.

The amount of treasure may be imagined from the fact that each seaman's share came to £850; the officers, of course, receiving much larger sums, in proportion to their rank. The owners' share was not less than £700,000; and the Scottish rebellion—"the '45"—having just broken out, they offered the money as a loan to the Government.

Captain Talbot is said to have behaved with great kindness and generosity to his prisoners, permitting the officers to retain all their valuables and their swords, and presenting each seaman with twenty guineas when they were landed. The enemy, we are told, was most anxious to ransom the ships, but this, of course, was out of the question; and subsequently some of the crews revealed hiding-places in which considerable treasure was stowed in the "linings," or double sides, receiving a handsome present for their pains. Furthermore, in overhauling the cargo, the British seamen every now and then came across a "wedge of gold."

After this Commodore Talbot decided to remain on shore and enjoy his fortune; he joined the body of merchants, who determined to fit out another squadron, the command being entrusted to a man of remarkable character, whose career as a privateer captain we shall now proceed to trace.

Among eighteenth-century privateersmen there is no more honourable name than that of George Walker. He was, of course, a contemporary of Fortunatus Wright, and Sir William Laird Clowes, the eminent naval historian, very truly remarks of these two men that they "did as much to uphold British prestige at sea as any captains of the Royal Navy"; the case might, indeed, be put in stronger language, for there were unhappily a good many instances at this period, in which naval commanders cut a somewhat sorry figure, and Walker himself, as we shall see, was witness upon one occasion of a lack of zeal and enterprise—to put it mildly—on their part which was in striking contrast to the intrepidity and resource displayed by him upon every occasion.

Beyond casual, but invariably complimentary allusions in naval histories, we should have known but little of George Walker, had it not been for the industry of an ardent admirer, who served under him on nearly all his cruises, and subsequently wrote an account of them. The writer withholds both his name and his rank, and tells his story with great simplicity, prompted solely by his admiration of his former chief, and the desire of vindicating his name as a great seaman and a born leader of men; for Walker was, at that time, in gaol for debt, owing to some dispute with his owners, who do not appear to have treated him with the generosity due to so faithful a servant. This is the sordid side of privateering, which, as has been before remarked, is too much in evidence; we need not, however, concern ourselves overmuch with the question of George Walker's financial dealings with his principals ; he may, for all we know, have muddled his accounts, but we are prepared to go bail for his honesty of intention. There is abundant evidence of his character in this little book, and no one who reads it will entertain a doubt as to his absolute integrity.

The narrator, in his Introduction, dwells much upon Walker's unwillingness to have his exploits discussed or published. It was with the utmost difficulty that he was persuaded to sanction the publication of this book, and when, in accordance with his strict injunctions, the copy was submitted for his approval before going to the printer, his deletions disposed of nearly one-third of the matter ; " at which," says the writer, " I am not so much disobliged by the shortening of the performance as at the loss of real truths which would have illustrated the chief personage of my work. And though this account may speak to the modesty of the gentleman himself, yet it is so far paradoxical that it takes greatly from his merit. . . . I will only say of him herein, as Mr. Waller does of good writers :

> Poets lose half the praise they would have got,
> Was it but known what they discreetly blot."

Nothing appears to be known of George Walker's birth and early training, save that he served in the Dutch Navy, and was involved in some engagement with, probably, Mediterranean pirates.

In 1739 he was commander and part owner of the

ship *Duke William*, trading to Gibraltar and South Carolina ; and, with the view of being able to defend himself in case of attack, he obtained a letter of marque, and provided his vessel with twenty guns. His crew numbered only thirty-two : but, with characteristic forethought and resource, he shipped a quantity of seamen's clothing, in order, should occasion arise, to rig up dummies ; and this, according to his biographer, he actually did on the approach of a Spanish privateer of superior force, crowded with men : " setting up all the handspikes and other provided utensils, and dressing them in the marine clothes, and also exercising the boatswain's call in the highest notes, as is usual in king's ships." This done, Walker proceeded to prepare for the grim realities of action, should it be forced upon him, he and his crew, as they busied themselves clearing away the guns, etc., going into fits of laughter at the grotesque appearance of the row of dummies, standing stiff and motionless amidships.   All being ready, Walker, consistently maintaining his game of bluff, fired a shot across the bows of the Spaniard, which was to windward of him. This invitation to fight was not accepted, and, though the Spaniard hung on for a couple of days, he eventually disappeared ; so we must suppose that the toy seamen and the boatswain's whistle carried the day !

Arrived at his destination, Walker, while waiting for a cargo, offered his services to the colonial authorities to put an end to the ravages of two Spanish privateers, which were having it all their own way on the coast of North Carolina. His crew was increased by nearly one hundred men, and several gentlemen volunteered their services. The tidings of an English privateer being abroad appears to have been enough for the Spaniards: "We could fall in with nothing which would stay for us upon the seas"; an English vessel was easily retaken from the enemy, a shore battery destroyed, and there was no more trouble. Walker received a tremendous ovation on the conclusion of this service, all the influential persons in the colony offering to sign a request that he might be given command of a king's ship. Upon his declining this, they tendered him an immense piece of land if he would remain amongst them; but Walker preferred to stick to his ship, and sailed for Barbadoes, and thence for England, in company with three traders who placed themselves under his convoy.

The vessels parted company in a gale, which blew with such violence that the *Duke William* started some of her planks, and leaked like a sieve. Walker was laid up in his cabin, and was indeed so ill that the surgeon despaired of his life. Things went on from bad to worse: all the guns save two—retained for signalling purposes, by Walker's orders, issued from his bunk—were thrown overboard; the boat was with difficulty preserved from following them, Walker being carried up from below to remonstrate and command; and when a section of the crew, despite his orders, were preparing to desert in the boat—a very desperate venture—a sail appeared; their signals were seen and heard, and she bore down—

then, evidently suspecting a ruse by an armed vessel, she hastily hauled off. While the crew were gazing at one another in despair, Walker coolly gave orders to cut away the mizzen-mast instantly; after a momentary hesitation his order was obeyed, and the meaning of it was immediately obvious. Another gun being fired, the stranger, convinced by the crippled condition of the ship, returned to the rescue, and proved to be no stranger, but one of their convoy. The transhipment of Walker and his men was safely effected at immense risk, and they reached home in a sorry plight, this vessel proving almost as unseaworthy as the other. And there Walker was greeted with very unwelcome tidings : he had lost his ship, and his agents had suffered the insurance to lapse ; he was a ruined man.

Before entering upon his distinguished career as a privateer captain Walker commanded for eighteen months a vessel trading to the Baltic ; and, returning from his last trip in 1744, just after war was declared against the French, he again most successfully adopted a policy of " bluff." Having shipped a number of wooden guns, and otherwise disguised his vessel, being chased off the coast of Scotland by a privateer, and finding she had the heels of him, he tacked, hoisted ensign, jack, and man-of-war's pendant, and fired a gun, as much as to say, " Come on ; I'm waiting ! " The enemy did not wait, and Walker proceeded quietly upon his homeward voyage.

In this same year, 1744, two fine vessels were equipped as privateers by some London and Dartmouth owners, and Walker was offered command of the *Mars*, of 26 guns and 130 men, her consort being the *Boscawen*, a vessel of similar armament, but of larger tonnage and with a more numerous crew.

When two days out from Dartmouth they encountered a French king's ship, of force about equal to the *Boscawen*, and Walker, of course, immediately engaged her, justly considering that, with his consort, he would soon overpower her ; indeed, he would have attacked had he been cruising alone. The captain of the *Boscawen*, however, was quite a different sort of man, with a strong dislike of hard knocks. Instead of seconding Walker's attack, he held off out of range, letting drive once or twice a futile shot, which dropped far short ; so Walker was left to fight alone, and after a severe tussle, he and the Frenchman parted, both ships a good deal knocked about. While his crew were repairing damages Walker went on board the *Boscawen* to have a little talk with her skipper—whose name is not mentioned —" but was never heard to throw any censure publicly on his behaviour." Walker was always a gentleman, and an instinctive disciplinarian. No doubt he gave the other, in private, a slice of his mind, but, as we shall see, without any good result.

A month later, in December, at midnight, with a fresh breeze and thick rain, they suddenly found themselves close to two large vessels. They could hear the people on board talking excitedly, in French, and apparently in a state of alarm, and, judging from these signs that they were treasure ships, Walker and his consort hung on their heels. At eight o'clock next morning the weather cleared and the two strangers were revealed as French men-of-war, the one of 74 and the other of 64 guns ; which was exceedingly awkward for the two Englishmen. The Frenchmen were, however, both treasureships as well as men-of-war, being bound from the West Indies with cargoes valued at nearly four millions sterling, were not in good fighting trim, and were very anxious to get into Brest with their treasure, so it is quite probable that they would have gone on their way and left the two privateers alone. The captain of the *Boscawen*, however, did not wait to see what they would do ; directly he realised their force he crowded sail, and disappeared from the scene without even a parting greeting to his consort ; and, seeing only one enemy left, and this a small one, the 64-gun ship—the *Fleuron*—was sent in chase of the *Mars*, rapidly gaining upon her. " Gentlemen," said Walker, " I do not mean to be so rash as to attempt a regular engagement with so superior a force ; all I ask of you is, to confide in me and my orders, to get away, if possible, without striking ; and, be assured, I shall employ your assistance neither in revenge nor vainglory, nor longer than I think it of use to our design. The ship which pursues is certainly the best sailer of the enemy, by being ordered to the chase ; if, by good fortune, we bring down a topmast or yard, or hurt her rigging so as to retard her pursuit, we may entirely get clear."

So he hoisted his colours and opened fire with his

stern guns, the enemy replying with his bow-chasers by the space of over two hours. The *Mars*, however, was not a brilliant sailer, and by this time the 74— the *Neptune*—had crept up, so that she was almost between two fires. There was nothing for it but surrender. " Well, gentlemen," said Walker, smiling, " we don't strike to one ship only—haul down the colours ! " And so he went on board the *Fleuron* to surrender his sword and his privateer commission. The French captain was not as polite as he expected : " How dare you, sir," he asked, in excellent English, " in so small a ship, fire against a force like me ? "

" Sir," replied Walker, " if you will look at my commission you will find I had as good a right to fight as you ; and if my force had not been so inferior to yours I had shown you more civil treatment on board my ship "—which was a very good specimen of English politeness.

" How many men of yours have I killed ? " demanded the Frenchman.

" None at all, sir." " Then, sir, you have killed six of mine, and wounded several ; you fired pieces of glass."

This preposterous accusation was, of course, denied ; but it turned out that some missiles of a very unusual nature *had* been discharged from the *Mars*. The captain of one of the stern guns, realising that they must surrender, took about sixteen shillings from his pocket, saying that " sooner than the French rascals should plunder him of all he had in the world, he would first send it among them, and see what a bribe would do." So he wrapped his shillings up in a rag, crammed them into the gun, and sent them humming and whistling through the Frenchman's rigging, which no doubt gave rise to the glass theory—neither Frenchmen nor any one else could be expected to recognise the " ring " of a coin under the circumstances ! The facetious gunner was an Irishman.

Well, the *Mars* was captive, while the *Boscawen* had prudently escaped ; but this was not the end of the incident. The action took place on a Friday, and at daybreak on Sunday morning four large ships were sighted astern ; it did not require a long period of observation to realise that they were coming up pretty fast, and in a couple of hours they were recognised as English men-of-war. Then the Frenchmen began to regret that they had stopped to capture the privateer, instead of making the most of their way homeward with their treasure, which now appeared almost inevitably destined to become English treasure.

The captain of the *Fleuron*—who by this time had learned that his prisoner, though only captain of a privateer, was worthy of respect—discoursed to Walker in some bitterness on this subject, and added : " It is seldom any great accident happens from single causes, but by a chain or series of things ; thus, if we be here overcome, our loss will be owing to the waspishness of a single frigate, which would not cease fighting so long as it had a sting in its tail "—a remark which, if somewhat bitter, was appreciative.

The English squadron gained steadily, and the French officer in charge of the *Mars* put his helm up and ran to leeward, hoping to draw off one of the ships after him ; in which he was successful, the *Captain*, a 70-gun ship, giving chase, and eventually recapturing the *Mars*.

The other three ships were the *Hampton Court*, 70 guns, and the *Sunderland* and *Dreadnought*, each of 60 guns. The *Sunderland* lost a spar, and dropped astern, but the other two were nearly alongside the French ships by sunset, the *Dreadnought*, a poor sailer, being somewhat astern.

The French captain thereupon, seeing an action inevitable, politely requested Walker and his officers to go below. " Sir," said Walker, " I go off with great pleasure on the occasion, as I am now certain of my liberty ; and I hope to have the satisfaction of seeing you again in being."

He was not destined, however, to regain his liberty so easily, for these naval captains, what with faulty tactics and absolute want of zeal and enterprise, entirely bungled the whole business, and permitted the French ships to escape, treasure and all. The *Captain* was commanded by Captain Thomas Griffin, senior officer of the squadron, who detached himself to chase the *Mars*, and gave, as an excuse, when he was tried by court-martial, that he thought the *Mars* was the only man-of-war, and the two larger vessels her convoy. The court apparently accepted this flimsy story—although the *Captain* was nearer than the other ships, and no one else had any such notion— but the Service generally did not.

Captain Savage Mostyn, of the *Hampton Court*,

hung about the French ships without firing a shot, waiting for the *Dreadnought* to come up, instead of endeavouring to disable them aloft; and he also cut an extremely sorry figure at the court-martial; but his lame and almost incredible excuses were accepted. He was acquitted, and said to have " done his duty as an experienced good officer, and as a man of courage and conduct." There seemed to be a determination to let off everybody just then; but the public did not let off Mostyn, for when he sailed from Portsmouth a year later, still in command of the *Hampton Court*, it was to the cry of " All's well! There's no Frenchman in the way!"

Now, it is a sad thing to have to say all this of naval commanders; and still more humiliating to reflect that, had George Walker, master-mariner and privateer skipper, been in command of that squadron, no such fiasco would have occurred; but this is most undoubtedly true. Walker would have had those French treasure ships had he been in command of the *Hampton Court*, as surely as he was then a prisoner on board one of them, watching with shame and disgust the paltry tactics of his countrymen, and compelled subsequently to listen to the boastful and disparaging comments of the Frenchmen.

Arrived at Brest, the Englishmen had no cause to complain of their treatment. Walker had by this time so ingratiated himself with the captain of the *Fleuron*, that the latter acceded to his request that the crew of the *Mars* might be landed at once, on the day after their arrival, and might receive every possible consideration until they could be exchanged ; and he resisted strenuously Walker's request that he might go and see personally to the comfort of his men, begging to know in what he had fallen short, to be thus deprived of his esteemed company. Walker politely insisting, the French captain gave him a most flattering letter of introduction to the Governor, who liberated the English captain and all his officers on parole, and treated them handsomely in every respect.

They left the *Fleuron* none too soon. On the following day, while Walker was in the act of writing to the captain to beg him to send him his letter of credit, which was in a tin box with his commission, people came running in crying that the *Fleuron* had blown up. It was, indeed, too true ; and the catastrophe was entirely due to the gross carelessness of the gunner, who, landing the powder, left some four or five barrels in the magazine for saluting purposes, and did not even have the loose powder, spilt in emptying the cartridges, swept up under his own eye. Some stupid fellows, engaged afterwards in this work, took a decrepit old lantern down with them ; the handle broke, the flame ignited the loose powder, and that was the end of the *Fleuron* ; she burnt to the water's edge, and then went down, treasure and all ; and the guns having been left loaded—it seems almost incredible, but we have the account of an eye-witness—kept going off at intervals, preventing the approach of boats, etc., which might have saved many of the crew. Walker had to mourn the loss of his friend, the courteous and generous captain, and also that of his letter of credit—a serious temporary inconvenience.

We must not dwell in detail upon the sojourn of Walker and his crew in France. Their exchange was arranged in a few weeks, Walker, by his courage, tact, and ability smoothing over every difficulty as it arose, and making many friends in the process. Indeed, the simple and straightforward account by the narrator of his cheerful and undaunted bearing under sundry incidental trials which arose, from lack of means, etc., fills one with admiration of the man. They arrived at Weymouth on February 28th, 1745, and Walker lost no time in reporting himself to his owners at Dartmouth, who, though they had heard, through the recaptured *Mars*, of his whereabouts, and had sent him fresh letters of credit, scarcely expected him so soon.

The *Mars* being repurchased, the two vessels were again fitted out for a cruise, the very cautious captain of the *Boscawen* being replaced by Walker's first lieutenant, who, however, was placed in command of the *Mars*. Walker selected the *Boscawen* as his own command, as being the finer vessel and the better sailer ; she was a French-built ship, a prize in the last war, mounting 28 nine-pounders. Walker increased her armament to 30 guns, twelve and nine-pounders, and shipped a crew of 314 men. Thus she was, as the writer says, " perhaps the most complete privateer ever sent from England " ; but she was not as good as she looked, and Walker had cause afterwards to regret that he had increased her weights, for she was structurally what an English shipwright would describe as a " slopped " ship ; cheaply built, and inefficiently fastened.

However, she was good enough for some brilliant work, with her able skipper and an enthusiastic crew, in the shipping of which there had been a passage of arms between Walker and one Taylor, captain of an Exeter privateer then fitting out, who found Walker in such favour that he could not obtain a full crew ; so he had recourse to some very underhand devices to decoy the *Boscawen's* men, one of whom, with address worthy of his captain, led him into a trap and made a complete fool of him, eventually taking nearly all the men he had succeeded in shipping to make up the *Boscawen's* crew ; while Captain Walker interviewed the owner—whose brother he had been instrumental in getting exchanged in France—and told him what he thought of him and his methods—and no one could talk straighter then Walker, when he found it necessary. There were some very amusing incidents in connection with these doings, which, however, must be omitted for lack of space ; we must get to sea again.

Without waiting for the *Mars*, Walker put to sea on April 19th, 1745, and a month later fell in with the privateer *Sheerness*, Captain Parnell, and kept company during the night. At daybreak, being then fifty miles west of the Lizard, they sighted eight vessels, evidently in company, and gave chase. The *Boscawen* left the other astern, and about nine o'clock the enemy formed line, and were soon made out to be armed vessels, awaiting attack. This was odds enough to discourage most men, and the *Sheerness* being hopelessly astern, no one imagined that Walker intended engaging, though all preparation was made for action.

Reading some suspense and anxiety in the faces of his officers, Walker called them together and addressed them : " Gentlemen, I hope you do not think the number of prizes before us too many. Be assured, by their being armed, they have something on board them worth defending ; for I take them to be mer-chantmen with letters of marque, and homeward bound. Without doubt we shall meet with some opposition, in which I have not the least doubt of your courage ; but I see we must here conquer also by a mastership of skill. Be cool, and recollect every man his best senses ; for, as we shall be pressed on all sides, let every man do his best in engaging the enemy he sees before him, and then one side need not fear nor take thought for the other. In a word, gentlemen, if you give me your voice for my leading you on, I pawn my life to you, I will bring you off victorious."

Was ever a more masterly speech from a chief to his subordinates ? But one reply was possible ; the men went to their quarters and the *Boscawen* sailed on into the thick of the enemy's line, strict orders being issued that, whatever fire they might receive, not a shot was to be returned until the captain gave the word. There were, unfortunately, sixty men sick, and these, with the exception of three, crawled on deck to render what assistance they could, or at least to see the fun.

Steering straight for the largest vessel, though already considerably damaged aloft by the fire of the others, Walker delivered his broadside, and then the enemy got round him, two on either side, one ahead and one astern ; the other two apparently decamped, and took no part in the action. The ship astern, after attempting to rake the *Boscawen*, was so roughly handled by her stern guns that she hauled off, and struck her colours. The fight was continued with the remaining five for the space of an hour ; and the writer asserts that it was maintained on board the *Boscawen* without any confusion or disorder, the men, under the officers' orders, banging away at whatever happened to be in front of their guns, " without fear or thought for the others." The flagship struck, and sank ten minutes later ; the remaining four stuck to it, hoping yet to subdue the sorely battered *Boscawen* ; but Walker's men remembered his pledge to them, and were resolved that he should not be stultified. In another half-hour every flag was down, and the *Sheerness*, at length coming up, chased and captured one of the runaways ; so the " bag " was one sunk and six captured.

The enemy is stated to have had 113 killed and drowned, while the *Boscawen's* casualties amounted only to one killed and seven wounded. The writer ascribes this comparative immunity to a protection, a raised bulwark, " man-high," of elm planking,

which Walker had caused to be erected, with a step
on which the marines could mount to fire, and stand
down to load ; and he says the elm did not splinter,
but kept out bullets, and closed up round the holes
made by shot.   With due allowance for this, however,
the Frenchmen must have made very wretched practice ; they were probably unpràctised and undisciplined merchant crews ; but it was a brilliant affair.
The vessels were all homeward bound " Martinico
men," as Walker had surmised, provided with letters
of marque.

An old lady, a person of some distinction, a passenger
in the commodore's ship, was picked up, floating
about on a bale of cotton ; she did not know how
she had got there.   The commodore was also rescued,
and Walker gave them the use of his cabin, and fitted
out the old lady with " a silk nightgown, some fine
linen waistcoats, cambric night-caps, etc., in which
she appeared a kind of hermaphrodite in dress " ;
a droll figure, indeed !   But a privateer skipper can
scarcely be expected to be provided with requisites
for such an occasion.   The poor old lady had a tragic
tale to tell, for her daughter, a young girl, went down
with the ship ; and her account of the scene between
decks, where she and her daughter retired during the
action, is ghastly enough : " Hither they brought
the poor bleeding sailors, one after another, without
legs, without arms, roaring with their pains, and
laid in heaps to be butchered anew by the surgeon,
in his haste and despatch of cure or death.   Here
several of the objects died at our feet.   Thus sur-

rounded by the ghastly prospect, all at once death himself came breaking in upon us, through the side of the ship ; cut down the surgeon and one of his mates, and shattered the whole medicine-chest in pieces. Here was a total suspension of all relief to the poor wounded wretches ; death coming, as it were, to reinforce his own orders and stop every means or effort to prevent him."

Arrived with his shattered vessel and equally dismantled prizes at King's Road, Bristol, Walker, reporting proceedings to the Admiralty, received a handsome congratulatory letter from the Secretary.

Sailing once more in July, Walker captured in August a vessel, the *Catharina*, which he subsequently bought as a tender, naming her the *George* ; and in the following month he found himself, as was so often the case in privateers, at loggerheads with his crew over a vessel—a Dutchman—which he overhauled, and, being satisfied that her cargo was not contraband, dismissed her. The crew, after grumbling among themselves, assembled on deck while Walker was at supper, demanding to see him.

He and his officers armed themselves and went on deck, and faced the three hundred angry men, who required to know why the Dutchman was not good prize. Walker's reply was admirable : " This is not the way to ask me. I am willing that the meanest man in the ship shall be satisfied of my conduct, but I will give that satisfaction in my own way, and not be called to account by you. I am sorry, indeed, that it should ever be said of me that

I was obliged to take up arms against my own people, in defence of conduct which can be so easily supported by words only. It will be a pain to me to reflect upon it, as long as I live, and a blot on the character I imagined I had gained. I am very willing to explain to you what rights we have over Dutch vessels, but I shall choose my own time for doing it ; and every man who does not instantly separate to his duty, when I give the word, I shall treat him as an associate in a mutiny."

Two of the men called out that it would be too late to explain when the chase was out of sight. " Bring those men aft, and put them in irons," said Walker ; and he was obeyed. Next morning he gave them a lecture on prize law and discipline, to which they listened in all submission.

CHAPTER XII

GEORGE WALKER—*continued*

IT was towards the end of this year—1745—after a visit to Madeira—where some of the crew got into trouble over a very foolish practical joke, putting a handful of soot in the holy-water fount at a church door—and a short cruise off the Azores, that Walker and his men were called upon to face death in a new form : not amidst the interchange of cannon-shot, the rattle of musketry, the clash of steel, but the gradual encroachment of the sea in a desperately leaky ship, threatening day by day to engulf them.

It was upon this occasion that George Walker displayed the noblest qualities, and by his fortitude, tact, and unwearying exertions kept the ship afloat and saved the lives of all on board.

The story is a thrilling one. The beginning of disaster was on November 12th, when the *Duke of Bedford* privateer had been for some days in company, and some hard gales had been experienced, the wind again increasing to a gale upon this day, with heavy rain. The mainyard, which should have been held aloft in its place by chain-slings, had been left, through carelessness, hanging by the tackle which was used to raise and lower it—termed the "geers"—and, upon the men being sent up to furl the mainsail, the strap supporting the upper block gave way, and the yard—the heaviest in the ship—came down, with all the men upon it. Strangely enough, no one was injured or thrown overboard ; but the narrator alleges that the shock of the yard falling shook up the ship, so as to open some of her joints. It may as well be pointed out, for the information of the non-professional reader, that no such result had any right to ensue in a ship with any pretension to being decently built ; the utmost damage should have been, perhaps, broken bulwarks, and probably some injury to the spar itself. However, whether by coincidence or from the vessel being really so shaky, she commenced, after this, to make water too freely, and two days later alarmingly, so that two pumps constantly going would scarcely keep her clear. The wind and sea increased, the ship laboured more and more, her planks working and seams opening everywhere. She was then off the Azores, some fifteen hundred miles from the Land's End, and Walker steered a course for the south of Ireland, intending to finish the cruise in those waters. On the 17th, however, the water increased enormously, and the officers, thoroughly alarmed, signed a petition to Walker to make for the nearest port. After some discussion, and a most disheartening report from the carpenter, he gave his consent, reminding them that his honour and his duty to the owners obliged him to speak every ship he sighted ; and recommending them to endeavour in every way to encourage the crew and keep their spirits up.

Vain endeavour! a day or two of constant pumping revealed the fact that all the power available would not keep the water under, and a large number of men had to be kept incessantly baling—dipping up the water in buckets from the hold, passing it from hand to hand, and emptying it on the deck, upon which the pumps also discharged, so that the scuppers would scarcely suffice to keep the deck free ; water below, water on deck, and a winter gale howling through the rigging, the ship labouring and lurching helplessly under reduced canvas. Almost mechanically the weary crew took their turns at pumping, baling, handling the ship ; despair began to grow upon them, and, after a week of toil and slow progress, it came to Walker's knowledge, through some men whom he could trust, that there was a plot to seize the arms, take the boats by force, with as many as they would hold, and leave the rest to perish. He responded with a counter-mine. At a given signal the officers, already disposed near where the arms were kept, suddenly threw every weapon overboard, except a sufficient number to arm themselves, thus turning the tables upon the astonished conspirators, who now imagined that they would receive the treatment they had designed for others ; but Walker, humane and sympathetic as he was brave, did not speak an angry word to them : " I sincerely forgive you your folly and rashness," he said, " which came rather from your fears than from deliberate disobedience. If you will now exert yourselves, and stick to the pumping and baling, we shall save the ship ; if not, we go to the bottom. And remember, that I have now the power to provide for myself and the officers alone, as you would so selfishly have done for yourselves ; but if you stick to us, we will stick to you, to the last."

The crowd of rough, sea-soaked, half-starved, wearied men, swaying on the slippery deck with the motion of the ship, had no words in which to reply to such a speech. Some of them were moved to tears, and when, as an earnest of their goodwill, one or two called for cheers for the captain, their voices, mingled with the dismal howling of the wind and the ominous sound of water surging about below, rang so quavering and feeble, that Walker turned aside to conceal his own emotion.

From that time forward he never left the deck, nor lay down for a week, sleeping as he stood, leaning on the rail.

Every eye was turned to that solitary, dauntless figure. Never a sign of fear or yielding did he show, and when he spoke words of encouragement as they toiled at the pumps, they would look up at him, some with a murmur of blessing and admiration, some with tears in their eyes.

Already six guns had been thrown overboard ; in a few days, the gale increasing, nearly all the remainder followed. The anchors were cut away, and also some spars which were superfluous in such a gale ; the sails were split by the violence of the wind, the rigging gave out, the masts swaying and threatening to go by the board, and never a sail appeared : not even a foe of superior force, which they would have welcomed in their dire extremity.

At length the word was beginning to be passed about that it was useless any longer to toil at the pumps. Nothing could save the ship, and the lassitude of despair was settling down upon them. The officers began to share the despondency of the crew, and Walker, looking round for those with whom he would consult, missed them : they had gone below to take eternal leave of one another.

Calling a seaman, Walker sent him aloft, with orders to cry " A sail ! " and then, sending for the drummer, he bade him beat to quarters.

Sudden animation ran through the ship. The men paused in their labour, looking round the horizon ; the officers ran on deck, and closed round the captain : " Sir, do you think of engaging ? " asked one. " Yes, sir," replied Walker, in a low voice. " When I see an enemy so near—your own fears, which attack the hearts of all my other men. I am willing to take my greater part of duty, but you leave too much to my share."

Ashamed, they endeavoured to emulate his fortitude, and this desperate ruse procured another respite from despair, and a night of renewed vigour at the pumps, in the hope of rescue in the morning. But there was no sail, and, though the wind had abated, despair returned ; Walker assured them positively that they would sight land next day, and thus induced them to turn to once more, though he was by no means confident that his word would come true : and when a man ran aft in a sudden panic, or sent by

others to tell the news, crying that the ship was just
about to sink, his patience gave way for a moment,
and he floored the scaremonger with a blow of his
fist. " You lie, you villain ! " he said ; " she told me
otherwise, as she rose on that last sea ! "

But it was over at last. On the following day the
coast of Cornwall was sighted, and in the afternoon the
battered and water-logged *Boscawen* ran into St.
Ives. Anchorless, she drifted helplessly, and, in spite
of the efforts of the Cornish boatmen, swept past the
pier and grounded on a rocky beach, where she instantly parted, her masts falling every way. All the
crew save four were got on shore in safety : Walker
remained to see the sick got out of the cabin window,
telling his men not to mind about him, as he would
presently swim on shore ; but two of the townsmen,
who had probably heard from some of the seamen
what sort of hero was in danger of perishing on the
wreck, came out and brought him off.

And that is the story of how George Walker, by
sheer undaunted courage and force of will and example,
kept his ship afloat and saved his own and over three
hundred lives from a horrible end in mid-ocean : the
noblest victory he ever won.

When he presented himself before his owners they
received him, says the writer, " with marks of esteem,
and a joy equal to what had been the claim of the
best success. One of the first questions Mr. Walker
asked was, whether they were insured ? The answer
was, " No, nor ever would be in a ship where he commanded "—a remark which, while exceedingly and

intentionally complimentary to the gallant Walker, scarcely represents a sound commercial attitude.

Walker's next command was a much more important one, for he was, as already stated, placed in charge of a squadron of privateers, all named after royal personages, and known collectively as " The Royal Family Privateers." The vessels were fitted out at Bristol, and were named :

	Guns.	Men.
King George, George Walker, Commodore ..	32	300
Prince Frederick, Hugh Bromedge, Captain..	26	260
Duke, Edward Dottin, Captain	20	260
Princess Amelia, Robert Denham, Captain..	24	150
	102	970

A formidable force, under such a commander. The *Prince Frederick*, however, got aground in the Bristol Channel, and was compelled to put back and dock : so the three others set forth in company at the beginning of May 1746, and had only been a week at sea when they encountered three French line-of-battle ships, from which Walker escaped in the dark by the ruse of leaving a lantern floating in a cask, while he extinguished all lights and altered his course ; but the *Princess Amelia* parted company and eventually put into Lisbon.

A little later, at Safia, on the coast of Morocco, having chased a small French vessel into the bay, Walker determined to cut her out that night with his boats—an operation not often undertaken by privateers, though numerous feats of the most daring description have been performed in this connection by the Navy. Walker considered, however, that he and his men were fully capable of planning and executing such an enterprise, and, having given detailed directions, he despatched three boats under the command of Mr. Riddle, his second lieutenant, on this dangerous service, about midnight. As is frequently the case with such undertakings, the original plan had to be modified, and they found the Frenchmen very much on the alert. The lieutenant in command was very severely wounded immediately, but nothing would stop Walker's men, and, after a tussle, they carried the vessel and brought her out in triumph. As she was a smart little craft Walker made her a tender in place of the *Princess Amelia*, naming her *Prince George* and putting his first lieutenant, John Green, in command. Mr. Green, we are told, would have been sent in charge of the cutting-out expedition, but that he had expressed the opinion that it would be better to wait until daylight. "Sir," says Mr. Walker, "though I have no reason to doubt your prowess, yet I never will send a man upon an expedition to which he has any objection." He gave him the command, however, of the new tender, displaying his customary fairness of dealing with all his subordinates.

During this eight months' cruise "The Royal Family" made some valuable prizes and put into Lisbon with more than £220,000 to the good, and without a single man having been killed.

Having overhauled and refitted his ships—now increased to six in number by the addition of the *Prince George* and the *Prince Edward*, a vessel purchased at Lisbon—Walker put to sea again on July 10th, 1747 and in October following occurred the most remarkable action in which he was concerned. He had, before this, lost one of his squadron, the *Prince Edward*, by a very extraordinary accident. Crowding sail to come up with her consorts, being astern, she was suddenly observed to reel, and immediately foundered, going down stern first. The survivors—her captain and two men only—stated that the mainmast had slipped out of the "step" in the bottom of the ship—or more probably had displaced the step by the strain upon it—and the heel of the mast had gone through her bottom, the mast, with all the sails set, falling over the stern.

On October 6th the squadron had been watering in Lagos Bay—that same harbour in which we saw Bernard D'Ongressill so scurvily treated by the Portuguese nearly five hundred years previously—and the *King George* and *Prince Frederick*, coming out about five o'clock in the morning, leaving the *Princess Amelia* still at anchor, saw a large sail standing to the northward. Walker made the signal to chase, and sent a small vessel, a recent prize, into the anchorage to hurry up the *Princess Amelia*. The *Duke* and *Prince George*, having completed their watering earlier, were in sight ; but, after chasing for about an hour, for some unexplained reason discontinued—or could not get up.

The chase, seeing she was likely to be hemmed in by the two nearest ships, kept away to the westward, making all sail ; and Walker, with his two ships, chased her until noon, when the *King George* was nearly up with her, the *Prince Frederick* some distance to the southward. They had not yet disclosed each other's nationality, but Walker realised by this time that the stranger was a very big ship, and he was within gunshot of her, practically alone ; and then it suddenly fell a flat calm, and the chase, hoisting her colours, ran out her guns, disclosing herself as a 74-gun ship.   The colours, however, hung down in the calm, and it was impossible to tell whether they were Spanish or Portuguese—for the two ensigns were very similar at that time, though they are not so now.   After about an hour, during which the *Prince Frederick* could get no nearer, and Walker and his big opponent were eyeing each other curiously, the latter ran in her lower deck guns, and closed the ports.   This looked as though she was a treasure ship, unwilling to fight if she could avoid it ; and, as a matter of fact, she was just that ; only she had already—after being chased by some English men-of-war—landed her treasure, to the value of some three millions sterling, at Ferrol, and was on her way to Cadiz.   However, seeing her somewhat shy, Walker's officers and men were all for fighting ; and when a light breeze sprang up about five o'clock, and the big ship again made sail on her original course, the *King George* at once continued the chase, leaving the *Prince Frederick*, which did not get the breeze so soon, yet further astern.

At eight o'clock, in bright moonlight, Walker was within speaking distance, cleared for action, his men lying down at their quarters.   He hailed in Portuguese : no reply.   Then he hailed in English, asking her name ; in reply, she asked his name, also in English. " The *King George* ! " replied Walker, and then came a thundering broadside, dismounting two guns and bringing down the maintopsail yard. Walker's men were on their feet and had their broadside in in a few seconds; and then this ridiculously uneven contest went on, the huge Spanish ship—her name, the *Glorioso* —towering above the other, and both letting drive with guns and small arms for all they were worth. Why the *King George* was not sunk it is impossible to say. The chronicler of the fight says that the Spaniards did not manage to fire their broadsides regularly but only a few guns at a time, while the *King George's* men got theirs in with great precision and regularity, and also maintained a very hot fire of musketry, under the control of the Captain of Marines.

This desperate conflict was maintained for three hours, at close range—so close at times that some burning wadding from the Spaniard's guns set fire to the *King George's* mainsail. The incident, as Sir John Laughton remarks, was unique in naval warfare; there have been instances in which a vessel of vastly inferior force has contrived to maim or delay her big antagonist until assistance arrived, and so to contribute very materially to her capture, advantage being taken of superior speed and handiness, or circumstances of wind and sea, and so on; but for a vessel of the *King George's* size to maintain a close ding-dong action with a 74-gun ship, in fine weather, for this space of time is entirely unprecedented. Had Walker been in command of a king's ship, he would certainly have been held blameless if he had run away; but running away, even from a vastly superior force, was not, as we have seen, a proceeding which found any favour in the eyes of George Walker ; and there was, of course, the strong inducement of the assumed treasure, which, after all, was not there.

The writer attributes their immunity from destruction and their trifling casualties—one killed and fifteen wounded—partly to the very closeness of the action, the Spanish ship's shot not hitting the hull ; and also, to the fact that, probably from the overloading of the guns with several shot, in the hope of knocking a huge breach in the *King George's* side, the shot came with such reduced force that, when they hit, they did not penetrate. Walker's device of high bulwarks of elm planking, before alluded to, he likewise considers had a share in their miraculous salvation.

Walker, he says, " fought and commanded with a calmness almost peculiar to himself " ; and his high example conduced to order and discipline even in the thickest of the fight. When the mainsail was set on fire he ordered some hands aloft to extinguish it, and when another man was somewhat officiously following, he called him down. " I have sent men enough aloft for the business, in my opinion ; if they fail in their duty, I'll send for you " ; such an episode, in the thick of a terrible engagement, is significant, indeed, of calmness and absolute self-possession, which is heroic in its measure.

The action was fought, we are told, so close under Cape St. Vincent that the castle on the Cape repeatedly fired upon the combatants, " as a neutral power commanding peace " ; in other words, as a protest against

From an engraving by Ravenet after a painting by Brooking.

ACTION BETWEEN THE "GLORIOSO," A SPANISH 74-GUN-SHIP, AND THE "KING GEORGE" AND "PRINCE FREDERICK," OF THE "ROYAL FAMILY" PRIVATEERS, UNDER GEORGE WALKER, OCTOBER 7, 1747.

[p. 182]

the action being fought in Portuguese waters, within gunshot of the coast.

By half-past ten the *Prince Frederick* came up to the assistance of her consort. At this time the *King George* had received so much damage aloft, that there was no choice but to remain, for she could not have run away. " All our braces and maintopsail yard were shot away, the foremast quite disabled, and the mainmast damaged. We could not work our ship, and bravery became now a virtue of necessity."

There was no mention of striking the colours, however ; and half an hour later the *Glorioso* desisted from action, and retired from the field. When, at daybreak, Captain Dottin, of the *Prince Frederick*, came on board, his first inquiry was as to whether the commodore was alive ; then, seeing the ship's company so nearly intact, and his friends among the officers unhurt, he embraced the gallant commodore in the enthusiasm of his joy and admiration.

Despatching the *Prince Frederick*, with the *Duke* and *Prince George*, in pursuit of the enemy, Walker set to work to refit ; and then a fresh alarm arose, for a large sail was seen approaching from the eastward. She proved, however, to be a friend, the *Russell*, an 80-gun ship, and Walker lost no time in acquainting her captain with the state of affairs.

Helpless in his dismantled vessel, Walker watched with his glass the progress of the chase, his own three vessels nearing the Spaniard, with the giant *Russell* crowding sail to join them ; but he could not account for a fourth vessel which now seemed to be in the fight.

The headmost ship, apparently the *Prince Frederick*, now engaged the Spaniard hotly, and Walker, speaking his thoughts aloud to his officers, deplored her captain's unwariness in not waiting for the others to come up ; for Dottin was blazing away for all he was worth, and Walker's experience immediately suggested a new danger. " Dottin will fire away all his cartridges at too great a distance, and afterwards be obliged to load with loose powder, by which some fatal accident may happen."

Scarcely had he spoken, keeping his glass upon the vessel, when simultaneously with the discharge of a broadside a pillar of smoke and flame shot up. " Good heavens, she's gone ! " cried Walker. " Dottin and all his brave fellows are no more ! " One of the officers suggested that it was merely the smoke of her last broadside. " It's a dreadful truth you tell," replied Walker, still looking through his glass, " for 'tis the last she will ever give ! " And when the smoke cleared away there was no ship to be seen ! This terrible incident so affected the ship's company that Walker called the officers aside into the companion-way in order to admonish them that they must keep up an air of cheerfulness before the men, who might otherwise be backward in fighting ; and while he spoke there was a series of sudden explosions, mingled with cries of alarm. Running out on deck, they found the crew in a panic, some clinging outside the ship, others climbing out on the bowsprit, in readiness to jump overboard when the ship should blow up. The alarm was caused by a seaman stepping upon a number of loaded muskets, which were covered with a sail, and firing one off, which quickly set the others going, some spare ammunition also exploding; bullets were flying about, the sail was on fire, and the men could not be persuaded to quit their temporary refuge, so completely scared were they by this sudden din, following closely upon the tragic occurrence they had just witnessed. The captain and officers extinguished the fire, assisted by the chaplain—" a very worthy gentleman "—apparently of the same type as that excellent parson described in " Midshipman Easy," who rendered such material assistance under similar circumstances, and was anxious to ascertain afterwards whether he had allowed his tongue too free play for one of his cloth ; he had, but Jack Easy consoled him. " Indeed, sir, I only heard you say, ' God bless you, my men ; be smart,' and so on."

Well, the *Russell*, aided by " The Royal Family," captured the Spaniard, of course, though she made a more stubborn fight than they expected, and the *Russell* was very short of men. The *King George*, however, had no decisive news on the subject for some days, when, encountering their consort, the *Duke*, what was the joy on board upon learning that the *Prince Frederick* was safe and sound ! The vessel which so unhappily blew up was the *Dartmouth*, a frigate which had come up, hearing the guns, to see the fun. Only seventeen of her crew were picked up by the *Prince Frederick's* boats ; one of them was an Irish lieutenant, O'Brien, who apologised to captain Dottin for his dress : " Sir, you must excuse the unfitness of my

dress to come aboard a strange ship, but really I left
my own in such a hurry that I had no time to stay for
a change." He had been blown out of a port !

It was not until he was introduced to the Spanish
captain, on board the *Russell*, that Walker learned
that the treasure was safe at Ferrol—a great blow to
him and his men ; and on arriving at Lisbon he was,
to his surprise, confronted by one of his owners, who
blamed him severely for venturing the privateers
against a man-of-war. Walker very justly replied,
" Had the treasure, sir, been aboard, as I expected,
your compliment had been otherways ; or had we let
her escape from us with that treasure on board, what
had you then have said ? "

Walker was then, in fact, treated very scurvily by
the owners, if we are to believe the quite simple and
apparently straightforward story of his friend and
former officer, and was at the last hustled out of his
ship, the *King George*, at Lisbon, by a scandalous
subterfuge. Probably avarice was at the bottom of
all this sordid business ; privateer owners had a very
keen eye for the main chance, and did not set too much
store by heroism—without profits !

Walker took his passage home in the packet, an
armed vessel, commanded by an elderly and somewhat
timid gentleman. They encountered an Algerine of
greater force, and some of Walker's men who were on
board were heard to remark that if their captain had
commanded he would knock her out of the water ; so
two English merchants, who were passengers, begged the
captain to turn over the fighting command to Walker.

This was actually done, and Walker, playing a clever game of bluff, sent the enemy off without firing a shot.

This is the last we hear of Walker at sea. We find him in gaol for debt, but the precise circumstances which induced his formerly very admiring owners to place him there are not quite clear. As we know, it was no disgrace in those days to be imprisoned for debt, and the process was, indeed, a remarkably easy one. As has already been remarked, it is impossible to believe that George Walker was otherwise than a man of strictest honour and probity: he proved himself almost quixotically so, in fact, for when, upon one occasion, a couple of rich East India ships offered him £1,000 to convoy them safely to Lisbon, he replied that " he would never take a reward for what he thought his duty to do without one "; nor would he accept the smallest present from them, after seeing them safely into port.

According to *The Gentleman's Magazine*, George Walker died September 20th, 1777. Where he buried does not appear; whether he was ever married or left any family is equally obscure.

One thing, however, is certain : he left behind him the reputation of a very noble and brave seaman, the idol of his men, the terror of his king's enemies. There is no eulogy which has been engraved upon the tombstones of our naval and military heroes which might not with justice have been included in George Walker's epitaph. So far as his opportunities went, he set an example which could scarcely have been improved upon.

SOME FRENCHMEN

CHAPTER XIII

JEAN BART

PRIVATEERING was very much resorted to in France, from the middle of the seventeenth century onwards; it was greatly encouraged by the State, and frequently men-of-war were lent to private individuals or corporations, who maintained them at their own cost, and of course pocketed the proceeds of the prizes captured. Some of these were large and powerful vessels, mounting fifty or sixty guns, and, having been built for men-of-war, were far superior to most privateers, which were frequently merchant vessels adapted for the purpose. Their crews were very numerous, not infrequently outnumbering those of our 64-gun ships, and it was not of much use for any vessel of less force than these to tackle them.

One of these big privateers, in the year 1745, was engaged off the south coast of Ireland with the 40-gun ship *Anglesea*, Captain Jacob Elton, with a very sad and tragic result. The *Anglesea*, having put into Kinsale to land some sick—her senior lieutenant being one—sailed again on March 28th, being one of the vessels ordered to command the entrance of the channel. On the following day, with a fresh breeze blowing, a large sail was reported to windward. Captain Elton, for some reason, assumed that this was his consort, the *Augusta*, of 64 guns; it was just twelve o'clock, so he ordered his boatswain to pipe to dinner, making no preparation for action. The stranger came down rapidly, displaying no colours, apparently—which should have aroused Elton's suspicion—and suddenly, when he was quite near, it was realised that the ornament on her quarter was in the French style.

Then, all in a hurry, they beat to quarters, and the English captain, in order to gain time for his preparations, made more sail, setting his foresail; but the wind was strong, with a lumpy sea, and the increased pressure of sail, as the gun's crews opened the lee ports, brought tons of water in on to the lower deck, threatening to water-log the ship.

The enemy—which was the *Apollon*, 50 guns, fitted out as a privateer—had it all her own way. Passing under the stern of the *Anglesea*, she rounded to on her lee quarter, and delivered a heavy fire. The guns were not cleared away, there was a lot of water below, and in a minute or two sixty men were dead or wounded. The captain and master were killed by the first broadside, and the command of the ship thus devolved upon the second lieutenant, a young and inexperienced officer. He was in a very tight place. The Frenchman being on the lee quarter, he could not bear up and run, as he would have fallen on board the enemy, which carried many more men, and his ship meanwhile was under a heavy fire, which could not be returned, his men falling fast. After consultation with the third lieutenant, he surrendered—and really it is difficult to see what else he could have done. Possibly an older man, of consummate skill and great experience, might have found a way of handling his ship so as, at least, to gain some respite ; on the other hand, no such man would have had any business to find himself in this predicament.

So the lieutenant—Baker Phillips by name—hauled down his colours, and in due course was tried by court-martial for the loss of his ship. The court " was unanimously of opinion that Captain Elton, deceased, did not give timely directions for getting his ship clear or in a proper posture of defence, nor did he afterwards behave like an officer or a seaman, which was the cause of the ship being left to Lieutenant Phillips in such distress and confusion. And that Lieutenant Baker Phillips, late second lieutenant of the said ship, by not endeavouring to the utmost of his power after Captain Elton's death to put the ship in order of fighting, not encouraging the inferior officers and men to fight courageously, and by yielding to the enemy, falls under part of the tenth Article.[1] They

---

[1] The tenth Article of War, at that time, read as follows : " Every flag-officer, captain, and commander in the fleet who, upon signal or order of fight, or sight of any ship or ships which it may be his duty to engage, or who upon likelihood of engagement shall not make the necessary preparations for fight, and shall not in his own person, and according to his place, encourage the inferior officers and men to fight courageously, shall suffer death, or such other punishment as from the nature and degree of the offence a court-martial shall deem

do sentence him to death, to be shot by a platoon of musqueteers on the forecastle ; . . . but . . . having regard to the distress and confusion the ship was in when he came to the command, and being a young man and inexperienced, they beg leave to recommend him to mercy."

That is to say, they felt bound, under the clause referred to in the Articles of War, to sentence him to death, but obviously hoped that the extreme penalty would not be inflicted under the circumstances—a very proper view to take. The recommendation, however, was ignored—it will be recollected that just at this period the British Navy was, for some reason, passing through a very unsatisfactory phase ; courage and energy appeared often to be lacking—as in the instance of the treasure ships, in the previous year, when George Walker was compelled to witness the outrageous incapacity and supineness of the captains of the men-of-war. These men were acquitted—Lieutenant Baker Phillips was not. Perhaps it may be permitted to ask, would Captain Elton have been shot had he survived the action ? His lieutenant was made an example of, and there is some story that a reprieve was refused on account of his Jacobite tendencies ; no evidence appears to be forthcoming in support of this view. Another and very terrible tale in connection with the incident relates that Phillips's

him to deserve ; and if any person in the fleet shall treacherously or cowardly yield, or cry for quarter, every person so offending and being convicted thereof by the sentence of a court-martial, shall suffer death."

wife, after a reprieve had been refused, went in person to Queen Caroline and obtained one, with which she posted in feverish haste to Portsmouth; but the unhappy young officer, desiring to avoid the terrible pain of a final interview with her, had, in ignorance of her mission to the queen, requested that the hour of his execution might be hastened. When she arrived, he had already been shot. One can only hope that this story is not true; it is too terrible to dwell upon.

Well, that is how the privateer *Apollon* scored off us. Five-and-thirty years later, in 1780, within a mile or two of the same spot, a still more powerful vessel, similarly commissioned—to wit, the *Comte d'Artois*, of 64 guns—was overcome and captured by the *Bienfaisant*, 64 guns, captain Macbride, after a smart action of over an hour. The *Bienfaisant* was countenanced, more than assisted, by the presence of the *Charon*, 44 guns, which took little or no part in the action. The French loss was 21 killed and 34 wounded, while the British lost 3 killed and 23 wounded.

It was one of these privately maintained king's ships which was selected to convoy the young Pretender to Scotland in 1745; indeed, both the *Elizabeth*, of 60 guns, and the *Dentelle*, a much smaller vessel, in which the prince embarked, were of this class. The two vessels encountered the British 60-gun ship *Lion*, off Ushant, and of course there was a fight. The *Lion* and *Elizabeth*, pretty equally matched, and each commanded by a doughty fighter, blazed away at each other by the space of four or five hours, when both had had enough. Captain Brett, of the *Lion*, while regretting that he had not been able to capture the *Elizabeth*, was pleasing himself with the reflection that he had " spoiled her voyage "—and so he had, for she had 65 killed and 136 wounded, while her hull was fearfully battered, and she was compelled to make for the nearest French port. Brett took but little notice of the smaller craft, which, endeavouring at first to assist the *Elizabeth*, was easily disposed of by the *Lion's* stern chasers, and hung about out of range until the big ships separated, when she proceeded on her voyage to Scotland. Brett must have been rather annoyed afterwards to think that he had not made a capture of the *Dentelle* ; but he had, in fact, spoiled their voyage very effectually, for the *Elizabeth* had on board all the stores and munitions for the campaign in Scotland, and Charles Edward Stuart landed very empty-handed in consequence.

One of the most prominent among French privateer captains is Jean Bart ; he is, in fact, perhaps somewhat unduly prominent, as it does not appear, from authentic accounts, that he performed any more wonderful or daring feats of seamanship and battle than some others. It may be that the many unfounded, or at least unsupported tales of his prowess —incredible tales, many of them—form the basis, to a large extent, of his immense popularity ; or, on the other hand, this very popularity may have given rise to these exaggerated anecdotes. He was, without doubt, a very fine seaman, and a determined and capable commander, very worthy of the public esteem, and his reputation gains nothing from wild inventions.

He was born in 1650, at Dunkirk, though his family is said to have been of Dieppe origin. He came of privateering, semi-piratical stock, and at the age of twelve he embarked as boy on board a Dunkirk smuggler, under a brutal, but capable ruffian named Jerome Valbué; his father's old boatswain, Antoine Sauret, accompanying him, apparently, as a kind of "sea-daddy"—and it appears to have been just as well that he had some one to stand between him and the skipper. After a four years' apprenticeship, young Bart, always enthusiastic and eager to learn, had acquired remarkable proficiency in seamanship and gunnery, and is said to have won the prize for the best marksman at the annual competition on the Dunes.

Thanks to Sauret's teaching and his own zeal, the lad was considered competent, at the age of sixteen, to fill the post of mate on a brigantine, the *Cochon Gras*, of which the redoubtable Valbué was appointed commander.

Jean Bart and his elderly adviser, Sauret, were, however, destined soon to find employ elsewhere, the occasion of their leaving the *Cochon Gras* being an exhibition of wanton cruelty on the part of their captain. The fact of the two having protested rendered it advisable that they should not remain.

M. Valbué, it appears, in common with many captains, both in the Navy and elsewhere at that period, still affected to be bound, together with his crew, by the Laws or Judgments of Oléron—a brutal code, dating from the twelfth century.

Valbué, half drunk, had been relating some wonderful tale of the miraculous intervention of a saintly bishop to save a fishing-boat, and proceeded to emphasise his own belief and his contempt for heretics by flinging his half-empty tin cider-mug at one Lanoix, a harmless Huguenot seaman. (Huguenots are habitually represented by the ordinary British writer as harmless, exemplary persons ; a large number of them were, in fact, bloodthirsty, cruel, and seditious ruffians, who richly deserved all they got.)

Lanoix meekly but firmly pointed out that the Laws of Oléron ordained that the captain was not to punish a seaman until his anger had cooled down. (It reminds one rather of Midshipman Easy walking about with the Articles of War under his arm, and admonishing his superior for using strong language !)

Valbué's rejoinder was a blow with a handspike, which narrowly missed braining the seaman. Antoine Sauret ventured to remonstrate, but was warned that he was in danger of similar treatment : for the Laws of Oléron allow the captain one blow, just as the law of England allows a dog one bite—only the skipper was apparently permitted one crack at each member of his crew. So Sauret said no more.

Lanoix, however, was as well up in the law as his captain, and, jumping over the iron rail which separated the forecastle from the after part of the vessel, reminded Valbué that if he followed him on to the forecastle and repeated the blow he would put himself in the wrong, and he, Lanoix, would have the right to retaliate.

Valbué immediately let loose a string of contemptuous and insulting epithets, and, passing the barrier, struck Lanoix two violent blows on the face.

Out came the seaman's knife, and in a second the captain's arm was badly gashed; but the instinct of discipline induced the crew to rush to the rescue, and they pinioned Lanoix—but not before he had killed one man, stabbing him to the heart.

Valbué thereupon sent his cabin-boy down to bring up a copy of the Laws of Oléron, Jean Bart, at the helm, looking on all this while with disapproval and horror very plainly expressed in his countenance. When the boy appeared with the book Sauret went aft and sat down by the helmsman.

Thinking to place Sauret and his young companion in the wrong, Valbué bade the former come forward and read out the law. He refused, pointing out that Valbué had himself broken the law, and that Lanoix was entitled to purgation of his offence by means of certain oaths and formulæ.

However, the protests of Jean Bart and the brave old man were of no avail. Ignoring their veto, and declaring that six out of eight of the crew agreed that Lanoix had wounded his captain and slain one of his shipmates, Valbué inflicted upon the unfortunate Huguenot the penalty for the first offence, lashing his arm to a sharp sword fixed to the windlass and then knocking him down, so that the flesh was stripped from his arm; and finally, ordering the dead body of the other man to be brought along, he caused Lanoix, sorely wounded but still alive, to be bound to it, and both were thrown overboard—which is also strictly in accordance with the Laws of Oléron, in the event of a seaman killing one of his comrades at sea—as he who runs may read.

Jean Bart and the boatswain acquired from that moment a strong distaste for the Laws of Oléron, and quitted the vessel upon arriving, the same evening, at Calais.

Valbué, consistent with all his brutality, reported the circumstances, as enjoined by the same code, to the authorities; and the incident, we are told, led to the framing of the Maritime Code of France.

Bart and Sauret were highly commended for their plucky protest, and a few days later the former was entrusted with the responsible task of conveying some French noblemen, in a half-decked sailing-boat, to join De Ruyter in the Dutch fleet, then lying off Harwich—so we are told in the account given by Mr. C. B. Norman, in "The Corsairs of France"; but Mr. Norman is very vague as to dates, and we can only conclude that this was during the interval between the "four days' fight," from June 1st to 4th, 1666, and the subsequent decisive action on July 25th and 26th. It is said that he distinguished himself in the "hard-fought action"—between Albemarle and De Ruyter—on August 6th following; but there is no record of any action on this date.

However, these matters are not of much importance, especially in the case of Jean Bart, concerning whom,

as has been stated, fables are plentiful. It appears
to be certain that he was some five years in the Dutch
service, his heart being all this time with France;
and when, in 1672, war was declared between France
and the States-General, he immediately returned to
Dunkirk, and entered upon his career as a privateersman. Commencing as a subordinate, he was given
his first command in 1674—when he was four-and-
twenty—a small vessel, mounting two guns, with a
crew of thirty-six.

In this vessel—the *King David*—Bart soon showed
himself to be a bold and capable captain; in four
or five months he captured six prizes. No fighting
was entailed, it is true; but those who knew Jean
Bart did not doubt that he could fight, should the
occasion arise; and his old friend and "sea-daddy,"
Antoine Sauret, loafing and chatting with his cronies
in Dunkirk, did not allow his young friend's exploits
to be forgotten.

Naturally, his next command was a larger vessel—
a brigantine, named *La Royale*, mounting ten guns,
and his success continued unabated. He cruised in
company with two other Dunkirk men, and made
many captures, the most important being the *Esper-
ance*, a States-General man-of-war, carrying 12 guns,
by which he appears to have won great renown—
though she was only overcome by the heavy odds
against her, Bart having the assistance of at least
one of his allies. However, there is no small merit in
always contriving to outnumber the foe.

Having taken four months' leisure in order to get

married, Jean Bart once more put out, in July 1675,
and met with immediate success ; and, capturing
quite a number of fishing-vessels, he permitted the
captains to ransom them for a handsome sum—a
much more convenient arrangement, in many instances, than bringing a number of prizes into port ;
it was, however, forbidden, as liable to lead to great
abuses, and Bart was deprived of half the proceeds
and warned to be more careful in future—a warning
to which he did not pay much heed. Ransoming was
subsequently forbidden to British privateers, and
other precautions against semi-piracy were instituted,
more or less copied from the French, who were always
in advance of us in their regulation of privateering.

So successful was Jean Bart in *La Royale* that
early in 1676 he was given command of a much more
important vessel—the *Palme*, of 24 guns, with a crew
of 150 men—a regular frigate of those times. Again
he was lucky in hunting in company, for he and his
consorts were opposed to eight armed whalers and
three privateers, which they fought for three hours,
when Bart boarded and carried the largest, while his
consorts secured the whalers, the two other privateers
finding it too hot to remain.

Bart was by no means satisfied with these exploits.
A genuine fighting man, he longed to be matched
singly against a man-of-war or a privateer of fully
his own force ; and this wish was gratified on September 7th, 1676, when he fell in with a fleet of fishing-
vessels, convoyed by the *Neptune*, a vessel carrying
32 guns. Bart sailed into the convoy, and, hoisting

From an engraving by J. Chapman.

JEAN BART, A FAMOUS FRENCH PRIVATEER COMMANDER;
B. 1650., D. 1702.

p. 202]

his colours, fired a gun for the enemy to bring to. Up went the Dutch colours, with a broadside by way of emphasis ; the Dutch captain was a man of Jean Bart's stamp—a foeman worthy of his steel—and they had a great fight.

For three hours, at close range, they battered each other, Bart all the while trying to get a favourable position for boarding, but being constantly frustrated by the good seamanship of the other. At length, however, the *Neptune* was so seriously damaged aloft that she was no longer under full command ; Bart, instantly and skilfully availing himself of the chance, got his vessel lashed alongside, and headed the boarding party, consisting of nearly all his crew. The Dutch captain, grievously wounded, sat on one side, like desperate Andrew Barton, and shouted to his men to lay on ; but they were demoralised by the banging they had had, and Bart and his boarders were not to be denied ; in a few minutes the affair was over, and the French flag replaced the Dutch. It was a proud moment for Jean Bart, and a proud day when he sailed into Dunkirk with the captured vessel in his wake, followed by the fleet of fishing-boats which his victory had thrown into his hands.

The fame of this exploit soon spread abroad, and one fine day Jean Bart received a gold chain from the king as a mark of appreciation of his prowess ; at the same time the authorities began to discuss the question of keeping a list, or roll, of the best fighting privateer captains, in order that they might be transferred to the Navy in case of need—not necessarily an advantage to a keen privateersman, as he would occupy at first a subordinate position, very irksome after the freedom of his former life, in command of his ship.

Colbert, the Minister of State, was very eager about the matter, and advocated giving the most efficient privateer commanders the rank of commodore among their brethren, so that they could operate in squadrons, and attack the enemy's men-of-war. He caused inquiries to be made at Dunkirk and other ports as to the character and capability of the leading privateersmen; and of course he received extremely favourable reports of Jean Bart, who meanwhile was again at sea in the *Palme*, doing great execution.

His employers soon displayed their appreciation of his services by providing him with a yet larger ship—the *Dauphin*, of 30 guns, with a crew numbering 200. In this vessel, a year later, he encountered another Dutchman of the same sort as the captain of the *Neptune*.

Sailing in company with two smaller privateers, on June 18th, 1678, a Dutch frigate was sighted. The smallest privateer happened to be nearest to the enemy, who immediately attacked, hoping to carry her before her consorts could arrive. The Frenchman, however, handled his craft so judiciously as to keep his big antagonist in play until Bart came up. The two larger vessels—the Dutchman was the *Sherdam*, Captain Ranc—at once got into action, while Bart's smaller consort stood off, awaiting a chance. Seeing his opportunity, Bart signalled to

her to bear down, and between them they got the
Dutchman in such a position that he could not avoid
being boarded. A crowd of men from both French
vessels was speedily on his deck; but they had no
kind of a walk-over; Ranc, though severely wounded,
rallied his men again and again, and it was not until
two-thirds of his crew were disabled or killed that he
at length surrendered.

Bart was wounded in the leg, and badly burnt by
the discharge of a gun, almost in his face, as he leaped
on board; six of his men were killed and thirty-one
wounded, while as for the saucy *Dauphin*, her
career was at an end. So well had the Dutchmen
plied their guns that her hull was shattered beyond
repair, and it was with extreme difficulty that she
was brought into harbour.

Bart, of course, had another ship at his disposal
immediately—such an invincible corsair was not
allowed to be idle—and he was at sea again in a
fortnight, in the *Mars*, of 32 guns; a few weeks later,
however, the war came to an end, and he returned to
Dunkirk to have a spell on shore.

And here the career of Jean Bart as a privateer
captain comes to an end; in January 1679 he was
given a commission as lieutenant in the navy. This
was not very much to his taste; besides the come-
down from captain to lieutenant, the aristocrats who
predominated among French naval officers regarded
a privateersman, thus pitchforked in among them,
with a very supercilious air, and made things decidedly
unpleasant for him.

However, Jean Bart pulled through this all right, and eventually had opportunity of displaying his capacity in the royal ships.

There are, as has been remarked, a number of romantic tales extant about Jean Bart; most of them are quite incredible, and for the others there is no reliable authority. One may be given here as a sample.

At Bergen, in the year 1691, it is said that Bart made the acquaintance of the captain of a large English vessel, who expressed a keen desire to meet him outside. Bart said if he would wait a few days his wish should be gratified, and sent word one day that he would sail on the morrow. The Englishman politely invited him to breakfast before they sailed to have it out, and Bart, after a little hesitation, accepted. After breakfast he lit his pipe, and soon remarked that it was time to go. " No," said the Englishman, " you are my prisoner! " " I am not your prisoner," replied Bart, " I will blow up your ship! " Rushing out of the cabin, with a lighted match, he ran to where stood a barrel of gunpowder which had most opportunely been hoisted up from the magazine—a cask with the head out, we must imagine, and the powder exposed. Here, of course, he had it all his own way; the Englishmen were afraid to touch him, lest he should put the match to the powder—and the crews of the French ships, having heard his shout of defiance, rallied on board the English vessel in numbers, cut down many of the crew, captured the ship, and carried her into Dunkirk.

It must be to this absurd story that M. Henri Malo alludes in " Les Corsaires," where he writes, in derision of privateering romances: " Privateers ! We read in these accounts the names of heroes of romance—Jean Bart, smoking his pipe, mark you, on a barrel of gunpowder ; Robert Surcouf, popularised in operetta."

Jean Bart deserves better than to be lampooned in this fashion ; and, though he rose to distinction in the Navy, and there has almost always been a French man-of-war named after him, it is chiefly as the indomitable corsair that his memory is cherished in Dunkirk.

CHAPTER XIV

DU GUAY TROUIN

ANOTHER hero, privateer first and naval officer later, was Du Guay Trouin—this being the name by which he was eventually known, and which has been bestowed upon more than one vessel of the French Navy in commemoration of his exploits. His family name was, properly speaking, Trouin ; his father was Luc Trouin, calling himself, after an estate which he owned, Trouin de la Barbinais. The future privateer captain and hero was the third son, and was born on June 10th, 1673, being named René, after his uncle, then French consul at Malaga—a post which had been held for some generations, apparently, by some member of the Trouin family. Little René, placed under the care of a nursing woman at the village of Le Gué, near by, became known as René Trouin du Gué, which was twisted about until it became Du Gué, or Du Guay Trouin.

René was by no means intended from the first to follow an adventurous career at sea ; his father had a very different aim in view. His uncle and name-sake, René Trouin the consul, who was also his godfather, was very friendly with the Archbishop at Malaga, and it was considered politic that the boy should become an ecclesiastic, and so benefit by the friendliness of the prelate towards his uncle ; and indeed, he was actually sent to the seminary at Rennes, as a very small boy, to commence his studies for the priesthood—very much against his will, but Luc Trouin was not to be trifled with ; and so, until he was fifteen years of age, René was held to be destined for the Church.

Then came a sudden change—his uncle and his father died within a year of one another, and he prevailed upon his mother to permit him to quit the seminary and study for the law. With this end in view he was sent to Caen, but we do not learn that he became a very diligent student—on the contrary, he displayed extreme precocity in getting into mischief of every kind, the only good thing he learnt, apparently, being the use of the sword ; and finally, having betaken himself to Paris to kick up his heels, he heard the waiter in a café order some wine for *Monsieur Trouin de la Barbinais*, his eldest brother, who imagined him to be engaged upon his studies at Caen—and thither young René fled incontinently. His brother had, however, got wind of his proceedings ; he was summoned home, a family court-martial held upon him, and he was sentenced to be sent off to sea, in a privateer of 18 guns, the *Trinité*, fitted out by the house of Trouin. As René was then only sixteen it was obviously a wholesome programme for a lad of such precocious proclivities ; he was soon to prove, however, that he was in advance of his age in other matters than dissipation.

There was not much doing for a year or two ; but, after having assisted to take a small prize into St. Malo, young Du Trouin soon had an opportunity of seeing hard knocks exchanged.

This was in a fight with a Dutch privateer, the *Concorde*, a vessel of equal force, but the *Trinité* had some thirty men absent in prizes.   However, the skipper, Fossart, was not a man who was afraid of odds, and, seeing the stranger to leeward, cracked on his canvas in chase, came up with her about noon, and fired a blank cartridge, followed by a shot across the Dutchman's bows.   This elicited the desired response—or, at least, the expected response—of a broadside, and they went at it, hammer and tongs, for over two hours, by which time the *Concorde* was considerably knocked about and the Frenchman thought it was time to finish the affair by boarding. Directly the two vessels touched the captain sprang on board.   Young Du Guay Trouin leaped beside him. As he did so, the vessels rebounded apart, and several Frenchmen fell between them, only to be crushed to death as the helmsman brought the *Trinité* up again.   An old acquaintance of Du Guay Trouin was among the number, being killed, to his horror, under his very eyes.   However, there was no time for lamentations over lost comrades.   René's skill with the sword now came into play, and he used it to good purpose, killing two out of three Dutchmen who were attacking his captain.   The Dutchmen yielded, after a creditable resistance ; and so Du Guay Trouin had his baptism of fire and sword.

On his next ship, the *Grenedan*, he took a prominent part in the capture of three out of a convoy of fifteen English ships off the south-west coast of Ireland. Young as he was, he was always in the front rank when fighting was going ; and on his return, the *Grenedan* entering the harbour at St. Malo with the three prizes in her wake, amidst enthusiastic cheers from the townspeople, his brother thought he might be entrusted with the command of a ship. This was in the year 1691, when he was not yet turned eighteen, and of course he would never have got a command at that age under ordinary circumstances. He had, however, proved himself to be something other than an ordinary lad, and his brother, as head of the house, had the power to appoint him captain of one of their privateers, if he was so minded. Accordingly, the young sailor was given command of the *Danycan*—not much of a craft, being a slow sailer and not heavily armed.

Caught in a gale of wind, the vessel was blown down Channel, and afterwards chasing some vessels— she could never catch them—into the Shannon, Du Guay Trouin landed his men in the night, burnt a couple of vessels on the beach, did a little pillaging, and alarmed the whole district. Messages were sent hot-foot to Limerick for the soldiers—it was a French fleet, an invasion in force ! Du Guay Trouin embarked his men just as the soldiers came in sight, up anchor, and got away cleverly. This was the only fun he had in the *Danycan*, for every vessel she encountered could "wrong" her, as they used to say in those days; that is to say, could sail round her; so there was not much honour and glory to be got out of her.

On his return to St. Malo Du Guay Trouin was given a better craft—the *Coëtquen*, of 18 guns. It is said that he held his commission from James II., the ex-king of England—it is certain that James did issue such commissions after his abdication, and indeed his consort, the *Saint Aaron*, commanded by one Welch, of Irish extraction, was thus commissioned.

Du Guay Trouin soon had some exciting adventures. Falling in with a fleet of English merchant vessels, under convoy of a couple of sloops, the two privateers captured five ships and the two men-of-war; but, as they were taking their prizes into St. Malo, an English squadron gave chase; then they had to get in where they could. Welch got safely into St. Malo with some of the vessels; Du Guay Trouin, being cornered, made a dash for the Isle of Brehat, behind which the navigation is of the most intricate and perilous description, with dozens of half-submerged rocks and a swishing tide. He managed to get in, and some of the English vessels which tried to follow him very nearly came to grief. He had been under fire some time, and unluckily his pilot was killed, and also some others who were familiar with the locality; so he contrived to find his way out without them, thus displaying that sort of intuitive skill in navigation and the handling of a ship which has almost always distinguished great seamen. He was not an accomplished navigator, having neglected his studies ; he was accustomed to trust entirely to " dead reckoning." Certainly, the means of observing the altitude, etc., of the sun and stars were very rude in those days ; but Du Guay Trouin was not expert even with these.

However, he got out of this trap, was presently blown into the Bristol Channel, and found an English 60-gun ship arriving about the same time. " Luckily," says one of his biographers, " there is an island in the middle of this estuary ; while the enemy came in on one side of it Du Guay Trouin went out on the other." This, of course, is Lundy Island ; and, getting a good start, Du Guay Trouin escaped cleverly—going out, so to speak, by the back door as his opponent came in by the front.

After this Du Guay Trouin had a bad time in the *Profond*, a very poor sailer, and altogether an unlucky ship, so that he was glad to see the last of her, and take command of the *Hercule*, of 28 guns.

After a little good fortune, he again fell upon evil days. No prey was sighted for two months, provisions began to run short, sickness broke out among the crew, discontent and insubordination soon followed. The officers and men demanded that he should return to France, but, partly by conciliation and partly by firmness, he persuaded them to keep the sea for eight days longer, promising them that, if they did capture a prize, they should pillage her and divide the spoil. On the last night at sea, Du Guay Trouin tells us, he had a vivid dream that two deeply laden ships hove in sight ; at daybreak he went aloft—and there they were ! He took them both ; they were rich prizes, and the crew were made happy by being allowed, as he had promised, to pillage one of them.

His next ship was the *Diligente*, of 40 guns ; and in her he was destined to experience the misfortune of defeat and capture. First, however, he came across the *Prince of Orange*, a hired armed vessel of considerable force—Du Guay Trouin says of 60 guns— convoying a fleet of thirty vessels. Having hailed one of them, and ascertained that they were laden with coal, he determined not to risk loss and damage for such a comparatively worthless cargo. Finding however, that his vessel easily " had the heels " of the other, he indulged in some aggravating antics, taking in sail so as to allow the English to come within gunshot, shooting ahead again, under English colours, which he hoisted " union down," *i.e.* as a signal " Am in need of assistance " ; then, dropping down once more, he so far forgot himself as to fire at the other while still under English colours—a gross breach of international law, accounted as an act of piracy. It was done, no doubt, through inadvertence, but the English captain did not forget it, and the Frenchman had cause to regret his carelessness.

And then came misfortune ; nine days later he fell in with a squadron of six English men-of-war cruising between Ireland and the Scilly Isles. They immediately gave chase. A hard gale blowing, Du Guay Trouin ran for the Scilly Isles, hard pressed by the *Adventure* and *Dragon*. In among the islands they ran, and by eleven o'clock the *Adventure* was near enough to engage, the *Diligente* replying with her stern guns. Still gaining in the heavy breeze, the *Adventure*—a 44-gun ship—was within easy range, the *Dragon*—46 guns—not far astern. Du Guay Trouin engaged the *Adventure* for nearly three hours, hoping all the time to escape ; however, at half-past two his fore and main topmasts were shot away, and the English vessel ranged up alongside, hauling up her courses, the *Dragon* at the same time signalising her arrival by a broadside.

This was a pretty desperate state of affairs, but the gallant Frenchman would not yet acknowledge himself beaten. Seeing the English vessel so near, he conceived the idea of suddenly boarding her, and carrying her off. He sent his officers to call the crew on deck, got the grapnels ready, and ordered the helm to be put over. The two ships were rapidly closing when one of the lieutenants of the *Diligente*, looking through a port, and not imagining for a moment that his captain really contemplated such a desperate measure, ordered the quartermaster to reverse the helm. The ships fell apart, but Du Guay Trouin shouted to jam the helm over again. It was too late ; the English captain, knowing that he and his consorts had the Frenchman secure, did not see the use of having a hundred and fifty desperate men jumping on board, so he set his courses, sheered off, and banged away again with his guns. The *Monk*, of 60 guns, now arrived, and the *Diligente* was fairly surrounded, two more ships coming up shortly.

Still the French flag was kept flying. The men, less heroic than their captain, began to run from their quarters. Du Guay Trouin cut down one, pistolled another, and was hustling them generally, when fire broke out below. He rushed down and had it extinguished, then provided himself with a tub of grenades, which he began throwing down into the hold, so that his crew found it too hot to remain below, and manned some of the guns. However, this could not go on against such fearful odds, and on gaining the deck once more he found that "some cowardly rascal" had lowered the colours. He ordered them up again, but his officers demurred; and then, with the last shot fired in the action, he was wounded severely in the groin and dropped senseless. When he came to himself the ship was in the possession of the English. He was taken on board the *Monk*, where Captain Warren treated him right well—"with as much care as though I had been his own son," says Du Guay Trouin—and he was probably quite old enough to have been father to the young French captain, who was then only one-and-twenty.

Arriving at Plymouth, the gallant young Frenchman became the object of much interest and favour; naval and military officers entertained him, civilians followed suit, and he was given, as he says, "the whole town for his prison"; in other words, he was placed on his parole, and allowed full liberty. Always susceptible to the attractions of women, he found, as he tells us, "une fort jolie marchande"—a sweetly pretty shop-girl, or shop-woman, with whom he formed a close acquaintance, and who was eventually mainly instrumental in procuring his liberty. Pretty girls, as we know, are reputed to be more abundant in Devonshire than in many other parts, and no doubt the Frenchman found her very seductive. It is curious what a diversity of parts this young woman is made to assume among the biographers of Du Guay Trouin. One makes her out just a shop-girl; another says she was " une jeune marchande qui preparait les repas de Duguay "—a young shop-woman who prepared his meals—while Mr. C. B. Norman, on what ground does not appear, calls her a " fair *compatriote* "—a Frenchwoman, married to a " Devonshire merchant," and has a good deal to say about the way in which she hoodwinked her good husband while she was obtaining information for the young Frenchman when he was in prison; we shall get him there directly. Du Guay Trouin, in his " Mémoires," simply speaks of her as already quoted; and " *marchande* " certainly does not mean " merchant's wife."

However, there she is, being entertained sometimes by Du Guay Trouin, and no doubt very proud of being the object of his attentions—just a shop-girl, he says; and he ought to know.

This delightful condition of affairs was, however, unexpectedly interrupted, for one fine day there arrived the *Prince of Orange*, to refit after seeing her colliers safe; and the captain soon recognised, in the prize lying at anchor, the vessel which fired at

him under the English flag.   He was in a great state
of mind, reported the circumstances to the Admiralty,
and demanded that Du Guay Trouin should be treated
as a pirate.   The authorities demurred to this request, but thought it advisable, during their delibera-
tions, that he should not have " the whole town for
his prison " ;   so they put him in gaol, allowing him,
however, to order his own food and entertain his
friends there.   The English officers who took turns on
guard at the prison were very glad to dine with him ;
and "my pretty shop-girl also came very often to
pay me a visit."

Too often, apparently, for the peace of mind of a
young French refugee officer, doing duty with an
English company of soldiers ;   and he actually came
to Du Guay Trouin and begged his good offices to
induce the girl to marry him—or, at least, to show
him favour.   Du Guay Trouin was at first disposed
to refuse indignantly, though he apparently wishes
to imply that his intimacy with her was quite innocent.   It occurred to him, however, that the young
soldier's infatuation might be turned to good account.

He would, he said, serve him with all his heart ;
but he was rather worried in his room, and could not
see his way to do much unless he could entertain her
in some more open place—the café close to the prison
would do very well ;   she could come there without
suspicion, and, if he had but one chance there, he
would use all his eloquence with her, and would even
arrange that the love-lorn young soldier should spend
the rest of the evening with her.

The bait was too strong for his loyalty. Du Guay Trouin, having established an understanding with " his gentle shop-girl," represented to her feelingly that the trial of imprisonment would soon cause him to succumb if she would not have the goodness to assist him to escape; which, of course, she did, first becoming his messenger to a Swedish captain, who sold him a good boat for £35, with sails and oars complete.

The whole scheme came off to admiration. Du Guay Trouin, with the connivance of the impatient lover, who had seen his lady enter the café, left his room and followed, the young officer only imploring him not to keep him long in suspense. " But," says Du Guay Trouin, " I scarcely gave myself time to thank and kiss that wholesome little friend "—he was out at the back, over the wall, and in the company of some of his officers and six stalwart, well-armed Swedish sailors before the French officer had any time to be anxious; and by ten o'clock they were in the boat, sailing by the men-of-war, answering " Fishermen " to the hail of the sentries, and so to sea. They reached the island of Brehat after a rough passage of fifty hours, and, after resting for a while, made their way to St. Malo, where Du Guay Trouin learned that his brother had a fine ship fitting out for him at Rochefort.

Whether the love-sick soldier went to look for " la jolie marchande " and what she said to him are not recorded; but it is to be feared that he experienced a rude awakening.

In his new command, named *François*, of 48 guns,

Du Guay Trouin was soon busy, taking several prizes
of considerable value off the coast of Ireland. He
was longing, however, for an opportunity of avenging
himself for his defeat and capture, and early in the
year 1695 he had his wish, encountering a large convoy
of vessels laden with huge spars, suitable for masts,
etc., bound from North America, under the protection
of the *Nonsuch*, of 48 guns. One of the convoy, the
Falcon, was also well armed, carrying 38 guns, according to Du Guay Trouin, and pierced for 72. He
calls the *Falcon* the *Boston*, and the *Nonsuch* by the
equivalent French name, *Sanspareil*.

He says that the inhabitants of Boston had
had the *Falcon* built, and loaded with valuable
mast-timber and choice skins, as a present to King
William III.

Sighting the enemy about noon, Du Guay Trouin
immediately attacked the *Falcon*, and with his first
few broadsides inflicted immense damage, sending her
main-topmast by the board, and smashing her mainyard. Leaving her for a time, he laid his ship on
board the *Nonsuch*, the two ships exchanging a hot
fire from great guns and small arms the while. The
Frenchmen discharged a number of grenades on the
decks of the *Nonsuch*, and then the boarders leaped
across; but fire broke out on the after part of the
English ship, and raged with such fury that Du Guay
Trouin was compelled to recall his men and disengage
his vessel. Seeing the flames nearly extinguished,
he closed again; but he was premature, for the fire
once more flared up, and caught his own maintopsail

and foresail. While both ships were busy tackling the fire night came on, and they fell apart, repairing damages on both sides.

At daybreak Du Guay Trouin renewed his attack upon the *Nonsuch*; but just as he was laying her aboard her fore and mainmasts fell with a crash, and he was compelled once more to sheer off—this time however, with the certainty that she was his. Seeing the *Falcon* making all sail in the endeavour to escape, he steered for her, and very quickly obtained her submission; meanwhile, the *Nonsuch* had lost her remaining mast, and was an absolute wreck, sorely damaged also in her hull.

Thus the determined young French captain had things all his own way; and he thoroughly deserved his success, which was the outcome of fine seamanship, backed by good gunnery and indomitable courage.

The captain of the *Nonsuch* was killed. The courtmartial which was subsequently held on the surviving officers found that he had not made adequate preparation for fighting, and so was overcome by a considerably inferior force, for the *Nonsuch* and the *François* were about equal. All the vessels engaged were very badly damaged, and, a gale of wind springing up immediately after the action, their position became very hazardous. The *Falcon* was recaptured by four Dutch privateers; the *Nonsuch* and *François* with difficulty managed to reach port.

On hearing of this achievement the King of France sent Du Guay Trouin a sword of honour, and his name was in every mouth.

He sailed next with a squadron under the Marquis de Nesmond which captured the English 70-gun ship the *Hope*, and subsequently he and a consort took three East Indiamen, with cargoes valued at about one million sterling.

After having been, to his great delight and exultation, presented to the king in Paris, he fitted out the *Nonsuch*, under the name *Sanspareil*, with an armament of 42 guns, and cruised off the coast of Spain. On this cruise there occurred an incident which was very characteristic of Du Guay Trouin's presence of mind and audacity.

Having news of three Dutch merchant ships lying at Vigo awaiting the escort of an English man-of-war, he took advantage of the English build and appearance of his ship, and hoisting English colours, appeared in the entrance of Vigo Bay. Two of the Dutchmen, completely deceived, immediately joined him, and were, of course, captured; the third, luckily for her, was not ready for sea.

This was all very nice; but one fine morning, at daybreak, he found himself close under the lee of a strong English fleet. Many men would have despaired of getting out of such a trap; but Du Guay Trouin instantly conceived a plan of action. Signalling to his prize-masters in the two Dutch ships to salute him with seven guns, and run to leeward, he calmly stood towards the fleet, as though he belonged to it, and had merely fallen out to overhaul the two Dutch vessels. Two large ships and a 36-gun frigate hauled out of line to inspect him, but, being completely deceived by his appearance and nonchalance, they desisted—the frigate, however, displaying undue curiosity with regard to the two Dutch vessels. This was very disturbing, and Du Guay Trouin was on tenter-hooks as he watched her approach them; however, he kept jogging along quietly with the English fleet, until, by edging away gradually, he was in a position to make a run for it. Setting all his canvas, he tried to place himself between the frigate and his prizes; and he rapidly conceived the glorious idea of boarding and capturing the frigate in view of the whole fleet—most likely he would have succeeded, as he had a far more numerous crew; but the English captain began to suspect, and, keeping a gunshot to windward, lowered a boat to board and question Du Guay Trouin. When it was half-way on its journey, the boat's crew suddenly realised the truth, and hastily returned; upon which Du Guay Trouin hoisted his colours and opened fire on the frigate. This woke up the Englishmen—who must, indeed, have been very sleepy—and several large ships detached themselves and came down upon the *Sans-pareil*; before they could reach her, however, the frigate, much damaged by Du Guay Trouin's fire, made urgent signals of distress, and while they were soothing the frigate and recovering her boat, Du Guay Trouin quietly made off and took his prizes safely into port! He was really a glorious fellow— and only now three-and-twenty.

Du Guay Trouin, shortly after this, had cause of complaint against a naval captain whom he encountered at sea, and who, evidently jealous of his successes, fired on his boat, and, calling him on board his ship, rated him in the most contemptuous and insulting manner, threatening to " keel-haul " him, and so on. This is a good example of the behaviour of the aristocratic naval officers towards privateersmen, and it is not surprising if the latter demurred to accepting commissions in the Navy. Du Guay Trouin, however, was destined ere long to take his place there, after a most tremendous and bloody encounter with some Dutch men-of-war escorting a fleet of merchantmen.

He was then commanding the *St. Jacques des Victoires*, and had in company his old ship the *Sanspareil*, commanded by his cousin, Jacques Boscher, and the *Leonore*, of 16 guns. Being joined, after sighting this fleet, under the care of two 50-gun and one 30-gun ship, by two large St. Malo privateers, Du Guay Trouin reckoned that he was strong enough to attack— with five ships to three, though the *Leonore* did not count for much in such an action. However, he despatched her to seize some of the convoy, told his cousin in the *Sanspareil* to tackle one of the 50-gun ships while he went for the other, and the two St. Malo men took care of the frigate in the middle. By the action of the Dutchmen Du Guay Trouin and his cousin exchanged antagonists; the ship destined for Boscher fell foul of the *St. Jacques*, and Trouin, with his customary promptitude and impetuosity, immediately launched half his crew on board and carried her. The Dutch commodore's ship, the *Delft*, proved a very hard nut to crack. The *Sanspareil* was repulsed with great loss, her poop on fire, cartridges exploding promiscuously, and nearly a hundred men blown up, shot dead, or wounded. She sheered off, and Du Guay Trouin ran alongside the *Delft*, to be received with even greater warmth. Her captain, an heroic man, fought like a demon, and the *St. Jacques* also was forced to haul off to breathe the men, who were getting somewhat disheartened, and repair considerable damages. Meanwhile, the larger of the St. Malo vessels, the *Faluère*, was directed to keep the redoubtable Dutchman amused, but she soon had enough of it, losing her captain, and running to leeward.

Du Guay Trouin was not going to give in, however. He rallied his men, and, summoning the *Faluère* to his aid, he went for the *Delft* once more—as he says, "with head down." He got her—but it cost him more than half his crew, and every one of the Dutch officers was killed or wounded. The commodore, Baron de Wassenaer, fell on his quarter-deck with four deadly wounds, his sword still grasped in his hand, and was made prisoner.

Then they had an awful night, for it came on to blow hard, on a lee shore ; all the ships were frightfully battered and leaking, masts and rigging cut to pieces, and the already exhausted crews had to turn to at the pumps for dear life. On board the *St. Jacques* the Dutch prisoners were set to work to lighten the ship by throwing overboard all her upper-deck guns, spars, shot—everything movable, to keep her afloat.

Day broke at length, the wind abated, and, with the assistance of boats from the shore, the ship was brought

in : a sorry wreck, indeed, but the fruits of her labour
soon came to hand—three Dutch men-of-war and
twelve ships of the convoy. The *Sanspareil* arrived
twenty-four hours later, having barely survived the
Dutchman's furious onslaught.

For this service Du Guay Trouin received a commission as commander in the Navy, and was again
presented to the king.

As a regular naval officer, he no longer remains
within the scope of these pages ; but there is one
incident which should not be omitted, even though it
be somewhat to the discredit of the English.

In the year 1704 Du Guay Trouin was in command
of the *Jason*, 54 guns, in company with the *Auguste*,
of equal force, when they fell in, at night, with the
English ship *Chatham*, an old antagonist, which had
before escaped them. At daybreak they were on
either side of her, blazing away, the English vessel
making every effort to escape, while maintaining
creditably her part in the fighting, and the three of
them ran into the English fleet. Then things became
serious for the two French ships : some of the fastest
sailers in the fleet were sent after them. The *Auguste*
was a poor sailer, so they agreed to separate. But the
English had force enough to pursue them both, and
the *Auguste* was soon disposed of. The *Jason* held on,
and presently was tackled by the *Worcester*, of 50
guns, which was considerably knocked about, and
dropped astern. Other ships came up, however, and,
supported by their presence, the *Worcester* again
attacked indecisively. With the dusk, the wind

René Duguay-Trouin.

RENÉ DUGUAY-TROUIN; A FAMOUS FRENCH PRIVATEER
COMMANDER; B. 1673, D. 1736.

p. 226]

dropped altogether, and there was the *Jason*, surrounded by foes in the darkness, only waiting for daylight to eat her up.

Naturally, her captain did not find it easy to sleep ; and it was characteristic of him that he still planned in his mind some desperate measure. He told his officers that he intended to go straight for the English flagship ; that he himself would take the helm and run aboard her, and that he thus hoped to perform a brilliant feat of arms, by carrying this ship, before they succumbed to superior force—and in any case, his flag was not coming down unless the enemy could get there to haul it down themselves.

With this heroic resolve in contemplation, he paced the deck. There was not a breath of wind. The ship rolled a little uneasily, the timbers creaking and blocks rattling aloft, while the few sails that were set slatted against the masts and rigging occasionally in that irritating fashion with which all seamen are familiar. At various distances round him were the enemy's vessels, few of them probably out of gunshot, and some very near.

About an hour before daybreak Du Guay Trouin noticed a dark line above the horizon ahead of his ship ; he watched it carefully, and felt convinced that a breeze was coming from that quarter. Calling the crew quietly on deck, he made sail, braced the yards up, and with one or two of the huge oars or "sweeps" provided in those days, he got the ship's head round so as to catch the breeze in a favourable manner in case it should come. And it did come : at first a

breath, which barely gave the ship steerage-way ;
then a little stronger—she steals ahead, two knots,
three knots ; the Englishmen are all taken aback, with
their topsails lowered, their yards braced anyhow.
Before they can make and trim sail the *Jason* is clear
of the ruck of them, a good gunshot clear !   The
Worcester was once more the only one to tackle her,
and was soon shaken off—by noon she was fast dropping
astern ; and, says Du Guay Trouin, " I looked on
myself as though risen from the dead."

Well he might do, too.   And what were all those
Englishmen thinking about, each ship with an officer
in charge of the deck ?   One would imagine that they
could see a breeze coming as well as a Frenchman
could.   But Du Guay Trouin had one essential element
of success about him—*he never threw away a chance.*

He died in 1736.   France may well be proud of him.
Think of a lad of one-and-twenty, pressed by half a
dozen ships among the Scilly Islands, conceiving that
plan of boarding and capturing the *Adventure* !   That
incident alone is sufficient to mark him as excelling
by many degrees the average—nay, the more than
average—fighting seaman.

CHAPTER XV

JACQUES CASSARD

AMONG the less well-known French privateersmen is Jacques Cassard, a native of Nantes, where there stands to this day a commemorative statue of him.

He was born in 1672, and so was a contemporary of Du Guay Trouin. The son of a seafarer, young Jacques was predestined to a similar life, but there is very little known of his early doings. He appears to have commenced as a privateer at the early age of fourteen, and he must evidently have established, during the following ten years, a reputation for skill and daring, for when he was five-and-twenty he was selected to command the bomb-ship in an expedition against Carthagena, under De Pointis, in 1697.

The sluggish and unseaworthy vessel which Cassard commanded parted company from the squadron while crossing the Atlantic, but in due course he arrived at St. Domingo, the rendezvous, where was assembled a formidable squadron, with 5,000 troops, and a contingent of 1,200 filibustering ruffians under Du Casse, Governor of St. Domingo.

The first assault by the ships on the forts at Carthagena was met with such a furious fire that De Pointis was glad to haul off for a time ; Cassard, however, backed up by Du Casse, was so insistent in urging an immediate renewal of the attack that they carried the day. Cassard distinguished himself throughout ; he took his little bomb-vessel close under the strongest fort and bombarded it mercilessly. When the Spaniards' fire began to slacken he and Du Casse led the assault on the battered defences, and, after a desperate conflict, carried the first fort. Cassard, prompt and resourceful, turned the guns upon an adjacent work, and by the evening the Spaniards, driven to the citadel, displayed the flag of surrender.

It was after the defenders had marched out, followed by numbers of the townspeople, however, that Cassard performed the most valuable service. A scene of horror ensued : the regulars and filibusters, mad with drink and lust, scoured the town, ransacked churches and houses, and perpetrated shocking outrages. Their officers lost all control, and were even shot down by the mad rioters when they attempted to remonstrate.

Then Cassard, having obtained permission to take the matter in hand, picked out a band of about three hundred Bretons from among the crews of the warships, and landed with them. He did not mince matters. He was well aware that the only course to pursue, with any hope of success, was to meet savagery with savagery, and the plunderers soon found themselves confronted with the alternative of submission or death. They fought it out in forty-eight hours, Cassard guarding the gates strongly, and searching systematically every quarter of the town. With his own hand he is said to have shot down a score of looters ; and when it was over he had to arrange for the burial of three hundred and seventy unhappy women, who had been ill-treated and murdered, often in the very churches.

De Pointis, on their return, strongly recommended Cassard for a commission in the Navy, but prejudice was too strong against his class, and it was not until nearly three years later, after some successful privateering, that he was summoned to the royal presence. " I have need," said the king, " of all the brave men I can find for my Navy, and as you, they say, are the bravest of the brave, I have appointed you a lieutenant in my fleet, and have given instructions that a sum of £2,000 be handed over to you, to enable you to support your position in a proper manner."

This was all very well ; but his newly earned honours sat heavily upon him, and the jealousy of the naval aristocrats made things unpleasant ; so it was in the capacity of commander of a private ship of war that he gained further laurels.

This was the *St. William*, fitted out by merchants of St. Malo in 1705, a small vessel, mounting only eight guns of insignificant power and manned by sixty-eight harum-scarum fellows picked up on the quays at St. Malo.

After a fruitless cruise he returned to refit, and then made a successful raid upon small traders off the south coast of Ireland, thereby gaining a little prize-money to encourage his crew. After a visit to Brest, he was returning to the coast of Ireland when he came across a Dutchman of greatly superior force, with which he had an heroic encounter.

The Dutchman fired the usual " summoning " gun, to which Cassard paid no heed. A shot across his bows followed, but he held on his course. The Dutchman cleared for action, crowding sail and rapidly overhauling the *St. William.* It looked like a foregone conclusion that she should succumb to this formidable adversary, carrying fourteen 9-pounders.

Cassard, however, had his own ideas as to the conduct of the engagement. As the enemy rapidly came up, pounding him with his bow-guns, the Frenchman suddenly shortened sail, squared his mainyard, and threw his ship aboard the other. A discharge of grape and chain-shot from the *St. William's* 3-pounders was instantly followed by a rush of sixty desperate men, headed by their captain.

A most bloody encounter ensued. Dutchmen are not easily beaten, and the deck had to be gained step by step. It is said that Cassard had told off one of his leading men to endeavour, the moment he gained a footing on board, to run in one of the Dutchman's guns and point it along the deck ; and while the remainder were at grips with the enemy, this man and half a dozen others contrived to effect this, loaded the gun with langrage—which means any odd bit of metal you can scrape up—and watched for a chance. Then they shouted, " Stand clear of the gun ! " The French suddenly parted to either side of the deck, and the shower of iron peppered the astonished Dutchmen. This was twice accomplished, the Frenchmen each time rushing forward in the smoke; and then the Dutch captain, wounded and bleeding, proffered his sword to Cassard. It was a good device, if the story be true; but not as easy of accomplishment as it is made to appear in the accounts of the action.

It is said that the Dutch loss, out of a crew of 113, was 37 killed and 51 wounded. Cassard had 16 killed and 23 wounded.

Some three or four years of success followed, during which Cassard adopted the illegal, but tempting device of ransoming his prizes and taking the captains as hostages for payment—a practice for which, like Jean Bart, he was brought to book, without very much practical result. However, he made a great deal of money, and in the year 1709 [1] he was appealed to by some merchants of Marseilles to convoy from Bizerta, on the north coast of Tunis, a fleet of grain-ships—an urgent business, as France was in very great need of grain. He was induced to put his hand in his pocket and fit out at his own expense two men-of-war—the *Éclatant* and *Serieux*—lent by the Government, the latter of which he commanded himself, and made sail for Bizerta, where he found the grain-ships safe enough. The difficulty was, to get them safely to Marseilles, the English fleet being on the alert. With this end in view he had recourse to a ruse, which is not very clearly set forth in the accounts; but in the end he enticed a frigate out of Malta and led her away from

---

[1] As related in " The Corsairs of France," by C. B. Norman; but it appears probable that it was in the previous year, for reasons to be stated later.

his convoy, which he had left in charge of the *Éclatant*, though it involved a desperate running action with a vessel of superior force, in which he nearly came to grief.

Arriving at length at Marseilles, he found that the grain-ships had turned up safely, which was really a great triumph ; but the wily merchants were too cunning for the simple seaman. There was, it appears, a clause in the agreement to the effect that Cassard should bring in the convoy—it is easy to imagine how such a document would be worded—and, because he had not personally conducted the ships into port, the merchants refused to pay him the stipulated sum for his services ! He appealed, but the merchants had too many friends at court ; so he found himself some £10,000 out of pocket in the long run, as a reward for averting a famine by his skill and courage.

He was destined, however, to repeat the exploit. In June 1709 a huge fleet of eighty-four merchant vessels, under convoy of six men-of-war, was despatched to Smyrna to bring back grain. The squadron consisted of the *Téméraire*, 60, *Toulouse*, 60, *Stendard*, 50, *Fleuron*, 50, *Hirondelle*, 36, and *Vestale*, 36, under the command of M. de Feuquières. Reaching Smyrna in safety, they sailed in October on the return voyage, with their precious freight ; but De Feuquières, learning that a strong English squadron was watching for him in the Gulf of Genoa, put into Syracuse, in Sicily ; and sent the *Toulouse* to Marseilles for additional force.

The people of Marseilles shamelessly appealed to Cassard, whom they had treated so scurvily; he refused at first to have anything to do with it. However, he was eventually placed in command of a little squadron, consisting of the *Parfait*, 70, with his flag; the *Toulouse*, Captain De Lambert; *Serieux*, 60, Captain De l'Aigle; and *Phœnix*, 56, Captain Du Haies.

With a fair wind, on November 8th he sailed for Syracuse, according to Mr. Norman, arriving there on the evening of the following day—a feat which may be safely put down as practically impossible, the distance being over 650 nautical miles, or knots. However, there is no doubt that Cassard arrived off Syracuse one day, and found only two English men-of-war watching for the grain fleet, instead of a strong squadron, as he expected. With these he resolved to deal at once, and bore down upon them.

The two English ships were the *Pembroke*, 64, Captain Edward Rumsey—not *Rumfry*, as Mr. Norman calls him, probably from some French document—and the *Falcon*, 36, Captain Charles Constable, the remainder of the squadron having gone to Mahon, in Corsica, to refit. The *Pembroke* had apparently had her turn there and returned to her station a few days previously, the *Falcon* joining her.

When Cassard's squadron hove in sight and Captain Rumsey, having failed to receive from them the acknowledgment of the private signal, realised that he was in for a serious business, he signalled the *Falcon* to shorten sail, and, running up alongside her, he asked Captain Constable what he made of the strangers, to

which the latter replied that one of them was a very
big ship, but he could not make much of the others.

" Shall we fight them ? " shouted Rumsey through
his speaking-trumpet. " Just as you please, sir ! "
bawled Constable. " That's no answer," rejoined
Rumsey. " With all my heart," said Constable, and
they cleared for action—none too soon, for the French
ships, bringing up a stronger breeze with them, were
already almost within gunshot.

Cassard had signalled Feuquières to weigh and convoy the grain-ships out while he engaged the two
English ships. Rumsey, realising that he was im-
peratively called upon to prevent, or at least to retard
their escape, had probably made up his mind before
he spoke to Constable. Leaving only two ships there
was a blunder, and he really had no choice about
fighting, for he could not well have escaped.

The action which ensued was one of the most stubborn sea-fights on record. Cassard attacked with three
ships, the *Parfait* ranging alongside the *Falcon*,
while the *Serieux* and *Phœnix* tackled the *Pembroke*.
If the Frenchmen expected an easy conquest of the
Falcon by the huge 70-gun ship they were very much
in error. With her crew of 740 men the *Parfait* was
run alongside, and her bowsprit lashed to the fore-
rigging of the *Falcon*. Instantly Constable turned
the tables on the foe, rushing on board at the head of
one hundred men. They were repulsed, with heavy
losses on both sides, and before Cassard could return
the compliment the two ships fell apart. The *Falcon's* flight was soon stayed by the heavy fire of the

French ship, which brought down spars and cut rigging extensively, and once more Cassard laid her on board. His first attack was repelled by the indomitable Constable and his men ; but the price was too heavy : something like 120 men had been killed or desperately wounded already, and Constable, taking counsel with his officers, was forced to the conclusion that it was useless to sacrifice more lives, and so hauled down his colours ; he had been badly wounded in the shoulder, but kept his place on deck. According to Captain Schomberg, in his " Naval Chronology," there were only sixteen men of the *Falcon's* crew able to stand at their quarters when she surrendered.

Meanwhile, the *Pembroke* and the other two ships were hammering each other at close range, and much damage resulted on both sides. After an hour and a half of fighting Captain Rumsey, who had behaved splendidly, was killed, and Barkley, the first lieutenant, came on deck and took his place. For two hours after the captain's death the unequal conflict was maintained : Cassard came down and joined the fray after the *Falcon* was captured, and had a tremendous cannonade with the *Pembroke*, yardarm to yardarm, while the *Serieux* pounded her on the other quarter. It could not last ; the English ship's mizzenmast went crashing by the board, her maintopmast followed, her rigging was nearly all cut away, her mainmast wounded and tottering, her decks lumbered with wreckage, which also rendered the ship almost unmanageable, and the crew falling by tens—to hold out longer would be worse than useless, so Barkley and his brother officers agreed, and the colours had to come down.

The losses on both sides afforded ample testimony to the splendid courage of the Englishmen and the gallant pertinacity of the French. Six months later Constable and the surviving officers of the *Pembroke* were tried by court-martial, were judged to have done their duty, and honourably acquitted.

It now remains to clear up some chronological discrepancies. According to Mr. Norman, this engagement took place on November 10th, 1710, and Cassard entered Toulon with his prizes on the 15th. Where he obtained these dates does not appear ; but, as a matter of fact, the court-martial took place on June 21st, 1710, and the sworn testimony of the officers of both ships places the engagement on December 29th, 1709 ; Captain Rumsey wrote from Mahon on December 10th, reporting to the admiral—Sir Edward Whittaker—that his ship had been careened, and was nearly ready for sea. These official reports being unimpeachable, it appears probable that the first affair with the grain-ships took place in 1708, as has already been hinted.[1]

However, this does not affect the actual facts with regard to the engagement, which was so creditable to both sides.

Promoted to the rank of commander, Cassard was appointed to command the military works in progress at Toulon ; but he was not happy in this post, and, after trying in vain to obtain restitution of the money

[1] See note, p. 233.

he had lost on the first grain venture, he took command of a squadron, consisting of nine vessels, men-of-war, but fitted out by private enterprise in St. Malo and Nantes.

With this force, and a proportional number of troops, he took St. Iago, in the Cape Verde Islands, then crossed the Atlantic and pillaged Montserrat and Antigua, ransomed Surinam and St. Eustatia, and, after some difficulties, treated Curaçoa similarly.

Despite his really brilliant achievements, Jacques Cassard was destined to spend his declining years in comparative poverty, and die in confinement. Jealousy on the part of the aristocrats, false accusations of misappropriation of prize goods, impudence amounting to mutiny in dealing with an admiral, and finally loss of temper and insolence to the all-powerful Cardinal Fleury—this was the end of all: he was imprisoned in the fortress of Ham, and there he died, in 1740, having survived Du Guay Trouin by four years.

CHAPTER XVI

ROBERT SURCOUF

ROBERT SURCOUF, another prominent French priva-teersman, was born on December 12th, 1773—just one hundred years after Du Guay Trouin, to whose family he was related.

Like his famous relative, he was intended for the Church ; but he speedily manifested a militant spirit by no means of an ecclesiastical quality—he was, in fact, an awful pickle at home and at school ; in-subordinate, always fighting with some one, tearing his clothes to pieces, and quite unamenable to parental or pedagogic admonition. Severity and entreaty were alike futile. However, he was sent to a seminary at Dinan, under a superior of great reputed strictness, and here for a time he raised his parents' hopes ; but he soon grew weary of the monotony of obedience, ceased to evince any interest in his studies, and speedily became the leader in every description of mischief.

The crisis arrived one day when the class-master seized young Robert with the intention of administering personal chastisement. The scholar proved to be exceedingly robust for his years, and resisted the operation with tremendous vigour ; and when at length the master had got him down, he seized his leg in his teeth, and compelled him to desist for the moment and seek for assistance. Surcouf's classmates loudly applauded him ; but, knowing that he would be ultimately compelled to yield to superior force, he got through the window, scaled the garden wall, and, without hat or shoes, started to walk home, the snow lying thickly on the ground. He had more than twenty miles to walk, and when it became dark he slipped about on the frozen snow, and at length, worn out and half perished with cold and hunger, he sank senseless by the roadside. Luckily, some fish-merchants found him and took him home, where he was nursed by his mother with the tenderest devotion during an attack of pneumonia. Thanks to his strong constitution, he recovered completely ; but he was not sent back to Dinan. It was obvious that there was nothing to be done but to recognise his vocation as a seaman ; and accordingly, at the age of thirteen, he was shipped on board the *Heron*, brig, bound for Cadiz.

This kind of coasting voyage was not at all to the mind of the impetuous and ambitious Robert. Some of the crew who had made distant voyages had wonderful tales to tell, and he longed to visit these far-off lands. It was two years, however, before his wish was gratified. In March 1789, at sixteen, he embarked as volunteer on board the *Aurora*, of 700 tons, bound for the East Indies. They had a gale of wind, with a tremendous sea, off the Cape, and young Surcouf displayed remarkable courage and aptitude in the various emergencies which are sure to arise on such an occasion, for which he was duly praised by his superiors on board. After touching at the Mauritius, they went on to Pondicherry; and during this latter portion of the voyage Surcouf became very friendly with the fourth officer, M. de Saint-Pol, who, having been born on the Coromandel Coast, was conversant with the Eastern seas, was a very good officer and a well-informed man. He took pleasure in imparting to his young shipmate the knowledge at his command, and the seed fell upon fruitful ground, young Surcouf drinking in with avidity every detail concerning the Indian Seas, which he was destined one day to hold for a while completely. Saint-Pol's enthusiastic description of the exploits of Suffren served to inflame his ardour. However, he had some unpleasant work before him ere he found the opportunity he sought.

The *Aurora*, having conveyed some troops from Pondicherry to Mauritius, sailed for Mozambique, and there embarked four hundred negro slaves for the West Indies. This was in February 1790, the season at which the tremendous cyclones of the Indian Ocean are most frequent and formidable. The *Aurora* fell in with one of these storms on the 18th, and, in spite of the brave efforts of master and crew, she was cast, dismasted and helpless, on the coast of Africa. The crew, together with the female slaves and children, were saved; but the negroes confined in the hold perished, every man, in that horrible death-trap, in spite of some brave attempts, in which young Surcouf took a part, to rescue them.

When the wind went down there was the terrible task to be performed of clearing out the ship, which appeared not to be damaged beyond repair; and in this work, which occupied fifteen days, Surcouf distinguished himself by his willing and untiring energy. Twice he was brought up fainting from that awful hold, but he continued to labour and set an heroic example until the end; and such fortitude in a lad of his age naturally attracted attention. He went back as mate in a vessel hired to convey the crew to Mauritius. She was driven terribly out of her course, and did not arrive until December; and Surcouf finished his first voyage as quartermaster, on board a corvette, the *Bienvenue*, for the homeward passage, reaching L'Orient on January 3rd, 1792. He made haste to visit his parents, who, no longer remembering the escapades of the school-boy, welcomed with pride and affection the stalwart, bronzed young seaman of eighteen, who appeared likely, after all, to do them credit.

The Indian seas called him again, and, after six months at home, he sailed as a lieutenant on board the armed ship *Navigator*, for Mauritius. After a couple of trading voyages between this island and the African coast, war broke out with England, and the *Navigator* was laid up.

Surcouf now became lieutenant on board another vessel, trading to Africa, in which he made several voyages. There was no opportunity of acquiring any honour and glory in action, so he applied himself to his profession, and became a very good seaman, with an excellent knowledge of the navigation of the Indian Ocean.

He was not as lucky, however, as he had been in the *Aurora*, with regard to his superiors. The first lieutenant was a Portuguese, and for some reason he conceived a deadly hatred of Surcouf.

One sweltering hot day, the ship being becalmed, the men obtained leave to bathe over the side ; after they had finished Surcouf thought he would like a dip, and took a header from the gangway. No sooner had he done so than he was seized with a sort of cataleptic fit, and found himself sinking helplessly. Luckily, it was noticed that he did not come up again, and some of the crew lowered a boat, while others dived for him, recovered him, and brought him on board ; but all their efforts failed to evoke any signs of life, and the Portuguese, obviously and brutally exultant, after declaring repeatedly that Surcouf was dead, seized the inert body and with his own hands dragged it to the ship's side.

Surcouf, conscious of all that went on around him, realised that, unless he could make some sign, he had only a few seconds to live. With a tremendous effort, he contrived a voluntary movement of his limbs— it was noticed, and the further exertions of his ship-mates sufficed to restore him.

The Portuguese, however, had not done with him. On their next visit to Africa some of the crew were laid up with malarial fever, and the first lieutenant caught it. He was very ill, and Surcouf earned the warm approbation of the captain for the manner in which he performed his senior's duties on the return voyage. After they arrived at Mauritius he was just going on shore when he received a message begging him to go and see the Portuguese, who said he must speak to him before he died. Surcouf did not much like the idea, but, after some hesitation, he went, having put a pair of loaded pistols in his pocket. The sick man made a sign to his servant to retire, and then said :

" I wish to speak to you with a sincere heart before I pass from this world, to relieve my conscience, and ask your forgiveness for all the evil I have wished to do you during our voyages."

Surcouf, touched by this appeal, assured him that he bore no malice. Just then the dying man appeared to suffer from a spasm which contorted his body, one arm stretching out towards a pillow near him. Surcouf quietly seized his hand and lifted the pillow, disclosing a couple of loaded pistols.

He seized them, and, pointing one at his enemy's face, said :

" You miserable beast ! I could have shot you like a dog, or squashed you like a cockroach ; but I despise you too much, so I'll leave you to die like a coward."

Which, we are told, the wretched man did, blaspheming in despairing rage.

After this, his ship being laid up in consequence of the blockade, he was appointed junior lieutenant of a colonial man of war, with a commission signed by the Governor.

Then came news of the death of Louis XVI. by the guillotine—news which astounded the colonists and seamen, who, in the Indian seas, were defending the " honour " of France—which they continued to do to the best of their ability, disregarding the deadly feuds and bloodshed at home.

In October 1794 a little squadron was despatched · from Mauritius to attack a couple of English men-of-war which were practically blockading the island— these were the *Centurion*, of 54 guns, and the *Diomede*, of the same force but fewer men ; and the French squadron consisted of the *Prudente*, 40 guns, the *Cybèle*, 44 guns, the *Jean Bart*, 20 guns, and the *Courier*, 14 guns. The Frenchmen attacked with great spirit, and the English vessels were practically driven off the station ; partly owing, it was said, to the extreme caution displayed by Captain Matthew Smith, of the *Diomede*, for which he was subsequently called upon to answer before a court-martial.[1]

In this spirited action, on the French side, Robert Surcouf took part as a junior lieutenant on board the

[1] Captain Smith appears, however, to have been very harshly used, through the implications, rather than any specific accusation, of his senior, Captain Osborn ; and upon his presenting a memorial to the King (George III.), setting forth the circumstances under which he was tried in the East Indies, the case was referred to the law officers of the Crown and the Admiralty Counsel, who declared that the finding of the court was unwarrantable, and should not be upheld. Captain Smith, who had been dismissed the Service, was thereupon reinstated ; but an officer who thus

Cybèle. The casualties were heavy, but he escaped without a single scratch, and was commended for his courageous attitude. But soon afterwards he found himself at a loose end, the volunteers being discharged ; so he presently accepted the command of the brig *Creole*, engaged in the slave trade, and made several successful voyages before the authorities realised that the traffic was, by a recent ordinance, illegal.

They gave orders to arrest Surcouf upon his arrival at Mauritius ; he, however, having got wind of this intention, steered instead for the Isle of Bourbon, and there landed his cargo during the night, in a small bay about ten miles from St. Denis, the capital of the island. At daybreak he anchored in St. Paul's Bay, in the same island.

About eight o'clock he had a surprise visit from three representatives of the Public Health Committee, who desired to come on board. Surcouf, concealing his annoyance, gave permission, and of course they were not long in discovering undoubted indications of the purpose for which the brig had been employed. They drew up an indictment on the spot, and warned Surcouf that he would have to accompany them to answer to it.

" I am at your service, citizens," he replied politely ; " but don't go until you have given me the pleasure of partaking of the breakfast which my cook has hastily prepared."

"scores" off his superiors is not readily pardoned, and he was never again employed. It appears to have been a shady business, with some personal spite in the background.

The invitation was accepted.   The conscientious
commissioners—"improvised negro-lovers, under the
bloody Reign of Terror," as Robert Surcouf's name-
sake and biographer contemptuously styles them—
were fond of good things, and the sea-air had sharpened
their appetites.   Surcouf had a short and earnest
conversation with his mate before he conducted his
guests below.

The cook's "hasty" efforts were marvellously
attractive, and the wine was excellent—Surcouf was
a bit of a *gourmet* himself, and liked to have things
nicely done—so what need was there for being in a
hurry ?

Meanwhile, the mate had dismissed the state canoe
of the commissioners, telling the coxswain that the
brig's boat would take them on shore.

Then the cable was quietly slipped, and the *Creole*,
under all sail, rapidly left the anchorage, and, opening
the headland, lay over to a fresh south-west wind.
The unaccustomed motion began to tell upon the
landsmen.   Surcouf invited them to go on deck, and
there was the island, already separated from the vessel
by a considerable tract of foam-flecked ocean—and
Surcouf was in command !   In reply to their threats
and remonstrances he told them that he was going
to take them across to Africa, among their friends
the negroes, and meanwhile they could come below and
receive his orders.

During the night the wind freshened considerably,
and the morning found the commissioners very anxious
to regain terra firma at any cost ;   Surcouf had it all

his own way. The indictment was destroyed, and a very different document was drawn up, to the effect that they had found no traces on board the brig of her having carried negroes, and that she had been suddenly driven from her anchor by a tidal wave—with other circumstantial little touches, which amused Surcouf and did them no great harm. Eight days later he landed them at Mauritius.

He had, however, had enough of slave trading. Of course, his exploit was the talk of the town, and most people were much amused over his impudent capture of the commissioners, who were compelled, in view of their written acquittal, to keep quiet. The general idea was that Surcouf had displayed qualities which would be extremely useful in the captain of a privateer ; and it was not long before he was offered the command of the *Emilie*, of 180 tons and 4 guns. Just when she was ready for sea, however, the Governor let it be understood that, for certain reasons, he did not intend to issue any privateer commissions. This was a very keen disappointment ; Surcouf obtained an interview with the Governor, who received him kindly but remained inflexible. Stifling his feelings, he sought his owners, and asked them what they were going to do. He received orders to go to the Seychelles for a cargo of turtles, and, failing these, to fill up with maize, cotton, etc., at these and other islands, and to fight shy of the cruisers that might be to windward of the island : a very tame programme.

However, he took comfort from the reflection that, although his ship was not a regular privateer, she was at least " an armed vessel in time of war " ; and, as such, was permitted to defend herself when attacked ; so he might yet see some fighting.

While at anchor at Seychelles, taking in cargo, two large English men-of-war unexpectedly appeared in the offing, and Surcouf only escaped by the clever manner in which he navigated the dangerous channels among the islands, to the admiration of his crew.

This incident set him thinking, and, calling his staff together, he drew up a sort of memorandum, setting forth how that they had been obliged to quit Seychelles on account of these two men-of-war, and could not return to complete their cargo ; and that they had therefore resolved, by common consent, to go to the coast of " the East "—*i.e.* Sumatra, Rangoon, etc.—for a cargo of rice and other articles ; " and at the same time to defend ourselves against any of the enemy's ships which we may encounter on the way, being armed with several guns."

This was signed by Surcouf and his officers and by some of the leading hands, No doubt it made him feel happier ; but he had quite made up his mind as to his future conduct.

They got in a cyclone south of the Bay of Bengal, and then steered for Rangoon, off which place they sighted an English vessel steering for them. She came steadily on, and, when within close range, fired a shot —the " summoning shot," for the *Emilie* to display her colours. It was not an attack, and Surcouf had no right so to consider it ; but that is what he chose to do. Hoisting his colours, he replied with three shots. The Englishman attempted to escape; but the *Emilie* was the faster, and, running alongside, delivered her broadside, upon which the other struck his colours.

" This was the first time," says his biographer, " that our Malouin had seen the British flag lowered to him, and though he had had only the commencement of a fight, his heart swelled with patriotic pride and beat with hope. The first shot has been fired; the captain of an armed ship in time of war gives place to the privateer commander. Surcouf arrives at a decision as to his future—he has passed the Rubicon ! "

All very fine; but it was an act of piracy, for which he could have been hanged at the yardarm. He repeated it shortly afterwards, capturing three vessels laden with rice, and appropriating one, a pilot brig, in place of the *Emilie*, which was losing her speed on account of a foul bottom. A few days later, having now thrown away all hesitation, he seized a large ship, the *Diana*, also laden with rice, and started to take her, in company with his stolen brig, the *Cartier*, to Mauritius.

On the voyage, however, Surcouf improved upon his former captures. A large sail was reported one morning, and it was presently apparent that she was an East Indiaman. The two French ships had not made much progress down the Bay of Bengal, and the English vessel was obviously standing into Balasore Roads, there to await a pilot for the river Hooghly, unless she picked up one earlier. The account given in *The Gentleman's Magazine* for June 1796 states that the Indiaman—the *Triton*—was at anchor in Balasore Roads when she was sighted. In the latest life of

Surcouf, however, written by his great-nephew and namesake, it is said that she was standing towards the Orissa coast, on the starboard tack—Balasore being, of course, in the province of Orissa, and the open anchorage a convenient place for picking up the Calcutta pilot. The difference is of some importance with regard to Surcouf's attack : it is one thing to board and carry a vessel at anchor, on a hot afternoon, when every one who is not required to be moving about is having a siesta, and quite another thing to board her when she is standing in to her anchorage, with the captain and officers on deck, and the crew standing by to handle the sails ; and this latter feat is what M. Robert Surcouf claims to have been performed by his great-uncle. It is possible, however, that both accounts may, in a measure, be correct ; that is to say, the *Triton*, when first sighted from aloft on board the *Cartier*, may have been standing in towards the anchorage, which she may have reached, and dropped anchor, before the Frenchman came alongside.

However this may be, Surcouf was quick enough to realise that the Indiaman, if fought in anything like man-of-war style, was far too strong for him. He had on board only nineteen persons, including himself and the surgeon, belonging to the ship, and a few Lascars who had been transferred from the *Diana* : a ridiculous number to attack an Indiaman.

Finding that he did not gain upon the chase, and knowing that his own vessel had been a pilot brig, Surcouf hoisted the pilot flag ; upon which the *Triton* immediately hove to and waited for him ; or, possibly, being already in the roads, dropped anchor ; but the story distinctly says, " met en travers, et permit ainsi de l'atteindre," which has only one possible interpretation. Surcouf was still some three miles distant, and kept an anxious eye upon his big opponent, or rather, upon his possible prey, for the *Triton* could scarcely be styled an opponent. He saw that she mounted some six-and-twenty guns, but that they were not ready for action. He saw also on deck " beaucoup de monde "—a great crowd of people, most of whom, he hoped, would prove to be Lascars ; but he very shortly discovered that they were nothing of the kind. He was now within gun-shot, and realised that the business might be serious for him ; but the Englishmen were as yet quite unsuspicious, so he harangued his crew :

" My lads, this Englishman is very strong, and we are only nineteen ; shall we try to take him by surprise, and thus acquire both gain and glory ? Or do you prefer to rot in a beastly English prison-ship ? "

It was cleverly put, from his own standpoint : he was spoiling for a fight, for an opportunity of displaying his masterly strategy and determined courage, to say nothing of the dollars in prospect ; but the implication was perfectly unjustifiable that the choice lay between a desperate assault and certain capture. If he did not want to fight, he had only to sheer off and run for it ; no Indiaman would initiate an action, or give chase, under such circumstances. However, he knew his audience, and his speech had the desired effect :

"Death or victory!" cried the eighteen heroes.

"Good!" replied their captain, "this ship shall either be our tomb or the cradle of our glory!"

It was really very fine and melodramatic—more especially since it was the prelude to an act of undoubted piracy.

This fact, however, does not detract from the merit of a very clever and bold attack, which was perfectly successful. Making his eighteen heroes lie down, while the Lascars stood about the deck, he took the helm and ran down for the *Triton*. The people on board only saw the expected pilot brig approaching, as no doubt they habitually did, to within a biscuit-toss, to tranship the pilot. Suddenly she hoisted French colours and let drive a heavy dose of grape and canister among the Indiaman's crew. A cry of dismay and astonishment rose from her deck, as every one instinctively sought shelter from the hail of iron. In another moment the brig was alongside, and Surcouf was leaping on board at the head of his small company. The surprise was so complete that there was but little resistance. The captain and a few others made a brave attempt, but were killed immediately; the rest were driven below, and the hatches clapped on. And so, with five killed and six wounded on the English side, and one killed and one wounded on the French, the thing was over. Really, it was a masterly affair.

Putting his prisoners on board the *Diana*, which he permitted her captain to ransom, he left them to make their way to Calcutta; and it is stated by contemporary Indian newspapers that he treated them with consideration, and was polite to the lady passengers.

The *Cartier* was captured by an English man-of-war, but Surcouf carried the *Triton* in triumph to Mauritius, where he was, of course, received with a tremendous ovation.

He was greatly dismayed, however, upon having it pointed out to him by the Governor that those who choose to go a-pirating are liable to be called upon to pay the piper. All his captures were condemned, and forfeited to the Government, as he had not been provided with a letter of marque. This was perfectly right and proper, though his biographer tries to make it out an injustice. There was a fearful outcry, of course, and eventually the matter was referred home, Surcouf appearing in person to plead his cause ; the appeal was successful, and all the captures were declared to be " good prize," which was very nice for Surcouf and his owners, who pocketed a good round sum of money. About the morality of the proceedings the less said the better.

During this period of litigation the privateer hero had, of course, revisited St. Malo and seen his family and friends ; and there he also fell in love with Mlle. Marie Blaize, to whom he became engaged. But the sea was calling him again, and he left her without being married.

His new command was the *Clarisse*, 14 guns, with a crew of one hundred and forty hardy seamen of St. Malo and elsewhere ; while Nicolas Surcouf, brother to the captain, and a man of similar type, was chief officer. She sailed in July 1798 for the old familiar cruising-ground in the Indian Ocean ; and just after crossing the Equator, fell in with a large armed English vessel, from which, after a sharp action, she parted, considerably damaged ; but Surcouf consoled himself for this failure—from which, as his biographer puts it, " there remained only the glory of having seen the flag of England flying before the victorious standard of France ! "—by the capture of a rich prize off Rio Janeiro ; and anchored in December 1798 at Port Louis, Mauritius, " where his expected return from Europe was awaited with impatience by those who had built great hopes upon the conqueror of the *Triton*."

Space does not admit of following the adventures of Robert Surcouf in detail ; his grand-nephew spares no pains, indeed, in this respect, spinning out his narrative, embellished with admiring outbursts of national and personal eulogy, in a somewhat tedious fashion. In the *Clarisse* Surcouf had more successes, capturing two armed merchant vessels very cleverly at Sonson, in Sumatra, not without damage, which rendered it advisable to return to Port Louis to refit : thence, putting out again, he was on one occasion chased by the English frigate *Sibylle* ; and so hard pressed was he that he was compelled to have recourse to desperate measures to improve the speed of his vessel : eight guns were thrown overboard, together with spare spars and other loose material, the rigging was eased up, the mast wedges loosened, the between-deck supports knocked away. It was a light breeze, of course, and these measures have a remarkable effect under such circumstances, rendering the vessel "all alive," as it were, and exceedingly susceptible of the smallest variation of pressure on the sails—and so the *Clarisse* escaped. Two days later she captured an English vessel, the *Jane*—which is misnamed *James* in French narratives—whose skipper wrote a long account of the affair. She sailed in company with two Indiamen, the *Manship* and *Lansdowne*, having been warned that Surcouf was on the prowl outside. The captain imagined that, by keeping company with the two large Indiamen —armed vessels, of course—he would be safe from molestation; but he was sorely mistaken, for when the privateer hove in sight, and he signalled his consorts, they calmly sailed on and left the *Jane* a victim, after a trifling resistance. Surcouf, being informed that these two large vessels, still in sight, were Indiamen, contemptuously remarked: "They are two *Tritons*," and he and his officers expressed the opinion that the captains deserved to be shot.

Next he encountered two large American ships: there was much ill-feeling between France and the United States, though war had not been declared, and when they met they fought like dogs of hostile owners. One of these vessels Surcouf captured by boarding, the other escaping; and this was his last cruise in the *Clarisse*.

It is in connection with his next command that Surcouf's name is, perhaps, most familiar. This was the *Confiance*, a new ship, and by all accounts a regular beauty. Before he got away, however, he had a quarrel with Duterte, another privateer captain of some note, commanding the *Malartic*, who had recourse to a ruse to obtain the pick of the available seamen in Mauritius for his own ship. Surcouf eventually contrived to circumvent him, and, after some high words in a café, they arranged a meeting with swords at daybreak. The Governor, General Malartic, however, intervened, commanding their attendance at the hour arranged for the duel, and, after an harangue from him, the two corsairs embraced and remained friends thereafter—they cruised, in fact, in consort for a time, in the Bay of Bengal, with much success.

Surcouf's great exploit in the *Confiance* was the capture of the *Kent*, East Indiaman, at the end of her voyage. M. Robert Surcouf, in describing this event, dwells upon every detail, from the moment the *Kent* was sighted, with most tedious prolixity, as though this was one of the decisive battles of the world. What happened is as follows :

On October 7th, 1800, a large sail was sighted at daybreak. After careful scrutiny, Surcouf decided that she was an Indiaman, a rich prize, and determined to have her if possible ; so he hailed from aloft, where he was inspecting the stranger : " All hands on deck, make sail—drinks all round for the men ! Clear for action ! "

Then, coming down from aloft, he mounted on the companion hatch, ordered everybody aft, and harangued them—he was great at a speech on an occasion of the kind, though probably his biographer has embellished it—told them the Englishman was very strong, but that he intended to board at once.

" I suppose each one of you is more than equal to one Englishman ? Very good—be armed ready for boarding—and, as it will be very hot work, I will give you an hour of pillage."

It was very hot work. The *Kent's* people certainly greatly outnumbered the privateer's ; she had on board a great proportion of the crew of the *Queen,* another East Indiaman, which had been destroyed by fire on the coast of Brazil. Surcouf says she had 437 on board, and the *Confiance* only 130 ; but the figures for the *Kent* are probably greatly exaggerated.

After the exchange of some broadsides, Surcouf at length out-manœuvred the English captain, his vessel being probably far more handy, and succeeded in laying him aboard. Captain Rivington, of the *Kent,* was a man of heroic courage, and fought at the head of his men with splendid determination ; but the privateer crew had all the advantage of previous understanding and association. The *Kent's* men were undisciplined and but poorly armed for such an encounter, while Surcouf's, we are told, had each a boarding axe, a cutlass, a pistol, and a dagger— to say nothing of blunderbusses loaded with six bullets, pikes fifteen feet long, and enormous clubs— all this, in conjunction with " drinks all round," and the promise of pillage !

As long as their captain kept his feet the " Kents " maintained the desperate combat ; but when at length he fell mortally wounded, though his last cry was "Don't give up the ship!" the flag was shortly lowered, though the chief officer made a desperate attempt to rally the crew once more.

And then commenced the promised pillage. Surcouf, hearing the loud complaints of the English, despoiled of their property, was on the point of angrily restraining his crew, when he remembered his promise, and stepped back, we are told, with a sigh of regret. But then came the screams of women.

"Good Lord! I'd forgotten the women!" he cried, and called his officers to come and protect them, which was very necessary. So hideous was the scene of plunder, amid the dead and wounded, that Surcouf exerted his power of will to cut short the time. He landed the prisoners in an Arab vessel, and arrived at Mauritius with his prize in November.

The French were accused of having behaved with great brutality, even wantonly poniarding the wounded and dying. This, of course, is denied; but it does not require a very vivid imagination to picture the scene—a crowd of half-disciplined men, excited with liquor, brutalised by bloodshed, elated with victory, turned loose to plunder; some word of remonstrance from a wounded man, finding his person roughly searched, and a knife-thrust, or fatal blow with the butt of a pistol, would be the only reply. Surcouf's protection of the ladies was, however, said to be effective; and this is probably true.

Surcouf took his flying *Confiance* back to France, with a letter of marque; he caught a Portuguese vessel on the passage, and arrived at La Rochelle on April 13th, 1801. His adventure in the East had not cooled the ardour of his feelings towards Mlle. Marie Blaize, whom he married six weeks later; and he now became in his turn the *armateur* or owner of privateers.

He was persuaded, however, to go to sea once more in 1807, when war had broken out again, in a vessel which he named the *Revenant—i.e.* the *Ghost*: and she had for a figure-head a corpse emerging from the tomb, flinging off the shroud.

With 18 guns and a complement of 192 men, the *Revenant*, a swift sailer, was quite as formidable as her predecessor; and so effectually did Surcouf scour the Bay of Bengal and the adjacent seas, so crafty and determined was he in attack, so swift in pursuit or in flight, that his depredations called forth an indignant but somewhat illogical memorial, in December 1807, from the merchants and East India Company to the Admiralty. The fact was that the British men-of-war on the station were doing pretty well all that could be done, but the *Revenant*, when it came to chasing her, was apt to become as ghostly as her figure-head—she had the heels of all of them, and her captain seemed to have an intuitive perception as to the whereabouts of danger.

Surcouf eventually settled down as a shipbuilder and shipowner at St. Malo. He had, of course, made a considerable fortune, and his business prospered, so he was one of the most wealthy and influential men in the place. He died in 1827.

Captain Marryat, in one of his novels, "Newton Forster," gives a vivid description of a fight between Surcouf and the *Windsor Castle* Indiaman, commanded by the plucky and pugilistic Captain Oughton. Such a yarn, by an expert seaman and a master-hand, is delightful reading, and the temptation to transcribe it here is strong. It must, however, be resisted, as the story is, after all, a fiction, and therefore would be out of place.

There are other French privateersmen well worthy of notice, did space permit, foremost among whom is Thurot, who, single-handed, contrived to harass the English and Irish coasts for months ; the brothers Fourmentin, the eldest of whom has the Rue du Baron Bucaille in Boulogne named after him, though his biographer informs us that he never called himself Bucaille, nor was he a baron—but somehow this title became attached to him.

M. Henri Malo, in " Les Corsaires," tells a story of him which is said to be traditional in his family, and is certainly entertaining ; so it shall be transcribed as related.

" One evening, several privateer captains were dining together. There was a leg of mutton for dinner, and a discussion arose as to whether French mutton was superior or inferior to English. Fourmentin said the only way to decide the question was to have the two kinds on the table ; they had French mutton, they only wanted a specimen of the English mutton—he would go and fetch it. Forthwith he proceeded to the harbour, and, according to his custom, summoned his crew by beating with a hammer on the bottom of a saucepan. Making sail, he landed in the middle of the night on the English coast, seized a customs station, and bound the officers, except six, whom he directed, pistol in hand, to conduct him to the nearest sheep-fold. Choosing the six finest sheep in the flock, he made the six customs officers shoulder them and take them on board his vessel. He gave his six involuntary porters a bottle of rum by way of reward for their trouble, and straightway made sail for France. He had left on the flood-tide —he returned on it, with the required sheep, which he and his colleagues were thus able to appreciate and compare with the others."

A very good family story, and probably quite as true as many another!

These Frenchmen of whom we have been discoursing were certainly fine seamen, and intrepid fighters; they had, no doubt, the faults common to privateers, but they were able and formidable foes, and left their mark in history.

CONCERNING THE FRONTISPIECE

On July 27th, 1801, capture was made of a remarkable vessel. There was no fighting, but the ship herself excited a good deal of interest at the time.

We learn from the captain's log of the British frigate *Immortalité* that, in the small hours of the morning, a large ship was observed, and sail was made

in chase.   At daylight the chase proved to be a four-
masted vessel, fully rigged upon each mast—a common
enough object nowadays, but then almost unique.
This was the French privateer *Invention*, a ship built
under the special supervision of the man who commanded her—M. Thibaut.   She was brand-new,
having sailed upon her first voyage only eight days
previously, and had already eluded one of our frigates
by superior speed.   She was probably a very fast
vessel, and might quite possibly have outsailed the
Immortalité ; but, very unhappily for Captain Thibaut,
another British frigate, the *Arethusa*, Captain W.
Wolley, appeared right in her path.   Thus beset,
Thibaut's case was hopeless, and so the *Invention's*
very brief career as a privateer came to an end, the
Immortalité—commanded by Captain Henry Hotham
—taking possession at eight o'clock.

Captain Wolley, as senior officer, reported the
circumstances to the Admiralty :

" She is called *L'Invention*, of Bordeaux, mounting
24 guns, with 207 men.   She is of a most singular
construction, having four masts, and they speak of her
in high terms, though they say she is much under-
masted.   I directed Captain Hotham to take her
into Plymouth.   I should have ordered her up the
river for their lordships' inspection, but I did not
choose to deprive Captain Hotham of his men for so
long a time."

The corner of the letter is turned down and on it
is written : " Acquaint him that their lordships are
highly pleased with the capture of this vessel."

There is an enclosure giving the dimensions of the vessel, as follows :

				Ft.	In.
Length of keel	..	..	..	126	10
Extreme length	..	..	..	147	4
Breadth of beam	..	..	..	27	1
Depth of hold	..	..	..	11	9
Draft of water	..	..	..	13	9

Mention is also made of a sketch enclosed, but this is not now with the letter. It is probable, however, that a small woodcut, on the first page of vol. vii. of *The Naval Chronicle,* is copied from this sketch, and the frontispiece of this volume is an enlargement and adaptation from the woodcut.

The *Invention* had less beam in proportion to her length than was usual in those days, and perhaps Captain Thibaut was afraid of masting her too heavily lest she should be " tender " under canvas. Her draft of water is moderate for her other dimensions, which would be an additional occasion of anxiety on this score ; but, with a large spread of canvas, she would have been very swift in moderate weather.

There does not appear to be any record to hand as to what became of the *Invention*, whether she was afterwards sent up the river for the inspection of their lordships, or taken on as a man-of-war ; possibly some dockyard archives may contain the information.

On August 25th, 1801, the Navy Board reported to the Admiralty that the *Invention* had been surveyed, and was a suitable vessel for the Royal Navy, and asked whether her four masts should be retained ; and September 1st following they ask that the sketch of the ship may be returned ; but there is no reply to be found to either of these letters in the proper place ; so the further correspondence must either have been lost or placed among other papers. Possibly the ship was not, after all, taken for the Navy ; if she was it would probably be under some other name.

SOME AMERICANS

CHAPTER XVII

CAPTAIN SILAS TALBOT

DURING the American War of Secession in the eighteenth century, as well as in that of 1812, American seamen took very kindly to privateering. There were many smart vessels afloat, commanded by intrepid and skilful men, with hardy and well-trained crews, and British naval historians are all agreed as to the success of their ventures and the immense amount of damage inflicted upon our sea-trade by them. Their fast-sailing schooners were usually able to outpace our men-of-war and privateers, and so to make their choice between fighting and running away ; and they do not appear to have been averse to fighting when there was the smallest chance of success, or even against considerable odds.

We find, nevertheless, among American writers, considerable diversity of opinion as to the advantages of privateering and the conduct of privateers.

In the *North American Review* for July 1820, six years after the conclusion of the last war, there is a most urgent appeal against privateering, denouncing all privateers, American and others, as practically pirates, and setting forth in the strongest possible terms the gross iniquity of the whole business.

Mr. Roosevelt, in his " History of the Naval War of 1812," alludes to their privateers in very disparaging terms, pointing out that they were far more keen upon plunder than fighting, and were utterly unreliable ; would fight one day, and run away the next.

Mr. George Coggleshall, in the introduction to his " History of the American Privateers during our War with England in the years 1812–14," says : " I commence my plea, soliciting public approbation in favour of privateersmen, and for those who served in private armed vessels in the war " ; and quotes Jefferson in support of his views.

Mr. E. S. Maclay, in his " History of American Privateers," says : " In general, the conduct of American privateersmen on the high seas was most commendable."

It is, of course, most natural that these writers should stand up for their countrymen, and Englishmen, as has already been stated, are not slow to acknowledge the prowess of American privateersmen. For the details of actions between these and British vessels we are indebted almost entirely to American accounts, and particularly to the two works above mentioned ; such engagements are usually only referred to in the briefest terms, or altogether unnoticed, in our naval histories ; and the American writers—especially Mr. Coggleshall—display a bitterly hostile spirit which is apt to be very detrimental to the merits of so-called history. And so, while there is no intention of questioning their good faith, one is at least at liberty to wonder where they obtained their information.

According to these writers, British naval officers and privateersmen habitually treated prisoners of war with shocking, wanton brutality : while the Americans exhibited invariable kindness, even beneficence, towards British prisoners : an allegation to which it is impossible to accord full credence, especially when statements are made without reference or authentication.

Moreover, the exploits of American privateersmen are frequently exhibited in an artificially heroic light ; the most trivial and obvious measures for the safety of the ship, for instance, related as though they demonstrated extraordinary qualities of courage and resource ; while the " long bow " is occasionally conspicuously in evidence, the author apparently not possessing the requisite technical knowledge to perceive the absurdity of some story which he has come across.

In support of his contention that the conduct of American privateers was admirable, Mr. Maclay tells the following story, which, he says, appeared in a London newspaper in December 1814—he does not tell us the precise date, or the name of the paper. Still, here is the story (page 15) :

" A trading vessel laden with wheat, from Cardigan, was taken in the Channel by an American privateer. When the captain of the latter entered the cabin to survey the prize, he espied a small box with a hole in the top, on which the words ' Missionary Box ' were inscribed. On seeing this the American captain seemed not a little astonished, and addressed the Welsh captain as follows :

" ' Captain, what is this ? ' pointing to the box with his stick. (Why a *stick*, at sea ?)

" ' Oh,' replied the honest Cambrian, heaving a sigh, ' 'tis all over now.'

" ' What ? ' said the American captain.

" ' Why, the truth is,' said the Welshman, ' that I and my poor fellows have been accustomed, every Monday morning, to drop a penny each into that box for the purpose of sending out missionaries to preach the Gospel to the heathen ; but it is all over now.'

" ' Indeed,' answered the American captain ; ' that is very good.'

" After pausing a few minutes, he said, ' Captain, I'll not hurt a hair of your head, nor touch your vessel ' ; and he immediately departed, leaving the owner to pursue his course."

There is no disputing the humanity of this American privateer skipper, if the tale be true ; but one would be disposed to wonder what his owners said to him about the business. They might want to know what he meant by allowing a Welshman to score off him by means of a pious fraud ! A privateer skipper, however religiously disposed, should not put to sea without his sense of humour.

" A still more forcible illustration of the humanity of American privateersmen," says Mr. Maclay (page 16), " is had early in 1782, when the private armed sloop *Lively*, Captain D. Adams, of Massachusetts, rescued the officers and crew of the British frigate *Blonde*, which had been wrecked on a barren and desolate island. The treatment which all American prisoners, and especially privateersmen, had received at the hands of the British would have almost justified the commander of the *Lively* in leaving these shipwrecked mariners to their fate. But the American jack tar is a generous fellow, and nothing appeals so strongly to his compassion as a fellow-seaman in distress, and on this occasion the people of the *Lively* extended every assistance to their enemies and brought them safely into port."

Really, they would have been no better than pirates if they had left them there. There does not appear to be any reason for supposing that American privateersmen were either more or less scrupulous than their British cousins ; there was always plunder in view on both sides, and, if plunder could be obtained without fighting, so much the better.

The editor of *De Bow's Commercial Review* (vol. i., page 518, June 1846), in a note appended to an article upon privateering, says : " Privateering constitutes a separate chapter in the laws of nations. Every nation has resorted to this method of destroying the commerce of the enemy, without questioning for a moment their right of doing so. Many have affected to consider it, after all, but legalised piracy, and calculated to blunt the finer feelings of justice and sear the heart to noble sentiments. We are at a loss, ourselves, to understand how the occupation of a mere privateer can be reconciled with any of the higher feelings of our nature : an occupation whose whole end and purpose is pillage upon the high seas and pecuniary gain out of the fiercest bloodshed. The love of country, patriotic self-devotion, and ardour, have no place in such concerns. . . . It cannot be doubted, that men estimable in other respects have been found in the pursuit of privateering ; but exceptions of this kind are rare, and could not, we think, occur again, in the improved moral sense of mankind."

With these preliminary remarks, let us now recount the doings of some of the American privateersmen, commencing with Silas Talbot.

CAPTAIN—OR COLONEL—SILAS TALBOT

" The Life and Surprising Adventures of Captain Silas Talbot ; containing a Curious Account of the Various Changes and Gradations of this Extraordinary Character." Such is the title of a small volume published in America about the year 1803 ; and the editor states that the bulk of the information contained therein was communicated personally by Talbot, and has since been substantially confirmed from various quarters.

Silas Talbot, we learn, was born at Dighton, Mass., about the year 1752, and commenced his career at sea as cabin-boy. At the age of twenty-four, however, he blossoms into a captain in the U.S. Army—or the rebel army, according to British notions—in the year 1776 ; and by virtue, we must suppose, of his nautical training, he was placed in command of a fireship at New York, and soon after promoted to the rank of major—but still with naval duties. He speedily attracted attention as a daring and ingenious officer, and was very successful in several enterprises, the most notable being the conquest and capture of a well-armed stationary British vessel, moored in the east passage off Rhode Island. He made the attack at night, and devised an ingenious plan for breaching the high boarding-nettings of the Britisher, fixing at the bowsprit end of his sloop a small anchor, which, being forcibly rammed into the net by the impetus of the vessel, tore it away. The attack was devised as a surprise, but the approach of the gallant Talbot was observed, and it was under a heavy fire that he and his men succeeded in their desperate enterprise.

In 1779, having meanwhile been promoted to the rank of colonel, he commenced his career as a privateer commander. The British had a considerable number of private ships of war afloat on the American coast at that time, and Talbot was placed in command of the *Argo*, a sloop of under 100 tons, armed with twelve 6-pounders, and carrying 60 men. She was very heavily sparred—with one mast, of course, and an immense mainsail, the main boom being very long and thick. She was steered with a long tiller, had very high bulwarks, a wide stern, and looked like a clumsy Albany trader ; we are told, however, that " her bottom was her handsomest part," which is only another way of saying that, with her big spars, she was, in spite of her uncouth appearance, a swift and handy craft.

In this little stinging wasp Talbot set forth, and, after one or two indecisive skirmishes, he encountered the *King George*, a privateer commanded by one

Hazard, a native of Rhode Island, who had been very busy. Captain Hazard had been greatly esteemed, until he elected to fight on the British side, " for the base purpose of plundering his neighbours and old friends " ; after which he was naturally regarded with the bitterest hatred, and Talbot approached to the attack, no doubt, with a grim determination to put a stop to the depredations of the renegade.

The *King George* was of superior force to the *Argo*, carrying 14 guns and 80 men ; but her captain apparently permitted Talbot to come to close quarters without opposition, for the writer tells us that he " steered close alongside him, pouring into his decks a whole broadside, and almost at the same instant a boarding party, which drove the crew of the *King George* from their quarters, and took possession of her without a man on either side being killed."

Talbot was, unquestionably, a born fighter and well versed in nautical strategy and attack ; but the writer of these records strikes one as being an enthusiastic and ingenuous person, without practical knowledge of seamanship or warfare, and consequently liable to be imposed upon by any one who could not resist the temptation to tell a " good yarn." Silas Talbot may have been afflicted with this weakness, for all we know. It is a genuine American characteristic, and by no means incompatible with the highest attributes of personal courage and skill in warfare. However, there is no cause to doubt the truth of the account of the capture of the *King George*, for which Talbot and his men deserve credit.

The next antagonist of the *Argo* was the British privateer *Dragon*, of 300 tons, 14 guns, and 80 men— rather a small armament and crew for a vessel of that tonnage, in those days.

This was a desperate engagement, carried on for four and a half hours, at pistol-shot. The gallant Talbot had some narrow shaves, for we are told that his speaking-trumpet was pierced with shot in two places, and the skirts of his coat torn off by a cannon-shot! We cannot avoid the conclusion that the gentle narrator was, in vulgar parlance, being " had " over this story. A modern small-bore bullet, with high velocity, would probably make a clean hole through a tin speaking-trumpet, which might possibly be retained in the hand, if held very firmly, during the process. But a clumsy, slow-sailing pistol or musket ball of that period would simply double up the tin tube and send it flying ; while as to the coat-tails— well, it is not stated that Captain Talbot experienced any discomfort in sitting down afterwards, or incon-venience for lack of anything to sit upon. It was a most discriminating cannon-ball!

Nearly all the men on deck—a vessel like the *Argo* certainly did not fight any men *below*—were either killed or wounded ; and the *Dragon*, losing her main-mast, at length struck her colours.

Then came an alarm that the *Argo* was sinking ; " but," says the gentle story-teller, " t he captain gave orders to inspect the sides of the sloop, upon which he found several shot-holes between wind and water, which they plugged up." And a very good device.

too, though a somewhat obvious one, to prevent a
vessel from sinking !

Having refitted his ship, Talbot put out again, this
time with the *Saratoga*, another privateer, of Provi-
dence, commanded by Captain Munroe, in company ;
and in due course they came across the *Dublin*, a very
smart English privateer cutter of 14 guns, coming
out of Sandy Hook. It was agreed that Talbot should
first give chase, for fear the sight of two vessels bearing
down upon him should make the Britisher shy : rather
a transparent device, since Munroe's craft was in sight,
at no great distance, the whole time. The Englishman,
however, awaited the attack, and a spirited duel
ensued by the space of an hour. When Munroe
thought it was time for him to cut in, he found that
his ship would not answer her helm. This is explained
as follows : " The *Saratoga* was steered with a long
wooden tiller on common occasions, but in time of
action the wooden tiller was unshipped and put out
of the way, and she was then steered with an iron one
that was shipped into the rudder-head from the cabin.
. . . The *Saratoga* went away with the wind at a
smart rate, to the surprise of Captain Talbot, and the
still greater surprise of Captain Munroe, who repeatedly called to the helmsman, ' Hard a-weather !
Hard up, there ! ' ' It is hard up, sir ! ' ' You lie,
you blackguard ! She goes away lasking ! Hard
a-weather, I say, again ! ' ' It is hard a-weather,
indeed, sir ! ' Captain Munroe was astonished,
and could not conceive what the devil was the
matter with his vessel. He took in the after-sails,

and made all the head-sail in his power. All would not do—away she went! He was in the utmost vexation lest Captain Talbot should think he was running away. At last one of his under-officers suggested that possibly the iron tiller had not entered the rudder-head, which, on examination, was found to be the case. The blunder was now soon corrected, and the *Saratoga* was made to stand towards the enemy; and, that some satisfaction might be made for his long absence, Captain Munroe determined, as soon as he got up, to give her a whole broadside at once. He did so, and the *Dublin* immediately struck her colours; yet, strange to tell, it did not appear, on strict inquiry and examination afterwards, that this weight of fire, which was meant to tear the cutter in pieces, had done the vessel or crew the least additional injury."

Here is a capital yarn, for the uninitiated; but it serves to illustrate the danger of entering upon technical details without adequate understanding. It may be true enough that the tiller was not properly shipped in the first instance; but, this granted, to begin with, any sailing-vessel that is properly trimmed will, upon letting go the tiller, come up into the wind, instead of running off it. Even admitting, however, that the *Saratoga* was so " slack on her helm," in nautical parlance, as to " go away lasking "—*i.e.* almost before the wind—under such conditions, the very last order the captain would give would be " Hard up," or " Hard a-weather," which would only cause her to run away worse than ever; while taking in the after-sail and piling on head sail would aggravate the evil! If the writer had represented Captain Munroe as shouting, " Hard down ! Hard a-lee, you blackguard !'" hauling in his mainsheet and taking off the head-sail, one might believe that Talbot or some other sailor-man had told the story. As it stands, it is ridiculous ; but it is repeated, word for word, in various accounts—among others by Mr. Maclay.

Well, the *Dublin* was captured, hauling down her colours after Munroe's innocuous broadside ; and Talbot's next antagonist was the *Betsy*, an English privateer of 12 guns and 38 men, " commanded by an honest and well-informed Scotchman." After some palaver at pistol-shot, Talbot hoisted the stars and stripes, crying, " You must now haul down those British colours, my friend !" To which the Scot replied, " Notwithstanding I find you an enemy, as I suspected, yet, sir, I believe I shall let them hang a little longer, with your permission. So fire away, Flanagan !'"

Had the honest Scot been of the same type of privateer captain as George Walker he would certainly have banged in his broadside before the stars and stripes were well above the rail, and perhaps altered the outcome of the action. As it was, Talbot took him, killing or wounding the captain and principal officers and several men.

The little *Argo* was subsequently put out of commission and returned to her owners ; and in 1780 Talbot was given command of another privateer, the *General Washington*. After making one capture, however, he was taken, we are told, by an English squadron off Sandy Hook, and sent on board the *Robuste*, Captain Cosby, where he was courteously treated. Being transferred, however, to a tender—name not stated—for conveyance to New York, the commander—" a Scotch lord," we are told, " put his gallant captive into the hold. The only excuse for this dastardly behaviour is to be found in the craven fears of his lordship. By a remarkable coincidence, the pilot he employed was the same formerly on board the *Pigot* (the stationary vessel captured by Talbot at Rhode Island), and this man so frightened his superior with the story of his prisoner's reckless daring that he—notwithstanding a written remonstrance which Captain Talbot forwarded to the British admiral—was thus kept confined below until they reached New York ; and the arm-chest was removed to the cabin."

This is quoted from " The Life of Silas Talbot," by Henry T. Tuckerman, published in 1850. The story is given for what it is worth. Had the name of the tender and of the so readily scared " Scotch lord " been given, it would have been more worthy of consideration.

After this Talbot was confined on board the *Jersey* prison-ship, off Long Island, where it is said that prisoners were treated with gross inhumanity ; and being eventually conveyed to England on board the *Yarmouth*, was kept in prison on Dartmoor, where he made four desperate attempts to escape. He was liberated in the summer of 1781, and found his way home to Rhode Island. He died in New York, June 30th, 1813.

CHAPTER XVIII

CAPTAIN JOSHUA BARNEY

AMONG the earlier privateersmen in the War of Secession was Joshua Barney, a naval officer, who, after having been a prisoner of war for five months, was released by exchange, and, failing naval employment, went as first officer of a privateer under Captain Isaiah Robinson—also a naval officer.

Barney had previously made a venture on his own account in a small trading-vessel, which was speedily captured, the English captain landing his prisoners on the Chesapeake.

After some difficulty, Robinson secured a brig named *Pomona*; she carried a scratch armament of 12 guns of various sizes and a crew of 35 men. The vessel was laden with tobacco for Bordeaux, and the primary object was to get the cargo through safely; but Robinson and Barney, with their naval training, were by no means averse to a fight, and they had only been out a few days when the opportunity arose, a fast-sailing brig giving chase and quickly overhauling the *Pomona*.

At 8 p.m. on a February evening, with a bright moon, the stranger came within hail, ran up her colours, and asked, " What ship is that ? " The

American ran up his flag, and the Englishman immediately shouted to haul it down.

Upon this Robinson delivered his broadside, which inflicted considerable damage upon the other, bringing down his foretopsail, cutting some of his rigging, and causing, we are told, much surprise and confusion on board—though why the Englishmen should be surprised it is difficult to comprehend, as it is to be presumed that they chased with the intention of fighting.

Then commenced a running action, which lasted until nearly midnight. The English captain, finding that the *Pomona* had no stern-gun ports, endeavoured to keep as much as possible astern and on the quarter where he could ply his bow-guns without receiving much in return ; but, we are told, the crew had been thrown into such confusion by the *Pomona's* first broadside that they were able to fire *only one or two shots every half-hour*—three or four rounds an hour ; so Robinson had a port cut in his stern, and ran out a 3-pounder gun there ; and, when the English vessel was coming up again for another of her leisurely discharges, she received a dose of grape which caused her captain to haul off—nor did he venture near enough during the night to fire another shot.

Daylight showed the English brig to be armed with sixteen guns ; and several officers were observed, displaying themselves in conspicuous places, in uniforms resembling those of the Navy. This was supposed to be a ruse, whereby the Americans were to be demoralised, imagining themselves to be engaged with a regular ship of war. " This, the English thought,' says Mr. Maclay, " would show the Americans the hopelessness of the struggle, and would induce them to surrender without further resistance " ; but he does not know what the English thought, or whether the officers in this privateer habitually dressed in some kind of uniform of their own.

However, the enemy, about sunrise, approached the quarter of the *Pomona* with the obvious intention of boarding ; and then the 3-pounder came into play once more. It was loaded with grape-shot, " and the charge was topped off by a crow-bar stuck into the muzzle." Waiting until the enemy was just about to board, Robinson, with his own hand, let go this charge of grape and crowbar, " and with such accurate aim " (at, say, ten yards range !) " that the British were completely baffled in their attempt, their foresails and all their weather foreshrouds being cut away."

Well, one cannot, of course, say that this is untrue ; but that 3-pounder was certainly a marvellous little piece. It carried a solid ball, the size of which may be judged by any one who will toss up a three-pound weight from an ordinary set of scales, and the bore of the gun was just large enough to admit it easily ; yet we are told that the charge of grape— small iron or leaden bullets—was equal to cutting all the foreshrouds, and all the headsail halyards—if this is what is meant by " foresails," which is a vague term, not in use among seamen.

This, however, is the story ; and the English captain immediately putting his helm " hard up " to take the strain off his unsupported foremast, Robinson took occasion to give him a raking broadside ; and this was the last shot fired, the Englishman failing to come up to the scratch again, and the *Pomona* proceeding on her voyage.

The British vessel was said to be the privateer *Rosebud*, with a crew of one hundred men, of whom forty-seven were killed and wounded ; we are not told the *Pomona's* loss. Captain Duncan, of the *Rosebud*, complained at New York that the Americans had not " fought fair," using " langrage "—*i.e.* rough bits of iron, old nails, etc. ; but this illusion was put down to the crowbar—quite a legitimate missile !

There is no British account to hand of this action ; but it is impossible to feel any great admiration of the " Rosebuds," in allowing a vessel of such inferior force to beat them off. They must have been sadly lacking in thorns !

The *Pomona* reached Bordeaux in safety, and there her captain, having sold his tobacco, purchased a more satisfactory lot of guns, powder, and shot, and raised his crew to 70 men ; and, having shipped a cargo of brandy, made sail on his return voyage to America.

On the road he encountered a British privateer of 16 guns and 70 men ; after several encounters, the Englishman all the while endeavouring to escape, Robinson captured her : British loss, 12 killed, and " a number " wounded ; American loss, 1 killed, 2 wounded.

The *Pomona*, however, was destined to have her career cut short by capture, and then there commenced a series of adventures for Joshua Barney as a prisoner of war. We are not told when or by whom

the *Pomona* was captured ; Mr. Maclay, on page 148,
says : " In the chapter on ' Navy Officers in Privateers,
mention was made of the capture of the armed brig,
Pomona, commanded by Captain Isaiah Robinson,
who had, as his first officer, Lieutenant Joshua Barney,
also of the regular service." There is nothing, however, to be found, in the chapter referred to, about
the capture of the *Pomona*. The final allusion is to
her safe arrival in America from Bordeaux, probably
in September 1779.

However, it appears that Joshua Barney became
a prisoner some time between September 1779 and
the autumn of 1780, and was placed in one of the
prison-ships. The arrival of Admiral Byron, it is
said, brought about a welcome change in the prison
administration ; some additional ships were ordered
for the accommodation of the American officers, and the
admiral personally inspected all the prison-ships once
a week; while some of the officers who belonged to the
regular navy were taken on board the flagship *Ardent*.

Barney, it appears, was selected for special consideration by Admiral Byron, having a boat placed at
his service, and being entrusted with the duty of
visiting the prison-ships in which his compatriots were
confined and reporting upon their condition to the
admiral. The only restriction placed upon his liberty
was the obligation to sleep on board the *Ardent* : he
was certainly a most highly favoured prisoner of war.

Upon one occasion, landing in New York in his
American naval uniform, to breakfast with one of
the admiral's staff, he was seized upon by an infuriated

mob, who were proceeding to throw him into a fire which was raging, alleging that he had originated the conflagration. A British officer fortunately intervened and explained the situation.

Upon the advent of Admiral Rodney, however, this pleasant time came to an end ; and in November —*not* December, as in Mr. Maclay's account—1780, Barney, in company with about seventy other American officers, was placed on board the *Yarmouth*, a 64-gun ship, under the command of Captain Lutwidge, for conveyance to England ; and here is Mr. Maclay's description of the treatment they received.

" From the time these Americans stepped aboard the *Yarmouth* their captors gave it to be understood, by hints and innuendoes, that they were being taken to England to ' be hanged as rebels ' ; and, indeed, the treatment they received aboard the *Yarmouth* on the passage over led them to believe that the British officers intended to cheat the gallows of their prey by causing the prisoners to die before reaching port. On coming aboard the ship of the line these officers were stowed away in the lower hold, next to the keel, under five decks, and many feet below the water-line. Here, in a twelve-by-twenty-foot room, with up-curving floor, and only three feet high, the seventy-one men were stowed for fifty-three days like so much merchandise, without light or good air, unable to stand upright, with no means and with no attempt made to remove the accumulating filth ! Their food was of the poorest quality, and was supplied in such insufficient quantities that, whenever one of the prisoners died, the survivors concealed the fact until the body began to putrefy, in order that the dead man's allowance might be added to theirs. The water served them to drink was so thick with repulsive matter that the prisoners were compelled to strain it between compressed teeth.

" From the time the *Yarmouth* left New York till she reached Plymouth, in a most tempestuous winter's passage, these men were kept in this loathsome dungeon. Eleven died in delirium, their wild ravings and piercing shrieks appalling their comrades, and giving them a foretaste of what they themselves might soon expect. Not even a surgeon was permitted to visit them. Arriving at Plymouth the pale, emaciated, festering men were ordered to come on deck. Not one obeyed, for they were unable to stand upright. Consequently they were hoisted up, the ceremony being grimly suggestive of the manner in which they had been treated—like merchandise. And what were they to do, now that they had been placed on deck ? The light of the sun, which they had scarcely seen for fifty-three days, fell upon their weak, dilated pupils with blinding force, their limbs unable to uphold them, their frames wasted by disease and want. Seeking for support, they fell in a helpless mass, one upon the other, waiting and almost hoping for the blow that was to fall upon them next. Captain Silas Talbot was one of these prisoners.

" To send them ashore in this condition was ' impracticable,' so the British officers said, and we readily discover that this ' impracticable ' served the further purpose of diverting the just indignation of the lands-folk, which surely would be aroused if they saw such brutality practised under St. George's cross. Waiting, then, until the captives could at least endure the light of day, and could walk without leaning on one another or clutching at every object for support, the officers had them moved to old Mill Prison."

This is a terrible picture of the treatment of American prisoners of war, in striking contrast to the generous conduct of Vice-Admiral the Hon. John Byron—to give him his correct title—towards Barney and his fellow-prisoners. If it is to be accepted as absolutely true, it should make Englishmen blush to read it, constituting a shameful record against us, as represented by Captain Lutwidge and his subordinates.

But is it absolutely true ? This question is suggested, in the first instance, by the utter wildness of the writer's chronology with regard to the pleasing episode in connection with Admiral Byron ; for it was during Joshua Barney's *first* period of imprisonment that he came in contact with Byron, in the year 1778. It could not have been after the capture of the *Pomona*, as Byron was in the West Indies in the summer of 1779, in pursuit of the French Admiral D'Estaing, and returned thence to England, arriving on October 10th in that year—he was not employed again. Moreover, during the time of Barney's second imprisonment, at New York, there was no *Ardent* on the Navy List : she was captured by the French on August 17th, 1779—while Barney was on his homeward voyage in the *Pomona*—and recaptured in April 1782.

Such reckless chronicling might well discredit the whole of this writer's account of the incidents ; fortunately—or unfortunately—for him, however, there is another source of information in a " Biographical Memoir of Commodore Barney," by Mary Barney—his daughter, perhaps—published in 1832, in which the dates are more consistent with possibilities. Probably Mr. Maclay derived his information from this volume, and, by an extraordinary oversight, confused the two periods.

From this record it appears that Barney was a lieutenant on board the frigate *Virginia* when she was captured by the British on April 1st, 1778, and that he was very kindly treated by two English captains, Caldwell and Onslow, under whose charge he found himself for a time and subsequently, as related, by Admiral Byron.[1] Moreover, it is here stated that it was while serving on board a regular warship, the *Saratoga*, that Barney was a second time made prisoner, being captured when in charge of a prize, and not on board the *Pomona* at all: so here is more recklessness of narration, which appears quite inexcusable, as the writer, it is to be presumed, had access to this memoir, which is said to be compiled from Barney's own statements to the author.

Now, with regard to the shocking treatment of the prisoners on board the *Yarmouth*.

---

[1] There still remains the question of Byron's flagship. She was certainly the *Princess Royal* when he arrived at New York ; but as the *Ardent*, 64, was one of the vessels of his squadron, it is, of course, possible that he may subsequently have hoisted his flag on her temporarily.

Mary Barney disclaims any wish to aggravate the case, declaring that she had the story from the lips of Joshua Barney, and appeals to his generous recognition of former kindness as a guarantee against wilful misrepresentation on this occasion.

Very good. But there is in existence the captain's log of the *Yarmouth*, also his letter to the Admiralty, reporting his arrival in England, and these official documents tend to discredit the dismal story in some important particulars.

The *Yarmouth*, we learn, sailed on November 15th, 1780, and arrived at Plymouth on December 29th— so she was forty-four, not fifty-three days at sea. The weather was very rough, and the ship developed some serious leaks, which increased alarmingly through the straining in the heavy sea. Under these circumstances, the ship's company being very sickly, with more than one hundred men actually on the sick list— one hundred and eleven, according to the " State and Condition " report on arrival—Captain Lutwidge states that he had the prisoners " watched "—*i.e.* divided into port and starboard watch, and set them to the pumps : " I found it necessary to employ the prisoners at the pumps, and on that account to order them whole allowance of provisions—the ship's company, from their weak and sickly state, being unequal to that duty."

According to the log, *five* prisoners, not eleven, died on the voyage, the deaths and burials at sea being precisely recorded.

So here we have the official record that, while the ship's company were too much enfeebled by sickness to work the pumps—in addition, of course, to constant handling of the heavy sails and spars in tempestuous weather—the American prisoners were sufficiently robust to perform this duty, and probably save the vessel from serious peril through her leaky condition.

In order to do this they must have been called on deck and mustered, placed in watches, and subsequently summoned in regular turn for their " spell " at the pumps.

This story is obviously incompatible with the other, and it is, to say the least of it, very remarkable that this pumping in watches, and full provision allowance, should have been entirely forgotten by Barney in his narration.

It is certainly open to any one, in view of this omission, to question the accuracy of other statements ; to hesitate before accepting the story of seventy-one men being confined in a space twenty feet by twelve and only six inches higher than an ordinary table ; of eleven of them dying in shrieking delirium, denied medical attendance, and six out of eleven deaths being suppressed.   The treatment of our American prisoners was undoubtedly sometimes unduly harsh, but it is impossible to accept this story as literally true.

Mr. Maclay's book and Mary Barney's memoirs are alike accessible to any one, and for this reason it is necessary that the other side should be heard—Joshua Barney having been a very prominent American privateersman.

While on the subject, it is as well to refer to the treatment of prisoners in Mill Prison, at Plymouth, of which Mr. Maclay has a good deal to say; and in support of his contention as to their being placed upon a different diet from other prisoners of war, he has two sentences in inverted commas (page 152), which are stated in a footnote to be quoted from the *Annual Register* of 1781, page 152; but no such passages occur there, nor in adjacent pages.

It is, however, perfectly true that a petition was presented, on June 20th, 1781, to the House of Lords, and discussed on July 2nd following, from these prisoners. The only complaint which was found to be substantiated was that the Americans were allowed half a pound less bread daily than the French and other nationalities. It would have been more accurate to put it that the French had half a pound more—for this was stated to be supplied, as being equal to the allowance to British prisoners in France. The question of increasing the allowance was put to the vote, and negatived; but it was shown that the American prisoners' diet was, as a whole, superior to that allowed to our own troops on board transports; and their health was stated to be excellent, which is borne out by the fact, as stated by Mr. Maclay, that they indulged in athletic games as a pastime. Men who are half naked and nearly starving do not indulge in such pastimes.

And now for the continued adventures of Joshua Barney, privateersman. Bold and resourceful, he determined to face the difficulties of escape, and the very unpleasant consequences of detection.

One day, playing at leap-frog, he pretended to have sprained his ankle, and for some time afterwards went about on crutches, maintaining the deception so skilfully as to throw the warders off their guard, and completely deceive all but a few of his intimate friends. He had already paved the way, by making friends with a soldier of the prison guard, who had served in the British army in America, and had there received some kindness, which he was willing to requite by civility to the Americans in Mill Prison.

On May 18th, 1781, this man was on sentry outside the inner gate—the prison being encircled by two high walls, with a space between—and Barney, hopping by on his crutches, whispered through the gate: " To-day ? " " Dinner," replied the sentry, with equal terseness, which meant one o'clock, when the warders dined. The friendly but disloyal soldier had provided Barney with the undress uniform of a British officer—which appears an unusual sort of thing for a private soldier to be able to lay hands upon without detection—and this Barney donned in his cell, putting on his greatcoat over it—his greatcoat, which, since he sprained his ankle, he had been wearing " for fear he should catch cold " : Barney was a man of details.

Still upon crutches, he left his cell, and, at a pre-arranged signal, some of his friends proceeded to engage the several sentries in conversation, while one, a stalwart individual, stood close by the gate.

Throwing aside his crutches, Barney walked across the enclosure towards the gate, and, first exchanging a reassuring wink with the sentry, sprang with cat-like agility upon the shoulders of his athletic accomplice, and in a moment was over the wall. Slipping off his greatcoat, and "tipping" the soldier to the extent of four guineas, he passed through the gate in the outer wall, which was usually left open for the convenience of the prison officials, but with an attendant on duty who, though we are not told that he had been "squared," obligingly turned his back as the escaping prisoner passed through.

So far, so good. And really Joshua Barney is to be congratulated upon the accommodating character of his custodians, which rendered it possible for him to cross the prison-yard at one o'clock on a May day and scale the wall, while the sentries conversed with his friends and the warders enjoyed their dinner, having previously been permitted to malinger with a sham sprained ankle. We are told that he had it bathed and bandaged for some time without being challenged and detected by the surgeon, though somebody in authority must have provided him with crutches. It appears somewhat absurd to insist upon the rigour of confinement in Mill Prison, in the face of this.

However, Barney was free, and he had friends near by who concealed him, and took him on to the house of an old clergyman in Plymouth in the evening. No immediate inquiry was made for him in the prison, for he had provided a substitute to answer his name at roll-call in the cell every day—a "slender youth," we are told, "who was able to creep through the window-bars at pleasure," and so crawled into Barney's cell and answered for him. We are not told who the "slender youth" was, or how, if he was an American prisoner, he contrived also to answer for himself in his own cell. Anyhow, this was an amazingly slack prison, for any such freak to be possible.

Finding two fellow-countrymen who had been captured as passengers in a merchant vessel and were looking for a chance of returning, they secured a fishing-smack, Barney rigged himself up in an old coat tied with tarred rope round the waist and a tarpaulin hat, and soon after daybreak they sailed down the River Plym, past the forts and men-of-war, and safely out to sea.

But they were not destined so easily to reach the coast of France, whence they hoped to find a passage to America. An inconveniently zealous British privateer from Guernsey boarded the smack, and the skipper was unduly inquisitive. Upon Barney opening his coat and showing his British uniform, the privateersman, though more polite, was obviously suspicious. What business had a British officer on the enemy's coast?—for Barney had stated that he was bound there. Barney made an official mystery of his " business," and refused to reveal it—a state secret, and so on.

No use ! The privateer captain's sensitive conscience would not permit him to let the smack go, and so the two vessels beat up for the English coast in company, and on the following morning came to anchor in a small harbour about six miles from Plymouth, probably Causand Bay. Here the privateer captain went on shore, on his way to Plymouth, to report to Admiral Digby, while most of his crew also landed to avoid the risk of being taken by the press-gang on board.

Barney, however, though he was treated with courtesy, was detained on board the privateer.

There was a boat made fast astern, and into this the American quietly slipped, hurting his leg as he did so, and sculled on shore, shouting to some of the idlers on the beach to help him haul up the boat.

The customs officer was disposed to be inquisitive and talkative, but Barney pointed to the blood oozing through his stocking, and said he must go off and get his leg tied up.

" Pray, sir," he said, " can you tell me where our people are ? "

He was told they were at the Red Lion, at the end of the village, which he discovered, much to his annoyance, that he was obliged to pass. He had almost succeeded in doing so unobserved, when one of the men shouted after him, and, approaching, gave him to understand that some of the privateer's crew had an idea of shipping in the Navy, and wanted some particulars from him ; showing that his disguise had deceived them.

Barney invited the man to accompany him to Plymouth, walking away rapidly while he spoke ; but, as Mr. Maclay puts it, the tar " seemed to think better of his plan of entering a navy noted for its cruelty to seamen," and accordingly turned back.

Barney now began to be very anxious about his safety. He was on the high road to Plymouth, where he might at any moment encounter a guard sent out to recapture him ; so he jumped over a hedge into Lord Mount-Edgecumbe's grounds, where the gardener, pacified by a "tip," let him out by a private gate to the waterside—and none too soon, for, as he passed out, the guard sent to seek him tramped along on the other side of the hedge he had jumped over. A butcher, conveying some stock by water, took him across the river, and that night he found himself back at the old clergyman's house from which he had started. His two friends of the fishing-smack adventure here joined him once more, and while they were at supper the town-crier bawled under the window that five guineas reward would be paid for the capture of Joshua Barney, a rebel deserter from Mill Prison.

Three days later, dressed in fashionable attire, Barney stepped into a post-chaise at midnight and drove off for Exeter. He was stopped at the Plymouth gate, and a lantern thrust in to see if he corresponded with the description of himself which had been circulated. Apparently he did not, for he was permitted to proceed, and eventually passed on to Bristol and London, France, and Holland; whence he shipped on board the armed ship *South Carolina*, which he saved, by prompt measures and good seamanship, from being wrecked on the Dutch coast—her officers being, apparently, timid and incompetent.

Eventually, having transhipped on board the *Cicero*, another American privateer, Barney reached Beverley, Massachusetts—the writer does not give the date, but it must have been in the autumn of 1781. At Boston, we are told, he met several of his fellow-prisoners who had also escaped from Mill Prison.

CHAPTER XIX

CAPTAINS BARNEY AND HARADEN

In April of the following year, 1782, Barney was again afloat in command of a privateer, the *Hyder Ali*(spelt *HydeA lly* in Mr. Maclay's book), fitted out, by merchants of Philadelphia, with sixteen 6-pounder guns and a crew of 110.

In this vessel he fought a remarkable and successful action against the *General Monk*, a British man-of-war, of alleged superior force, though this is not borne out by British accounts. She was formerly the *General Washington*, was captured by a British squadron in 1780, and renamed upon being added to the British Navy. She was commanded on this occasion by Commander Josias Rogers, an officer of great courage and resource, and was armed with sixteen 9-pounder carronades and two 6-pounders. A 9-pounder carronade was a foolish little piece, very short, and addicted to jumping violently and capsizing when it became at all hot : and it would be quite outranged by a long 6- or 9-pounder.

We are not told, either in the British or American account, the tonnage of the two vessels, but in the latter the *General Monk* is described as being pierced for twenty guns : and in the former the *Hyder Ali* is said to have carried eighteen guns, 6- and 9-pounders (proportion of each not stated), while her crew is put down as 130 men.

Dropping down the river Delaware with several merchant vessels under convoy, Barney had reached Cape May Roads, just inside Delaware Bay, where he anchored, and was there discovered by a blockading squadron under Captain Mason, of the *Quebec* frigate.

Sending Rogers in to reconnoitre, and, if possible, attack, Mason endeavoured to sail a little higher up the bay, to prevent the American vessels running for the Delaware River, while Rogers, engaging the assistance of the *Fair American*, a privateer, went straight for the convoy. No sooner had he rounded Cape May, in sight of the Americans, than Barney, signalling his convoy to run for the river—the *Quebec* not having yet got far enough up to head them off, on account of the shoal water—endeavoured to put his ship in the way of the pursuers. The *Fair American* ran past him, with a broadside which was not returned, captured one vessel, chased another on shore, and then, in the endeavour to cut off three others, ran aground herself.

This cleared the field for a duel between the *General Monk* and the *Hyder Ali*, and they had a very pretty fight.

Barney, as the *General Monk* came on with the intention of boarding, delivered his broadside at pistol-range, and then frustrated the Englishman's plan of boarding by a ruse. Bidding the helmsman

interpret his next order by " the rule of contrary,"
he shouted, as the vessels were on the point of fouling,
" Hard a-port !   Do you want him to run aboard us ? "
—the intention being that the order, distinctly audible
on board the British vessel, should convey a false
impression ; for the helmsman, in accordance with the
hint just received, put the helm *hard a-starboard*,
the result being that the English vessel's jibboom
became entangled in the *Hyder Ali's* fore-rigging.
This is all very possible, and Barney was just the
kind of man to have recourse to a ruse of this kind ;
but the relative positions of the ships at the moment
are not technically described, so it is impossible to
judge of the feasibility of the manœuvre, or of its
efficacy.   However, we are told that the Americans
lashed the head-gear of the *General Monk* to their
rigging, and raked her with their fire, to which she
could make no effective return.

Rogers called his men to board, but the American
defensive measures were too strong, and they fell back.
Then ensued a conflict chiefly with small-arms, and
there are some little stories in connection with it.
Barney, it appears, had among his crew a number of
backwoodsmen, crack shots, but little accustomed to
the amenities of discipline.   One of these men kept on
asking his captain, whenever he came within earshot,
where the musket which he was using was made.
Barney, annoyed by this freedom, ignored him for a
time, then asked him sharply why he wanted to know.
" W-a-a-l," drawled the backwoodsman, " this 'ere
bit o' iron is jes' the best smoothbore I ever fired in

my life "—and he went on picking off the Britishers.
Another drew Barney's attention to his next shot.
" Say, Cap., do you see that fellow with the white
hat ? "—and in another moment the individual in the
white hat leapt three feet in the air, and fell to rise
no more. It was found, after the action, says the
narrator, that every one of the Englishmen killed or
wounded by musketry was struck either in the head
or breast.

The Britishers, however, were not idle with their
small-arms ; Barney, jumping on the compass stand
to see better what was going on, had his head shaved
by a ball which perforated his hat. Another tore off
part of his coat-tail. Upon this he ordered his Marine
officer to direct his men's fire at the enemy's tops, and
in a few minutes the tops were cleared.

Then a round-shot struck the binnacle, or compass
stand, upon which Barney stood, and sent him flying.
Just before this occurred he had had a vision of one
of his officers, with the cook's axe uplifted, in act to
floor a seaman who had got nervous, and was hiding
behind the mainmast. The next moment Barney
turned an involuntary somersault, and found the
officer, who had dropped the cook's axe, standing over
him in apprehension. Finding his captain unhurt—
most of us would have been a good deal hurt under
the circumstances, but perhaps Captain Barney came
down on the spot, like a sixpence when a billiard-ball
is knocked from under it—the stern officer resumed
his murderous weapon, and made for the timid seaman again. But the latter had by this time realised

that the cook's axe was a certainty and the enemy's fire a chance, so he returned to his quarters.

And so, with these little amenities, the fight went on ; but it was a losing fight for the British. Rogers could not get his ship away. His guns—his stupid little carronades—were behaving in a fiendish manner, tumbling about and shooting anywhere except in the right direction ; and his men were falling fast. His masts and rigging were so damaged that he could not handle the sails, and he was at length compelled to yield, himself severely wounded and many of his officers and men dead and dying around him ; and so the *General Monk* changed hands again, and became once more the *General Washington*.

Captain Barney, without doubt, fought his craft with immense pluck and dexterity, and thoroughly deserved the victory ; but it is extremely doubtful whether the superiority of force was not on his side. Neither account gives the tonnage of the two vessels. Robert Beatson, a good authority, gives the *General Monk's* armament as above described, and gives also a very different account of the action, ascribing Rogers's defeat chiefly to the inefficiency of his guns. He says, at the commencement, that the *Hyder Ali* " cut her boat adrift, and did everything else to get away, *notwithstanding her superior force.*" The reader can take his choice.

This ends Joshua Barney's career as a privateer during this war. He was placed in command of the *General Washington*, and subsequently visiting Plymouth, he entertained on board his ship the friends

who had aided his escape and a number of British
officers, and bestowed a purse of gold upon Lord
Mount-Edgecumbe's gardener, who had so opportunely
opened the little gate for him.

There are other privateer heroes of this period who
richly deserve notice, but space does not admit of a
detailed account of their doings.

There was Jonathan Haraden, of Salem, for instance, conspicuous by his seamanlike skill and marvellous coolness under fire, as well as by his bold tactics
in the presence of a superior force.

It is related that, upon a dark night in the Bay of
Biscay, being then in command of the privateer
General Pickering, of 180 tons and 16 guns, he came
across the British privateer *Golden Eagle*, of 22 guns—
as was afterwards discovered.   Haraden was not aware
of her name and force when he sighted her—at no
great distance, of course; but, having neared her,
as is stated, unobserved, he concluded that she was a
vessel of superior force to his own.   In the words of
the narrator, " having formed a fairly accurate idea
of her force," he resolved to have recourse to a ruse
—it was a very foolhardy proceeding, but it was
justified by success.   Running up alongside the English
vessel, he hailed the captain while the two ships, at
close quarters, plunged along together.   " This is an
American frigate of the largest class ; if you don't
surrender immediately, I'll blow you out of the water ! "

Now, Haradan's craft was of 180 tons, and an
American frigate of the largest class at that time—the
year 1780—would be at least 800 tons ; the two

vessels were close together, and we have seen that the American captain had, some time previously, been able to estimate the size and probable strength of the other ; so what was the use of shouting such a fable to the Britisher ? Any seaman of moderate experience would ridicule the idea of mistaking a vessel of 180 tons, close alongside, even at night, for a first-class frigate, with her comparatively large hull and immense, towering spars. Some of the English privateer captains whom we have been discussing would have had a very short reply for Haraden—" Frigate, be d——d ! " and a broadside ; and it was really very lucky for the American that he had dropped upon a " soft thing " in finding a British skipper so extremely unsophisticated as to be deceived for a moment. However, the captain of the *Golden Eagle* chanced to be the one man in a thousand who would be so taken in, and he hauled down his colours without firing a shot ! Had he been a naval officer, he would have had to answer at a court-martial for his conduct, and it is impossible to imagine any punishment for such an offence, short of death. However, nothing succeeds like success ; Haraden—according to the story, as narrated by Mr. Maclay—made good his piece of " bounce," and took possession ; and the most appropriate comment appears to be that each captain got what he deserved.

Shortly afterwards Captain Haraden engaged a privateer—the *Achilles*—of vastly superior force, off Bilbao, so close in shore that the Spaniards crowded the headlands in hundreds to see the fun. Haraden, by superior seamanship, succeeded in beating off his big antagonist and in recovering the *Golden Eagle*, which the enemy had recaptured but could not hold, and which had on board an officer and prize crew from the *Achilles*. So the balance was in the American's favour.

An onlooker—one Robert Cowan—is reported to have said that the *General Pickering* looked like a long-boat in comparison with the *Achilles*, and that " Haraden fought with a determination that seemed superhuman ; and, although in the most exposed positions, where the shot flew around him, he was all the while as calm and steady as amid a shower of snowflakes."

Another of Captain Haraden's exploits was the capture of " a homeward-bound king's packet from one of the West India islands," under very dramatic circumstances, the American captain, his watch in one hand and a lighted match in the other, with only a single round of ammunition remaining, giving the battered Britisher five minutes in which to surrender. But surely some less vague relation is due before such a story can be accepted—the name of the packet, her force, the date, latitude and longitude, and so forth.

However, Captain Haraden was, no doubt, a fair specimen of a very fine class—the Salem skippers—and Americans have every cause for being proud of him.

CHAPTER XX

CAPTAIN THOMAS BOYLE

UPON the declaration of war with England in 1812 Americans naturally inaugurated at once a vigorous privateering campaign.

War was declared on June 18th, and by the end of the month two privateers had put out from Salem, and a dozen more were almost ready for sea; while New York had sent out, by the middle of October, twenty-six vessels, mounting some three hundred guns, and manned by more than two thousand men.

On July 10th occurred a curious episode, quite impossible in these days, when the earth is tied up in every direction with telegraph cables. The British man-of-war schooner *Whiting* was lying in Hampton Roads; her commander, Lieutenant Maxey, ignorant of the declaration of war, was in his boat, going on shore, when the American privateer *Dash*, Captain Carroway, arrived upon the scene. Carroway, better informed, seized the English commander and his boat, and, running alongside the *Whiting*, called upon the officer in charge to surrender—which he did.

The American Government, however, in view of the English captain's ignorance of the commencement of hostilities, ordered the *Whiting* to be returned. A similar incident is said to have occurred in the case of the *Bloodhound*, an English sloop of 12 guns, captured by the 8-gun privateer schooner *Cora*. Neither of these events is chronicled by British naval historians.

One of the most daring and skilful privateer captains during this war was Thomas Boyle. His first command was the *Comet*, a staunch, fast-sailing schooner, and he lost no time in getting to work, starting upon his first cruise in July 1812, within a month of the declaration of war.

Returning in November, after capturing several vessels, he refitted his craft and prepared to set forth again. There was more difficulty, however, in getting out upon this occasion, as the English had a strong squadron blockading Chesapeake Bay.

Waiting for a dark, squally night, Boyle made his venture on December 23rd, and all went well until near daybreak, when he suddenly found himself under the guns of a frigate, which let drive a broadside at him. The *Comet* sustained but little damage, however, and got clear away, heading for the coast of Brazil, where Boyle learned that some English vessels were about to sail from Pernambuco.

This information proved to be correct, and on January 14th they were discovered, standing out to sea—three brigs and a ship—*i.e.* a larger vessel full-rigged. Boyle was prepared to find the merchant vessels armed, but did not reckon upon a very obstinate resistance from them. He stood out to sea, so as to be able easily to get between the English vessels

and the coast; and about three o'clock he put his
helm up and gave chase. The fast schooner soon
neared the other ships; and then Boyle discovered
that he was in for a more exciting adventure than he
had anticipated, for one of the brigs was obviously
a man-of-war, of formidable strength, though he had
been informed that there were no British war-vessels
in the neighbourhood.

However, he put a bold face on, cleared for action,
and steered for the cruiser, hoisting his colours as he
came abreast of her. She replied with Portuguese
colours, and hailed that she would send a boat on board.
Boyle, distrustful, but wishing to ascertain the real
nationality of the stranger, hove to and awaited her
boat; for he did not see what a Portuguese man-of-
war had to do with convoying British vessels. Well,
nobody else can see it, either; but she turned out
to be a genuine Portuguese, and the officer gave Boyle
a great idea of her force, telling him that the merchantmen were under his charge, and must not be
molested.

Boyle, producing his commission from the American
Government, replied:

" This is an American cruiser, here are my papers,
and I am going to take these English vessels if I can.
I don't recognise your right to interfere, and I shall fire
upon you if you do."

To this plain statement of the case the Portuguese
officer replied that his ship had orders to protect the
merchantmen, and that he would be very sorry if anything disagreeable occurred.

" Oh, so shall I," said Boyle ; " very sorry ; but if you oppose me, I shall fire into you."

The Portuguese officer returned to report to his captain, promising to come back presently. This, however, he did not do. It was by this time quite dark, and Boyle, hailing to know when he might expect the boat, was asked to send his boat ; but he did not quite like this plan—indeed, it was highly suspicious ; so he replied that he did not care about sending his boat away in the dark.

" And now I'm going to take those English vessels."

Accordingly, he " let draw " his sails, and was soon among them, hailing the ship to heave-to as he romped past her, having great way on the schooner. Finding no attention paid to his demand, he tacked and came alongside the ship, and opened fire upon her and one of the brigs—the man-of-war being close on his heels, and speedily joining in the fray.

All five vessels, under a press of sail, were now running together in a ruck, the *Comet*, from her superior sailing qualities, being compelled to tack and manœuvre to maintain her position. There was a bright moon, but presently the smoke from the guns accumulated in a great cloud, obscuring the view, so it was difficult to tell one vessel from another. This was quite an agreeable arrangement for Captain Boyle, as he could make no mistake, while the others were in constant dread of hitting a friend—and probably did so occasionally.

This running fight lasted until nearly midnight. The Portuguese fired away whenever he could do so without risk of hitting his convoy, but made wretched practice, while Boyle took but little notice of him, sticking to his prey tenaciously, until the ship and one brig surrendered, much cut up; but the *Comet's* boat, going to take possession, was struck by a broadside from the Portuguese, and returned, almost sinking. Then the privateer and the man-of-war had a set-to alone, the latter eventually sheering off, but hovering near, evidently watching for a chance.

Boyle, however, managed to send a prize crew on board the brig. The captain of the ship hailed that he was severely damaged, almost sinking, and his rigging cut to pieces; but he would endeavour to follow, as ordered, if he could get his ship under command.

Standing by his prize until daybreak, Boyle saw the war-brig again bearing down upon him; he immediately tacked and went to meet her. But the Portuguese had apparently had enough of it; she managed to take the ship and one brig with her into Pernambuco, the two merchantmen in an almost sinking condition, masts tottering, sails cut to pieces, leaving Boyle with his one prize—a rich one. It was altogether an extraordinary affair, for the *Comet* only carried 14 guns and about 120 men; and the Portuguese brig, seen afterwards by some Americans at Lisbon, was found to be a very formidable vessel, heavily armed. Why she was convoying British vessels, Portugal not being at war with America, does not appear to have been explained. Her name is not given.

This incident affords a good indication of the character of Thomas Boyle; he found the *Comet* so superior

in speed, as a rule, to any vessel, small or great, which
he encountered that he used sometimes to sail round
a ship of superior force, just out of range of her guns—
thereby vastly amusing himself and his crew, and
greatly annoying the other man. By pursuing these
tactics upon one occasion, he secured the retreat of a
prize, keeping a British man-of-war brig engaged in
trying to catch him, while the prize got safely away.

The *Comet* made seven-and-twenty prizes; and
Captain Boyle was then placed in command of the
Chasseur, a more formidable vessel, mounting sixteen
long 12-pounders. She is said to have been one of
the fastest and most beautiful vessels afloat, and in her
Boyle had a most successful career. The last and most
important action he fought was with the British man-
of-war schooner *St. Lawrence*, of 13 guns—an American-
built vessel, formerly the *Atlas*, privateer, and captured
by the British in July 1813.

This was on February 26th, 1815, off the coast of
Cuba, when Boyle, about 11 a.m., gave chase to a
schooner apparently running before the wind. She
was discovered to be a man-of-war, with a convoy,
just visible from aloft, as was imagined, in company.
The *Chasseur* gained, though not very fast, and the
stranger presently hauled nearer to the wind, apparently anxious to escape. At 12.30 Boyle showed his
colours and fired a gun, but the other made no sign,
continuing her efforts to escape, and losing her foretopmast through the press of sail she carried. The
Chasseur now came up rapidly, and at one o'clock the
chase fired a gun and hoisted English colours.

Watching her narrowly, Boyle made out only three gun-ports on one side, and there appeared to be very few people on deck. So he cracked on his canvas, anxious to get alongside and make short work of her ; and, not anticipating serious fighting, made no great preparations for action.

When, however, he ran up within pistol-shot, about half-past one, a sudden change came over the English vessel—port-covers were triced up, showing her full armament, with a crowd of men at quarters, who gave three cheers and promptly put in a broadside. Boyle had been caught napping for once.

He and his men did not take long, however, to recover themselves. The *Chasseur* at this time had only 14 guns on board, according to American accounts, having sacrificed some on a former occasion in escaping from a British frigate. She is put down in Sir W. Laird Clowes's " Royal Navy " as carrying 24 guns. This, however, is an error.

However this may be, Boyle got to work, hammer and tongs ; came to close quarters, ran his foe aboard, and, in a quarter of an hour from the first shot, the Englishman surrendered !

The equality of the two vessels, or rather, to be precise, the slight preponderance of force in the *Chasseur's* favour, is dwelt upon in detail by Mr. Maclay (page 296). " Here," he says, " we have an admirable opportunity to compare the relative merits of American and British man-of-warsmen ; for the *St. Lawrence*, being built and equipped by Americans, deprives our friends, the English, of their oft-repeated cry that our vessels were better built, etc. The *Chasseur* carried 14 guns and 102 men as opposed to the *St. Lawrence's* 13 guns and 76 men. Both vessels were schooners."

In view of the categorical statement which ends this paragraph, Mr. Maclay would have done well to take into consideration the illustration of the action which appears opposite page 298, a replica of that in Mr. Coggleshall's book, in which the American vessel is clearly a brig. One does not, of course, place much reliance upon details in illustrations of this class, as proving or disproving important statements, and the draftsman has represented the British schooner " all on end " aloft, whereas she had lost her foretopmast before the action commenced. But what says Mr. Coggleshall ? " The *Chasseur* was a fine, large brig " (page 367) ; and he was a seaman, so he took care that his illustration should be technically correct and in agreement with the text, with regard, at least, to the rig of the vessels.

This discrepancy naturally arouses some suspicion as to other details, and a perusal of the minutes of the court-martial upon Lieutenant James Edward (*not* Henry Cranmer) Gordon,[1] held at Bermuda, April 21st, 1815, throws considerable light upon the matter.

Lieutenant Gordon describes the *Chasseur* as a large brig, registering upwards of 400 tons, British measure-

---

[1] Mr. Maclay is not, however, responsible for this error, as Gordon is so named by Sir W. Laird Clowes, vol vi., p. 155. The mistake does not recur in the list of British losses, p. 555, the name being given as James Edward Gordon, as in the official report of the court-martial.

ment, and much superior to our 18-gun brigs. Making every allowance for unconscious exaggeration on the part of an officer upon his defence, this description accords with that of the American seaman, Coggleshall. Gordon further states that he had on board 52 seamen and officers, 6 passengers, and 6 boys, total 64, which was 12 short of his complement. Compare Captain Boyle's statement, in his letter to one of the owners, that the *St. Lawrence* had on board " a number of soldiers, marines, and some gentlemen of the navy, passengers "; in another place "eighty-nine men, beside several boys." The crew of the *Chasseur*, according to the evidence of some officers of the *St. Lawrence*, admitted in conversation that they had 119 on board, though some were away in prizes.

The officers of the *St. Lawrence*, on their oath, state that there were 48 men at quarters, and that the long 9-pounder was not in action, *as they had not the men to man it.*

There is no mention, either in Gordon's letter or the evidence, of any attempt to disguise the force of the schooner. She had no convoy with her, and simply tried to get away on account of the important despatches, which were weighted and thrown overboard before surrender.

Gordon and his officers were honourably acquitted, the court being satisfied that they had done their best against heavy odds, handicapped as they were by the loss of the foretopmast. The duration of the action is stated as half an hour, or more, by the schooner's officers ; this, however, is not of very much importance.

Captain Boyle was, no doubt, a very brave man and a fine seaman, and the capture of a regular British war-vessel was a great feather in his cap; but it is really no very extraordinary feat for a large brig to take a schooner, fighting two guns less, and with a crew, including boys, in a minority of about forty—accepting the American statement as to the *Chasseur's* crew—and partially crippled aloft.

Captain Boyle, rendered more and more bold and enterprising by success, sent a " Proclamation of Blockade" of the British coast to be posted in Lloyd's Coffee House. This was a joke, said to be in imitation of the farcical " paper " blockades of the American coasts issued by British admirals, when they had not the ships present to enforce it. The British blockade, however, was no farce as a whole, as American writers testify.

CHAPTER XXI

THE "GENERAL ARMSTRONG"

ONE of the most formidable American privateers during this war was the *General Armstrong*, a large brig, armed with a heavy long gun amidships, and eight long 9-pounders.

The last action in which she was engaged was of a most desperate nature, against the boats of a British squadron. The privateer was lying, on September 26th, 1814, at Fayal, in the Azores, and her commander, Samuel Chester Reid, having been on shore to see his Consul and arrange about a supply of water, returned on board about 5 p.m., accompanied by the Consul and some friends.

They were chatting on deck, and the captain was informed that no British cruisers had been seen in the vicinity for several weeks, when their conversation was most unexpectedly broken in upon by the appearance of a large British brig-of-war rounding the northern point of the anchorage, within gunshot of the privateer.

Reid at first contemplated cutting his cable and making a bolt for it, confident in the sailing powers of his fine craft. The wind, however, was light and uncertain, and the British brig had most of what there was at the moment, so he abandoned the idea, being informed by the Consul that he would not be molested as long as he remained at anchor—which was, of course, a very correct and proper assumption, Fayal being a Portuguese possession, and therefore a neutral port. So Captain Reid and his friends watched the brig, which was the *Carnation*—of 18 guns, commander, George Bentham—standing in through the gathering dusk. After the pilot had boarded her, she came on and anchored within pistol-shot of the *General Armstrong*.

The American did not feel at all easy as to the efficacy of neutral protection ; and, while he discussed it, an English 74-gun ship and a 38-gun frigate appeared round the point—to wit, the *Plantagenet*, Captain Robert Lloyd ; and the *Rota*, Captain Philip Somerville—and the brig immediately commenced signalling furiously to them.

This was getting a little too hot ; and, seeing the brig presently send her boats to the line-of-battle ship, Captain Reid resolved, escape seaward being impossible, to be prepared for the worst. So, the wind having dropped, he got out his sweeps and slowly pulled his vessel further inshore.

The *Carnation* immediately got under way and followed ; but the wind was too light, and she was unable to close the privateer.

About 8 p.m. the Americans—to give their version first—perceived four boats, armed and full of men, approaching. Captain Reid thereupon dropped his anchor with a spring on the cable, and swung his broadside upon the boats. When they came within hail he warned them not to approach nearer, on pain of being fired upon ; they came on, however, and the privateer opened on them with cannon and small arms. " The boats promptly returned the fire, but so unexpectedly warm was the reception they got from the privateer that they cried for quarter and hauled off in a badly crippled condition."

Captain Reid says he had one man killed and his first officer wounded. Being convinced that he had not seen the last of the British boats, he hauled so close in that the vessel was almost touching the rocks, right under the castle, and anchored head and stern.

The *Carnation* was observed, about nine o'clock, towing in a number of boats ; she could not, however, get close enough in to co-operate with them, as the wind was baffling and the tide was adverse ; so the boats cast off and remained for some time under cover of a low reef of rocks.

There were eleven of them, according to the British official report—twelve, the Americans say—and they must have contained at least two hundred men ; probably more, as some would be very large boats, pulling fourteen or sixteen oars. Such a force would have been considered far more than adequate for the cutting out of a French vessel ; indeed, much larger vessels than the *General Armstrong* have often been captured by British boats with considerably less force than was despatched upon this occasion. We rather

" fancied " ourselves in this matter of cutting out vessels from a harbour, and some splendid feats have undoubtedly been performed in this way. It was a sort of adventure which was considered essentially British in character ; and justly so, as our enemies certainly never ventured much in the way of attempting to cut out our vessels.

Captain Lloyd and his merry men were now to learn the difference between French or Spanish seamen and Americans.

Meanwhile, the Governor had sent a letter to the British captain begging him to respect the neutrality of the port and abstain from further attack upon the privateer. Captain Lloyd replied by pointing out that the Americans had broken the neutrality of the port by firing into his boat without the least provocation. That he had intended to respect it, but was now determined to seize the privateer, and hoped the Governor would direct the fort to assist him.

About midnight the flotilla of boats advanced to the attack. They were allowed to approach within what used to be termed " point blank " range—a vague term, but equivalent, probably, to longish pistol-shot, and then came the round and grape from the privateer, doing considerable execution. The British responded with the guns mounted in their boats ; then, with loud cheers, they raced for the *General Armstrong*, boarding her in several different places.

A most bloodthirsty and terrible conflict now took place. The British seamen, with characteristic dash and courage, climbed up the vessel's side on all hands, nothing daunted by the fierce resistance of her crew. The Americans, armed with every kind of weapon which would serve at close quarters, met them at arm's length with such ferocity that the boats were soon cumbered up with wounded and dying men, hurled back with pistol, pike, or cutlass. Wherever an English head cropped up above the bulwarks it was a target. And still they continued the attack, and with so much success in the bow that a number gained a footing on the forecastle, and the two American officers in charge forward were killed or disabled. Learning the state of affairs forward, Captain Reid, who, with the after-hands, had pretty well disposed of the attack at the stern, rallied his men, and, leading them forward on the run, drove the British over the bows into their boats—and that was the end of it. The fight lasted forty minutes—a tremendous time for such a desperate affair, proving the stubborn courage on both sides.

Two of the frigate *Rota's* boats, the American account states, were taken possession of, loaded with dead and dying men. "Of the forty or fifty men in these boats only seventeen escaped death, and they by swimming ashore. Another boat was found under the privateer's stern, commanded by one of the *Plantagenet's* lieutenants. All the men in it were killed but four, the lieutenant himself jumping overboard to save his life."

These details appear to corroborate the description of an eye-witness, given by Mr. Maclay; he says: "The Americans fought with great firmness, but more like bloodthirsty savages than anything else. They rushed into the boats sword in hand, and put every soul to death as far as came within their power."

The estimate of killed and wounded, as given by Mr. Maclay, respectively 120 and 130, is greatly exaggerated; the official account, with names of officers, seamen, and marines, gives it as 36 killed and 84 wounded—and quite enough, too !

The affair was disastrous for the British; but Captain Reid had, of course, to lose his ship. He received a communication at 3 a.m. from his Consul that Captain Lloyd was determined to have him, and at daybreak the *Carnation* stood in and engaged him. But, being unable at the moment to pick up the best berth for operations, the British vessel hauled off again, with some small damage from the American long gun. A second time she was more successful, and, bringing her heavy short guns to bear at close range, sealed the fate of the *General Armstrong*. Reid and his men, prepared for this ending, scuttled their ship and went on shore, upon which the English set her on fire, completing her destruction.

Captain Lloyd, in his report, declares that the *General Armstrong* was so close inshore that the attacking boats had not room to board on the inside; and that " every American in Fayal, exclusive of part of the crew, being armed and concealed in these rocks, which were immediately over the privateer, it unfortunately happened when these brave men gained the deck they were under the painful necessity of returning to their boats, from the very destructive fire kept up by those above them from the shore, who were in complete security."

This is rather a wild story, to which the thoughtful reader will not be disposed to yield full credence. With regard to the breach of neutrality, there is an affidavit, sworn before the British Consul, by Lieutenant Robert Faussett, of the *Plantagenet*, to the effect that he approached, unarmed, in the pinnace, for the purpose of ascertaining what vessel it was ; and that the Americans warned them off when they were so close that the boat was shoved off with a boathook, and then opened fire ; that Faussett called for quarter, shouting, "Don't murder us !" and they continued their attack ; that he had no means of returning a shot, and could only retire, with two killed and seven wounded. He says nothing about the proximity of other boats, armed or otherwise ; and so the Americans would appear to have been technically guilty of the initial breach of neutrality. Captain Lloyd, by way of showing that American privateers were addicted to this kind of thing, encloses a copy of the affidavit of William Wilson, late master of the transport brig *Doris*, which was captured, in defiance of the law of neutrality, on June 25th preceding, in the anchorage of Flores, another island of the Azores.

Captain Lloyd, however, got no credit out of this affair. The Lords of the Admiralty expressed very strong disapproval of the whole business ; told him he ought to have known that the sending of a boat after dark was sure to lead to some such incident ; that, if the Americans broke the neutrality of the

port, his first business was to make representation to
the Governor, and not take the law into his own
hands; that the honour of the flag and the prestige
of the British Navy, represented by a 74-gun ship,
a frigate, and several sloops, was not likely to be
endangered by the presence of one privateer—with
other home truths and doses of common sense. And
really, one cannot help agreeing cordially with their
lordships, and heartily deploring the loss of so many
brave men in a fiasco due to thorough bad manage-
ment.

A fortnight later the boats of the British frigate
Endymion, Captain Henry Hope, made an attempt
to carry the *Prince de Neufchatel*—a very successful
privateer, but why such a clumsy name ?—off Nan-
tucket, with very similar results. The fight was even
more desperate than in the case of the *General
Armstrong*, the privateer having only nine of her crew
untouched, while the British casualties amounted to
fully half of the men engaged. The privateer escaped.

Such are some of the incidents of the two American
wars ; of this type were the men—or many of them—
who commanded the privateers. The British records
of the period, during the war of 1812, bear full testimony to their success, and the officers of the Royal
Navy come in for some rough handling by the Press
—as in *The Times* of February 11th, 1815 : " The
American cruisers daily enter in among our convoys,
seize prizes in sight of those that should afford protection, and, if pursued, ' put on their sea-wings ' and

laugh at the clumsy English pursuers. To what is this owing? Cannot we build ships? It must indeed be encouraging to Mr. Madison to read the logs of his cruisers. If they fight, they are sure to conquer; if they fly, they are sure to escape."

That the Americans have the knack of building faster sailing-vessels than ours is a fact which we have been compelled to accept. Not that our smartest clippers would be beaten, as a matter of course, by any of theirs; but, taking it all round, an American who wants to turn out a specially swift sailing vessel will almost always eclipse our efforts in the same direction. Are we not still trying in vain to win back the "America" Cup? The long, rakish craft, of comparatively small beam and tapering lines, was no doubt originally an American production.

These swift vessels, sailed by such men as Boyle, Haraden, Barney, Coggleshall, and others, were both hard to catch and bad to beat. The sentence quoted above from *The Times* sums up the situation pretty accurately; and, this being the case, it is all the more to be regretted that the accounts of their exploits should so constantly be tainted with obvious exaggerations, or embellished with incredible little anecdotes.

SOME MORE ODD YARNS

CHAPTER XXII

THE "PRINCESS ROYAL" PACKET

IN the days of sailing-vessels the mails were regularly carried by fast-sailing brigs, which were known as packets. They were virtually men-of-war, but were not heavily armed, nor did they carry a numerous crew. The captain's first duty was to convey the mails with expedition and safety, and he was not expected to go out of his way to engage an enemy, but to escape if possible. Some fire-eating commanders of packets required, indeed, to be admonished as to their duties in this respect. The brigs were usually very heavily masted, and it was considered a point of honour to "carry on" their canvas, sometimes to a dangerous extent. More than one of these craft has unaccountably disappeared, having no doubt foundered in a storm.

They were very fine little vessels, however, and there was probably a certain amount of "swagger" attached to belonging to them—a sort of craft that was not under anybody's orders, and was not to be interfered with ; and when they were attacked, and found escape impossible, their "swagger" assumed the form, in many instances, of a most heroic defence

—while the mails were always sunk before surrendering.

Here is a very interesting letter, describing an
action between the *Princess Royal* packet, Captain
John Skinner, and a French privateer of vastly superior
force. It is written by one of the passengers, who
" plied the small arms with much effect."

" NEW YORK, *August 25th,* 1798.

" I have at last the pleasure to inform you of my
arrival here, the 14th instant, after a very tedious
passage. We left Falmouth on June 12th, in company with the *Grantham* packet, bound to Jamaica,
which kept with us five days. Four days after,
on the morning of June 21st, we fell in with a
French privateer ; at five o'clock she made sail
after us. We had light airs and a smooth sea—
all sails set. At midday, we triced up our boarding-
nettings and made clear for action, with our courses
up. The privateer, towards the afternoon, came
up with us fast, by the assistance of her sweeps.
At 7 p.m. our men were all at quarters. She
hoisted English colours, firing a shot,[1] which we
returned, and she answered by a gun to leeward.
At this time she was within cannon-shot, but, it
growing dark, kept in our wake ; and we turned in,
not expecting an attack till next morning. However,
before daylight, at half-past three in the morning,
she came within pistol-shot, and fired a broadside
of great guns, swivels, etc., which we immediately

[1] An illegal and piratical act ; she was bound to show her
own colours before firing.

returned, and kept up a general fire with our cannon and small arms. Our force was only two 6-pounders, and four 4-pounders; of which six guns we got five on one side to bear on them. We mustered thirty men and boys, exclusive of Captain Skinner and his master, besides thirteen passengers and four servants: in all forty-nine.

"The privateer was a low brig, apparently mounting twelve or fourteen guns, and full of men. Our guns were extremely well plied; a lieutenant, going to join the *St. Albans* man-of-war, was captain of one of our 6-pounders, and the rest of us passengers plied the small arms with much effect. The engagement continued, without intermission, for two hours, when she out with her sweeps, left off firing, and rowed off, for it was near calm, there not being wind enough to carry us a knot through the water. As she was rowing off we got our two stern-chasers, the 6-pounders, to bear upon her, and hit her twice in her counter, which must have gone through and through, for it caused great noise and confusion on board, and soon after we saw two men at work over her stern. At six o'clock, being out of cannon-shot, we ceased firing, and set about repairing our damage. She had some swivels fixed in her tops, which would have done us considerable mischief, had they not been drove from them early in the action, which was Captain Skinner's first object at the beginning of the engagement.

"Thank God, we had no one killed; most of their shot went above us. The boarding-nettings, directly over our quarter-deck, were shot away, as their principal force seemed to aim at the passengers, who plied fourteen muskets to some advantage, and annoyed the privateer much.

" Captain Skinner conducted himself well ; it was no new business to him. His orders were given coolly and everything done with great precision and regularity. I believe you know that he lost his right arm in an engagement on board of a frigate last war.

" I cannot omit mentioning that a lady (a sister of Captain Skinner), who, with her maid, were the only female passengers, were both employed in the bread-room during the action making up papers for cartridges ; for we had not a single four-pound cartridge remaining when the action ceased.

" Our sails were shot through, rigging very much cut, our spars and boat upon deck shot through, several grape and round-shot in our bows and side, and a very large shot, which must have been a 9- or 12-pounder, in our counter. The ship proved a little leaky after the action, but she got pretty tight again before our arrival. Captain Skinner was slightly wounded, but is now well.'

This plain and very credible story was afterwards supplemented by the independent testimony of an American gentleman, who was a prisoner on board the privateer during this engagement. She was the *Aventurier*, and this gentleman states :

" That her force was fourteen long French 4-pounders, and two 12-pounders ; that she had eighty-five men on board at the time, of whom two were killed and four wounded in the action. That all her masts were shot through, her stays and rigging very much cut ; that when she got to Bordeaux she was obliged to have new masts and a complete set of new rigging. They supposed, on board the privateer, that there was not a single shot fired from the packet that did not take effect : which seems probable, for, though so low in the water, she had nineteen shot in her bottom under her wale.[1] At the time there were on board thirty English and American prisoners. She was so peppered that she would certainly have been made a prize of, could the packet have pursued her ; and was so cut to pieces by the action that she after-wards ran from everything until she got into Bordeaux to refit ; the shots that raked her as she moved off went quite through, and caused much confusion."

This is a very pretty tale of pluck and skill com-bined. The reproach which has been laid against the British Navy in this—1798—and subsequent years of inexpertness in gunnery, certainly could not have been levelled against the crew of the *Princess Royal*, who put in their 4- and 6-pounder shot in such businesslike fashion, while the passengers picked off the dangerous swivel-men in the tops. The two un-daunted women quietly making cartridge-bags in the bread-room rounds off the picture very agreeably.

TWO COLONIAL PRIVATEERS

Here are two instances in which privateers fitted out by our colonies have performed very brilliant

[1] Wale, or wales, sometimes termed " bends " ; the thickest outside planking of the ship, at and above the water-line.

services ; and the first is introduced by Vice-Admiral Sir Roger Curtis, Bart., Commander-in-Chief of His Maesty's ships and vessels at the Cape of Good Hope, who writes from Capetown on December 20th, 1801, to Evan Nepean, Esq., Secretary to the Admiralty, as follows :

" SIR,—The private ship-of-war, the *Chance*, belonging to Mr. Hogan, of this place, and commanded by Mr. William White, having been a cruise on the coast of Peru, returned on the 11th instant. The Commander of the *Chance* addressed a letter to me containing an account of his proceedings during his cruise. He appears to have uniformly acted with great propriety ; but his conduct, and that of his officers and men, was, on two occasions, so highly creditable to them that I send his account of these occurrences for their lordships' information.

" I am, etc.,

" ROGER CURTIS."

Extract of a letter from Mr. William White, commander of the *Chance* private ship of war, fitted out at the Cape of Good Hope, to Vice-Admiral Sir Roger Curtis, Bart :

" At four p.m. on August 19th (1801), the island St. Laurence [1] bearing N.E. two leagues, saw a large ship bearing down upon us. At nine brought her to close action, and engaged her within half pistol-shot for an hour and a half, but finding her metal much heavier

---

[1] There does not appear to be an island under this name on the west coast of South America, in any modern atlas. It must have been close to Callao, the sea-port of Lima, as he sent his prisoners on shore there next day.

than ours, and full of men, boarded her on the starboard quarter, lashing the *Chance's* bowsprit to her mizzenmast, and, after a desperate resistance of three-quarters of an hour, beat them off the upper deck; but they still defended from the cabin and lower deck with long pikes in a most gallant manner, till they had twenty-five men killed and twenty-eight wounded, of whom the captain was one. Getting final possession, she was so close to the island that with much difficulty we got her off shore, all her braces and rigging being cut to pieces by our grape-shot. She proved to be the new Spanish ship *Amiable Maria*, of about 600 tons, mounting fourteen guns, 18, 12, and 9-pounders, brass, and carrying 120 men, from Concepcion bound to Lima, laden with corn, wine, bale goods, etc. On this occasion, I am much concerned to state, Mr. Bennett, a very valuable and brave officer, was so dangerously wounded that he died three days after the action; the second and fourth mates, Marine officer, and two seamen badly wounded by pikes, but since recovered. On the 20th, both ships being much disabled, and having more prisoners than crew, I stood close in and sent eighty-six on shore in the large ship's launch to Lima. We afterwards learned that seventeen of the wounded had died.

"At 4 a.m. on September 24th, standing in to cut out from the roads of Puna, in Guaiquil Bay, a ship I had information of, mounting twenty-two guns, fell in with a large Spanish brig, with a broad pendant at maintopmast-head. At five she commenced her fire on us, but she being at a distance to windward, and desirous to bring her to close action, we received three broadsides before a shot was returned. At half-past five, being yardarm and yardarm, commenced our fire with great effect, and, after a very severe action of two hours and three-quarters, during the latter part of which she made every effort to get away, I had the honour to see the Spanish flag struck to the *Chance*. She proved to be the Spanish man-of-war brig *Limeno*, mounting eighteen long 6-pound guns, commanded by Commodore Don Philip de Martinez, the senior officer of the Spanish Marine on that coast, and manned with 140 men, sent from Guaiquil for the express purpose of taking the *Chance*, and then to proceed to the northward to take three English whalers lying in one of their ports. She had fourteen men killed and seven wounded; the captain mortally wounded, who died two days after the action. The *Chance* had two men killed and one wounded, and had only fifty men at the commencement of the action; mounting sixteen guns, 12- and 6-pounders.''

Captain White's little argument in favour of boarding the *Amiable* (?) *Maria* reads rather quaintly : " Finding her metal much heavier than ours, *and full of men* " : a good argument for reversing the boarding operations, one would imagine ; but the *Amiable Maria* was not equal to the occasion—was not, in fact, if the pun may be pardoned, *taking any chances* !

The other colonial privateer about which good things are recorded was the *Rover*, of Liverpool, Nova Scotia. This loyal province, it appears, fitted out some fifteen privateers in 1794 and the three following years ; and of these seven or eight hailed from the little town of Liverpool. Captain Godfrey shall be allowed to tell his own simple and straightforward tale :

" The brig *Rover*, mounting fourteen 4-pounders, was the present year (1798) built and fitted for war at Liverpool in this province. She sailed under my command June 4th last on a cruise against the enemies of Great Britain, being commissioned by His Excellency Sir John Wentworth, Bart. Our crew consisted of 55 men and boys, including myself and officers, and was principally composed of fishermen."

" On the 17th of the same month, in the latitude of 23 N. and longitude 54 W.[1] we fell in with six sail of vessels, whom we soon discovered to be enemies, one being a ship, with four brigs and a schooner. The schooner showed 16 guns, one of the brigs 16 guns, another 6 guns. These six vessels drew up close together, apparently with an intention of engaging us. On consulting with my ship's company, we determined to bear down and attack them, but so soon as the enemy perceived our intentions, they by signal from the schooner dispersed, each taking a different course, before we got within gun-shot of them. After a few hours' chase we took possession of the ship and one of the brigs. The ship proved an American, bound from the South Seas, laden with oil, and the brig an American, laden with wine, from Madeira. From them we learned that they had been captured some

[1] That is, to the north-westward of the northernmost of the Windward Islands, in the West Indies.

short time before by a French privateer, which was the schooner in company ; that she mounted sixteen guns, two of which were 9-pounders and the rest sixes, and carried 155 men ; and that the other three were American vessels which she had taken, one of which was from the East Indies. Night coming on, we were prevented from taking any more of them.

" On September 10th, being cruising near to Cape Blanco, on the Spanish Main, we chased a Spanish schooner on shore and destroyed her. Being close in with the land and becalmed, we discovered a schooner and three gunboats under Spanish colours making for us. A light breeze springing up, we were enabled to get clear of the land, when it fell calm, which enabled the schooner and gunboats, by the help of a number of oars, to gain fast upon us, keeping up at the same time a constant fire from their bow-guns, which we returned with two guns pointed from our stern ; one of the gunboats did not advance to attack us. As the enemy drew near we engaged them with muskets and pistols, keeping with oars the stern of the *Rover* towards them, and having all our guns well loaded with great and small shot, ready against we should come to close quarters. When we heard the commander of the schooner give orders to the two gunboats to board us, I waited to see how they meant to attack us, and, finding the schooner intended to board us on our starboard quarter, one of the gunboats on our larboard bow, and the other on our larboard waist, I suffered them to advance in that position until they came within about fifteen yards, still firing on them with small-arms and the stern-guns. I then manned the oars on the larboard side, and pulled the *Rover* round so as to bring her starboard broadside to bear athwart the schooner's bow, and poured into her a whole broadside of great and small shot, which raked her deck fore and aft, while it was full of men ready for boarding. I instantly shifted over on the other side [*i.e.* sent the men over] and raked both gunboats in the same manner, which must have killed and wounded a great number of those on board of them, and done great damage to their boats. I then commenced a close action with the schooner, which lasted three glasses [an hour and a half], and, having disabled her sails and rigging much, and finding her fire grew slack, I took advantage of a light air of wind to back my head-sails, which brought my stern on board of the schooner, by which we were enabled to board and carry her, at which time the gunboats sheered off, apparently in a very shattered condition. We found her to be the *Santa Rita*, mounting ten 6-pounders and two 12-pounder carronades, with 125 men. She was fitted out the day before by the Governor of Porto Cavallo, with the gunboats, for the express purpose of taking us. Every officer on board of her was killed except the officers who commanded a party of 25 soldiers ; there were 14 dead men on her deck when we boarded her, and 17 wounded ; the prisoners, including the wounded, amounted to 71.

My ship's company, including officers and boys, was only 45 in number, and behaved with that courage and spirit which British seamen always show when

fighting the enemies of their country. It is with
infinite pleasure I add that I had not a man hurt ;
from the best account I could obtain, the enemy
lost 54 men. The prisoners being too numerous to
be kept on board, on the 14th ult. I landed them all
except eight, taking an obligation from them not to
serve against his Majesty until regularly exchanged.
I arrived with my ship's company in safety this day
(October 17th) at Liverpool, having taken during my
cruise the before-mentioned vessels, together with a
sloop under American colours bound to Curaçao, a
Spanish schooner bound to Port Caballo, which have
all arrived in this province ; besides which I destroyed
some Spanish launches on the coast."

A very successful four month's cruise. Godfrey's
crew of Nova Scotian fishermen would be very difficult to beat : they were stalwart, hard-bitten fellows,
well used to hardship in their calling, and not afraid of
anything ; much the same type, in fact, as those Salem
men who gave us so much trouble in the war of 1812.

To the initiated, Captain Godfrey's handling of his
craft on the approach of the three Spanish vessels
will commend itself. It was an exceedingly pretty
bit of seamanship, only possible at such a moment
to a captain of consummate coolness, with his crew
well in hand.

The Spaniards appear on this, as on so many other
occasions, to have made the wildest practice with their
firearms ; Godfrey had not a man touched, after an
action of one hour and a half, with a hand-to-hand
fight at the end of it !

CHAPTER XXIII

THE AFFAIR OF THE "BONAPARTE"

In the year 1804 there was a very formidable French privateer cruising in the West Indies, by name the *Bonaparte*, carrying 18 guns and a crew of over 200. This vessel encountered, in the month of August, the British ship of war *Hippomenes*—a capture from the Dutch at the surrender of Demerara in the previous year—of 18 guns, commanded by Captain Kenneth McKenzie, who had in some measure disguised his ship in order to entrap privateers. The Frenchman was so far deceived as to invite a conflict, believing the *Hippomenes* to be a "Guineaman," or African slave-trader, which were almost always armed, but which the *Bonaparte* would have no cause to fear.

Having caught a tartar, the French captain did not on that account endeavour to avoid battle, and a sharp action ensued. After some time, the French ship fell aboard the *Hippomenes*, upon which Captain McKenzie instantly had the two ships lashed together, and, calling upon his men to follow him, sprang on board the *Bonaparte*. He appears, however, to have been very unfortunate in his crew, many of whom, it is said, were foreigners, and only eight men had the stomach to follow him. This little band, however, under their captain's gallant leadership, actually drove the Frenchmen from their quarters for a time, no doubt under the impression that this was merely the vanguard of a formidable force of boarders. Finding themselves opposed by such insignificant numbers, however, they rallied, and the plucky Englishmen were terribly cut up, McKenzie receiving no less than fourteen wounds, while the first lieutenant and purser were killed and the master wounded. There was nothing for it but to scramble back on board their own ship, which they barely succeeded in doing when the lashings gave way, and the vessels swung apart, Captain McKenzie almost missing his leap, and falling senseless into the " chains " of his own ship. The Frenchman had had enough, so the action ended indecisively, and the *Bonaparte* was free to continue her depredations. Had the whole of the English crew been of the same kidney as the gallant eight her career in the French service would certainly have been ended then and there.

A month or two later the *Bonaparte* fell in with three British armed merchantmen, to wit the *Thetis*, *Ceres*, and *Penelope*, which had sailed in company from Cork in October, John Charnley, captain of the *Thetis*, being commodore of the little squadron.

The *Bonaparte* was sighted at 7 a.m. on November 8th, to windward of Barbadoes, and the three English ships at once hauled their wind and prepared for action. What ensued shall be told in the language of the three captains, as illustrating the curious diversity of views which may result from distorted vision in the heat of action—for that one or other of these captains had his vision so distorted there can be no doubt. All three letters are dated November 10th, 1804, from Bridge Town, Barbadoes, and are addressed to the owners—though whether all three ships were owned by one firm does not appear.

The captain of the *Ceres* writes :

" I am happy to inform you of my safe arrival here, in company with the *Penelope* and *Thetis*. The day we came in we fell in with the *Bonaparte*, French privateer, of twenty guns, which bore down upon us, and commenced a very heavy fire, which we returned as warm as possible. She attempted to board the *Thetis*, and, in the act, lost her bowsprit, and soon after her foremast went over the side—a fortunate circumstance, as I understand she was the terror of the West Indies. She sent a challenge here by an American, the day before we arrived, to any of our sloops of war to fight her. We understand she had beaten off one of them. The action was very smart for about two hours ; we began firing at nine o'clock in the morning, and did not leave off till half after twelve. My ship was on fire three times by neglect of the people with their cartridges. She once got on fire in the cabin ; but, by the exertions of the crew, it was soon extinguished. They behaved with the greatest spirit ; and, I believe, would have fought to the last, though half of them were foreigners. I had several shots in the hull and my rigging and sails were very much cut. The small shot and grape came on board us like hail, though they did not hit one man. I had two men blown up by the cartridges taking fire, who are very much burnt."

The *Penelope* account comes next :

" I arrived here safe, after a passage of thirty-three days, in company with the *Ceres* and *Thetis,* and shall be detained here some time to refit : having on the 8th inst., in lat. 13.26 N., long. 57.30 W. had an engagement with the *Bonaparte* privateer, of 22 guns and 250 men, for three hours ; in which engagement we had ten of our guns dismounted, which I must repair here, and likewise replenish our powder. I suppose I shall be ready for sea by the 13th. I am sorry to say Mr. Lindo was killed in the engagement, and his poor wife is very disconsolate. I wish her to return home from hence, but she refuses. I send this by the *Burton,* of Liverpool, who is now under weigh, or otherwise would be more particular. The action commenced at 9 a.m., and we engaged until half-past meridian, when we left off chase. The privateer lost her bowsprit and foremast in attempting to board the *Thetis,* who had two men killed and five wounded."

Captain Charnley's report is as follows :

" MESSRS. STUART, HEESMAN, & CO."
" GENTLEMEN,

" I arrived here, in company with the *Ceres* and *Penelope,* last evening. On the 8th instant, at 7 a.m., seeing a strange sail and a suspicious one (being commodore), I made a signal for an enemy, and to haul our wind on the larboard tack to meet her. At nine we met ; she kept English colours flying till after firing two broadsides. Seeing him attempt to lay us alongside to leeward, thought it better to have him to windward, so wore ship on the other tack. He was then on our quarter, and lashed himself to our mizzen chains ; the contest then became desperate for one hour. They set us on fire twice on the quarter-deck with stink-pots and other combustibles, and made four very daring attempts to board, with at least eighty men, out of their rigging, foretop, and bowsprit, but were most boldly repulsed by every man and boy in the ship. At the conclusion, a double-headed shot, from our aftermost gun, carried away his foremast by the board ; that took away his bowsprit and maintopgallant-mast. He then thought it was time to cast us off. No less than fifty men fell with the wreck. We then hauled our wind as well as we could, to knot, splice, and repair our rigging for the time, which gave the other ships an opportunity to play upon the enemy ; but, being a little to leeward, had not so good an effect. A short time afterwards wore ship for him again, with the other ships, and engaged him for about an hour more ; but, finding it impossible to take him, owing to his number of men, and no surgeon to dress our wounded, I thought it best to steer our course for this island. Her name is the *Bonaparte*, of 20 9-pounders and upwards of 200 men. I had 18 6-pounders and 45 men, 19 never at sea before, boys and landsmen. As to the behaviour of my whole crew, to a man they were steady, and determined to defend the ship whilst there was one left alive. I had two killed and nine wounded. On our arrival Commodore Hood paid us every attention, sent the surgeon and mate to dress the wounded, also men to assist the ship to anchor, and gave me a written protection for my crew.[1] I cannot conclude without mentioning the gallant and spirited conduct of Mr. Dobbs, a midshipman (passenger with me), who acted as Captain of Marines, and during the action fought like a brave fellow, as well as exciting in the minds of the crew unconquerable zeal. We are much shattered in our hull, sails, and rigging; it will take us two days before we can be ready for sea."

"I remain, in haste, gentlemen,

"Your very obedient servant,

"JOHN CHARNLEY."

In another letter to a friend, a day or two later, Charnley says:

"The *Bonaparte* privateer is the completest ship in these seas. She made too certain of us. Freers, my first mate, behaved most gallantly, and fought like a lion; so did Lambert, my second mate. Indeed, I cannot say enough for every man and boy in the ship. The greatest part of them stripped

---

[1] That is, indemnity from having the crew pressed by any man-of-war which was short of hands. As a regular privateer, she would be exempt from this; but apparently she and her consorts were merchantmen, armed and probably provided with what were loosely termed letters of marque for protection in case of attack.

and fought naked, and I am sure would have died sooner than have been carried. There was one hour's hard work, I assure you. I was near going frequently, as they fired several musket-balls through my clothes."

This appears to be a straightforward account, and though it differs from the others, in respect of the parts played by them in the action, Captain Charnley does not attach any blame to them for lack of zeal or enterprise.

The Barbadoes *Mercury* headed the account of the action—"Defeat of *Bonaparte*! *not* the Great, but celebrated privateer of Guadaloupe!"

Four months later Captain Charnley deemed it necessary to publish, in the *Bristol Journal* of March 16th, 1805, the following justification of himself:

" On our arrival in this port, observing a paragraph in the London papers respecting a late action between the *Bonaparte*, French privateer, and the ships *Thetis*, *Ceres*, and *Penelope*, off Barbadoes, which makes it appear to the public that the two latter did wonders, and the *Thetis* little or nothing; I now think it incumbent on me, and a duty I owe to my crew, as commander of the *Thetis*, to state a few facts, and confute any reports that have been made of the action; which would have been passed over in silence by me, had they not resorted to the means they have of obtaining unmerited credit at the expense of others. The three ships sailed in company from Cork, the *Thetis* to act as commodore. Nothing material occurred till November 8th, when at 7 a.m. the man at our mast-head called out, 'A sail!' It

soon appearing a suspicious one, I made a signal for
an enemy, and to haul our wind on the larboard tack
to meet her ; which was answered by our consorts.
At nine the privateer and the *Thetis* met ; the other
ships not sailing so fast, were at this time about one
mile astern in her wake. The privateer hailed us in
English twice, with English colours flying ; the latter
we answered with a broadside from our larboard
guns. Seeing him determined to board us, we wore
ship and sailed large ; in the act of doing which
she raked us twice, ran up alongside under a press
of sail, and made herself fast to our mizzen-chains.
By this time the other ships were nearly up ; but,
instead of coming into action on the enemy's quarter,
which ought to have been their station, bore up before
they reached us, fired five or six guns (the contents of
which we shared with the enemy) ; and during the
whole time (upwards of one hour) we were lashed
together they were sailing ahead of us at about half
a mile distance, although the crew of the *Penelope*
went aft to their commander and told him it was
a shame to see the *Thetis* so mauled and render no
assistance : this was their report on board his Majesty's
ship *Centaur*. At the conclusion of the fight a fortunate double-headed shot from our aftermost gun
carried away the enemy's foremast, bowsprit, and
maintopgallant-mast ; upon which he cut us adrift,
when we hauled our wind to the northward, with
an intention to gain so far to windward as to get on
his weather-side, where all the wreck was lying. On
examining my crew, I found two killed and seven

wounded, our sails and rigging so much cut that the ship was ungovernable ; however, by uncommon exertions, we got her wore on the other tack, but only fetched under the enemy's lee, when we passed almost shaving her, and gave her two broadsides, at the same time receiving one from her which wounded two more men and disabled four guns. Afterwards spoke the *Ceres*, whose commander inquired into the state of our ship and men ; he and his passengers drank my health, and he expressed himself more than once (through his trumpet), that he was very sorry it was not in his power to give us any assistance. I then urged a wish to further annoy the enemy, as she would be an easy capture. His answer was, " It is impossible ; she has too many men." During this time, for about half an hour, the enemy was lying a complete log, while our consorts had received no damage. However, at length all three of us made sail together for her again, and engaged her at a distance for about an hour. My wounded being in great agony, I shaped a course for Barbadoes, where we all arrived next evening.

" When we anchored I was visited by Captain Richardson, of his Majesty's ship *Centaur*, who immediately sent for a surgeon, Mr. Martin, who has my thanks for his particular attention to the wounded. Commodore Hood very handsomely gave me a protection for my crew, and took the wounded into the Royal Hospital.

" So little credit was given to the account of the action given by the captains of the *Ceres* and *Penelope* at

Barbadoes, that they resorted to the means of obtaining the captain of the *Bonaparte's* signature to a letter, in direct contradiction of his statement to a naval officer who captured him, which was in the fullest manner corroborated by the surgeon who was stopped at Dominica on his way to Guadaloupe.

"The action speaks for itself. Neither of the vessels, the *Ceres* or *Penelope*, was in the smallest degree injured, although one of them reported he expended *six barrels* of gunpowder. Double that quantity might have been expended with equal effect, as a large proportion of it was set fire to in the barrels. The *Penelope*, I understand, lost a passenger by a chance shot, yet I believe was equally as fortunate as the *Ceres* in escaping without damage.

"The steady behaviour of the *Thetis's* officers and crew in this action, and their conduct during the voyage, demand my highest esteem, and will be for ever imprinted on my memory."

The inhabitants of the island of Dominica, in presenting Captain Charnley with a handsome sum of money and a piece of plate, allude to his gallant defeat of the *Bonaparte* as " thereby protecting two valuable ships under your convoy " : which is significant of the version of the affair which had got abroad, either through Charnley or the French captain.

However, it was not done with yet, for Daniel Bousfield, captain of the *Ceres*, arrived in England in April and immediately proceeded to enlighten the editor of the *Bristol Journal* as to the " true facts " of the case, enclosing a copy of the letter which he had received from the captain of the *Bonaparte*, and which readers are requested "to compare with the partial and pompous account of the action inserted, on the authority of Mr. Charnley, in the public papers."

"Sir, I have been astonished at the account given against you of the engagement we had together; the manner in which you conducted yourself obliges me, upon my honour, to inform the public of the fact. On my arrival here, I was surprised to find that the captain of the *Thetis* took to himself all the merit of having fought with me. It is true that, during the heat of the action, he was the nearest ship to me, but that was from necessity, as it was him that I attacked first, and which I did because I saw that he was the best armed of the three. He commenced the fire, which was soon followed up by you and the other letter of marque. The courage you have all three shown cannot be too much admired. Your manœuvres convince me that they were the result of reflection and experience; and the national character which you have manifested certainly merits the eulogium of the public.

"Your fire was tremendous for me; and I can with truth affirm that it was you who did me most damage, and who dismasted my vessel, which was the reason that I was unable to capture the *Thetis*. A single ship, then, has not all the honour of the fight, but certainly all three. In short, sir, I thank the accident that has procured me the pleasure of your acquaintance, and to express the satisfaction that I feel in my heart in writing this letter. I leave you full liberty to make it public among your countrymen. In proving my particular esteem for your person, it will no doubt, at the same time, ensure you the public approbation, and preserve you from those malicious tongues who shall dare attack your respectable character.

"I have the honour to be, with consideration and esteem, sir, your obedient servant,

"PAINPENY."

The Frenchman declares that it was the *Ceres* which dismasted his ship, though both the captains state in their letters that she lost her foremast, etc., in boarding the *Thetis*. Captain Charnley says the two other ships stood off, and came out of the fight undamaged, whereas they both report considerable injury, and the captain of the *Penelope* states that ten of her guns were disabled. The only casualty, however, appears to have been one passenger killed, while the *Ceres* had only two men injured, through their own careless handling of the ammunition—though " the small-shot and grape came on board like hail."

Now, when we are told that a ship has ten guns disabled in action, and that the only person touched was a passenger, presumably not stationed at a gun, the question inevitably presents itself—where were the guns' crews? Also, when grape and case are coming on board like hail, it seems odd that nobody is hit. Every one who has any experience or knowledge of battle is aware, of course, that the saying that " every bullet has its billet " is rank romance ; a vast majority of bullets discharged in hot action find no other billet than the bottom of the sea—unless, indeed, they are swallowed by inquisitive fish while sinking—or the nearest hillside. Still, these two good men do not appear to make out their case very well ; let us hope that they did not deliberately lie to their owners. The Frenchman was, of course, interested in demonstrating that he was beaten off by three, rather than by one ship ; still, he was perhaps a very truthful man : and there we must leave it. The only thing quite clear is that the *Bonaparte* made rather sure of catching three good prizes, and was considerably sold.

CHAPTER XXIV

THE "WINDSOR CASTLE" PACKET

ONE of the most brilliant instances of the defence of a packet is that of the encounter of the *Windsor Castle* with the French privateer *Jeune Richard*. The packet was outward bound to the West Indies, and fell in with the privateer not far from Barbadoes, about half-past eight on the morning of October 1st, 1807. The privateer immediately gave chase, being probably well aware of the class of vessel she would encounter, and confident in her very great superiority in numbers. The packet, commanded by acting-Captain W. Rogers, cracked on sail, as in duty bound, to escape ; but the big privateer schooner of those days was among the fastest craft afloat, and it was speedily apparent that some fighting would have to be done. Rogers had only twenty-eight in his crew, all told, men and boys— sufficient to work the brig fairly well, but not, one would imagine, to fight her against a schooner crowded with men. However, he beat to quarters and made all his arrangements, not forgetting to place some responsible persons in charge of the mails, to shift them about to a place of safety as required, and, in the last resort, to sink them. This, of course, reduced his little fighting force still further.

The privateer was within gunshot at noon, and, hoisting French colours, opened fire, the packet returning it with her stern-chasers. Arriving within hail, the French captain, who appears to have been sadly deficient in that politeness which is characteristic of his countrymen, demanded, in rude and contemptuous terms, the lowering of the British colours. He could very plainly see, by this time, how scanty was the crew of the packet compared with his own, and, upon Rogers declining to surrender, he immediately ran aboard the *Windsor Castle*, intending to finish the affair off at once by sheer weight of numbers— for he mustered no less than ninety-two, against the British modest twenty-eight, minus the mail-tenders.

However, they did not get on board ; so sharp and stubborn was the resistance offered, that they were glad to return to their own decks, eight or ten short in their number, and immediately cut the grappling-ropes to get clear. The vessels, however, had got locked by their spars, and a desperate encounter ensued. The men in charge of the mails, upon whom the captain, in spite of the fighting, contrived always to keep an eye, were running about from one place to another with them ; but they did not prematurely sink them, though matters must have looked hopeless enough.

About three o'clock, seeing the enemy about to attempt boarding again, Rogers crammed one of his 6-pounder carronades with grape, canister, and a bagful of musket-balls, and let drive just as the Frenchmen commenced their rush. The result was tremendous, a great number being killed and wounded. "Soon after this," says Captain Rogers, in the most matter-of-fact style, as though it were quite an ordinary kind of affair, " I embraced the opportunity of boarding, in turn, with five men, and succeeded in driving the enemy from his quarters, and about four o'clock the schooner was completely in our possession. She is named the *Jeune Richard*, mounting six 6-pounders and one long 18-pounder, having on board at the commencement of the action ninety-two men, of whom twenty-one were found dead upon her decks, and thirty-three wounded. From the very superior number of the enemy still remaining, it was necessary to use every precaution in securing the prisoners. I was obliged to order them up from below, one by one, and place them in their own irons as they came up, as three of our little crew were killed, and ten severely wounded, the mizzen-mast and main-yard carried away, and the rigging fore and aft much damaged. It is my duty to mention to you, sir, that the crew of the packet, amounting at first to only twenty-eight men and boys, supported me with the greatest gallantry during the whole of this arduous contest."

So runs the bare narration, in a service letter to Rear-Admiral the Hon. Sir Alexander Cochrane, who, in forwarding it to the Admiralty, remarks: " It is such an instance of bravery and persevering courage, combined with great presence of mind, as was scarcely ever exceeded."

From an engraving by William Ward after the painting by
S. Drummond, A.R.A.

THE CAPTURE OF THE FRENCH PRIVATEER "JEUNE RICHARD" BY
THE "WINDSOR CASTLE" PACKET, ACTING CAPTAIN W. ROGERS,
OCT. 1ST., 1800.

p. 356]

No one will feel disposed to quarrel with this verdict. Rogers would have done well, if, against such odds, he had beaten off his opponent, and saved the mails; the boarding and carrying of the privateer by six men was certainly something outside the bargain!

THE "CATHERINE"

The *Naval Chronicle* for December 1808 contains a copy of a letter from the mate of an armed ship, the *Catherine*, the property of Messrs. Hogg & Co., of London, giving an account of a severe action with a French privateer. The mate—whose name was Robertson—writes very simply and convincingly, and shall tell his own story:

MALTA, *September 26th*, 1808.

" GENTLEMEN,

"I do myself the honour to inform you of the safe arrival of the ship *Catherine* in this port from Gibraltar, which place she left on the 8th instant; but I am sorry to add that Captain Fenn was very badly wounded, on the 13th inst., in latitude 38 deg. 35 min. N., longitude 3 deg. 20 E.,[1] by a shot in an action with a French privateer. On that day a sail hove in sight on the larboard bow, on a wind, standing for us. We hoisted ensign and pendant, and fired a gun. She showed St. George's flag and pendant, and stood on until she got into our wake, then bore up directly for us. We prepared everything for action,

---

[1] That is, a little south of the island of Majorca.

being suspicious of her ; and as soon as it was possible to be understood, by Captain Fenn's order, I hailed and asked from whence she came ? She answered, from Gibraltar, and was in distress for water. I ordered her to haul her wind immediately, or we should fire into her. She still cried out, 'Water! water!' and came on, when I immediately pointed one of the stern guns, and ordered fire. I then jumped to the opposite gun, pointed it, and ordered fire. This order was countermanded, in consequence of her crying 'Mercy!' and 'Water!' But as soon as the smoke of the first gun cleared away, Captain Fenn saw with his glass that they were getting ready to change their colours, and were pointing their bow-guns. He called out, 'It is a Frenchman, fire away!' He no sooner spoke than he got the contents of the second ; but before our guns could be fired again he grappled, and commenced a heavy fire with grape and musketry. I immediately seized a musket and shot the captain, who was going to give orders through his trumpet. I sung out, 'I have shot the captain ! Victory, my boys!' and we gave him three cheers to advance. They returned the same, and came on bravely ; when poor Fenn, with his boarding-pike in his hand, was shot through the body. He addressed himself to me : 'I am shot ; but fight on, my dear fellow.' I encouraged my men, and soon repelled the boarders with very great slaughter.

" In about half an hour, like savages, they sang out and came on again ; but were again repulsed with considerable loss. This caused such great confusion among them that they got their grapplings unhooked and took a broad sheer off; which I improved immediately by sheering likewise, and got two of the great guns into him before he could get to again. This, no doubt, damped their courage; but they again boarded, with three cheers, and several succeeded in getting over our nettings into the poop; but our men, like heroes, made a bold push, and either killed or wounded every man who made his appearance; and those poor devils who had the impudence to come on the poop were all shoved overboard with the pikes fast in their bodies. This was the sickening job, for they made a terrible noise, and got their grapplings unhooked; when I ordered the man at the wheel to luff the ship to give a broadside. Unfortunately, the ship was unmanageable, her sails and running rigging flying in all directions; but, as a substitute, we gave them the stern-chasers, entirely loaded with grape, as long as it could be of service. I then gave all the hands a good glass of grog, and, like smart fellows, they soon got the vessel on her course again. This being done, I ran to the captain and dressed his wounds. He was then apparently dying; but, through a miracle, we have preserved his life. He is in a tolerably fair way, and on shore, under the doctor's charge.

" The privateer was a fine, lateen-rigged vessel, carrying two large sails, and her decks as full of men as possible—we judge from seventy to eighty. We must have killed a great number, as a great quantity of blood rose on the water. It appeared to me a miracle that none of our men were killed, as the grape and musket-balls came in like hail. We had only two men slightly wounded, one of whom was at the wheel."

Little comment is necessary to supplement this narrative, except that the *Catherine's* loss was very trivial for so severe an action. It is impossible to explain these things, which so frequently crop up in the reports of battles, both by land and sea. A whole company or a ship's crew comes almost unscathed out of a " hail of lead and iron." Well, either the " hail " was not quite as thick as was imagined in the heat of action or the balls found every gap between the men. The *Catherine* would not, of course, have more than about five-and-thirty hands, if as many, and they would be scattered about at the guns until the Frenchmen endeavoured to board. Mr. Robertson's graphic and circumstantial story is quite worthy of credence, and he was certainly an able second in command.

Another spirited incident of a similar description is the defence of the *Fortune*, armed ship, Captain Hodgson, against a French privateer, on April 13th, 1811. The odds were, as usual on such occasions, very greatly in favour of the privateer, which was a brig, carrying 16 guns and about 120 men ; while the *Fortune*, which was not intended for aggression, had 8 small guns and 2 swivels, and 19 persons on board, all told.

The action took place in the Atlantic some distance west of Ireland, and lasted for an hour and twenty minutes. The Frenchman, as usual, hoisted English colours at first, and, getting within hail, desired Captain Hodgson to send his boat on board. This was too stale a trick to meet with any success: " If you have any business with me, send your boat here," was the reply.

Failing in his ruse, the privateer captain immediately hoisted French colours and fired, first a single shot between the *Fortune's* masts and then a broadside, which was promptly returned with 100 per cent. interest. Then the enemy, very naturally, sought to bring matters to a conclusion by boarding; but, in spite of their numbers, they could not obtain any footing on the *Fortune's* deck. Eight of them managed to get into the jolly-boat, which hung from the stern—a very convenient method of boarding, provided that no one happens to be handy with a sharp knife. Unluckily for the eight Frenchmen, an English seaman with a cool head and a keen knife happened to be close by—possibly he was steering—and in a moment the jolly-boat's tackles were cut, and she disappeared with her freight. On the forecastle, however, a considerable number had got on board at one moment, but Hodgson, nothing daunted, ordered a volley and led a charge with such impetuosity that the enemy was driven from the deck—mostly overboard.

The *Fortune's* colours were shot away twice, and, after the second time, were nailed to the gaff by a young lad, who, of course, immediately became a mark for the enemy's small-arms; but it is said that he very coolly completed his operations, encouraging the Frenchmen to " fire away." This is very probably true; it is just the kind of thing an English boy delights in doing—more readily, perhaps, than one of more experience.

The *Fortune*, however, in spite of the sustained and courageous resistance of her company, was soon in a bad way: her sails riddled, her rigging cut to pieces, and too large a proportion of her crew wounded or killed, it seemed inevitable that she must surrender; but a lucky shot—or rather, let us say, a skilful shot, and give the gunner the credit, instead of " luck " —brought down the privateer's foretopmast. The " Fortunes " raised a hearty cheer, and the enemy, hampered by the wreck, sheered off, receiving a parting kick in the shape of a broadside. Hodgson and his men hurried up to repair damages, expecting a renewal of the attack; but the privateers had had what is known in sporting circles as a " bellyful," and did not come up to the scratch again. Out of her small ship's company, the *Fortune* had four killed and six wounded—which only leaves nine to fight!

THE "THREE SISTERS"

Captain George Thompson, of the merchant ship *Three Sisters*, addressed the following letter to his owners on September 18th, 1811, being then off the Isle of Wight:

" I have to acquaint you with a desperate engagement I have had with a French privateer, Le Fevre, mounting 10 guns—six long sixes, and four 12-pound carronades—with swivels and small arms, manned with 58 men, out from Brest fourteen days, in which time she captured the *Friends* schooner, from Lisbon, belonging to Plymouth, and a large sloop from Scilly, with codfish and sundries, for Falmouth. On the 11th, at nine p.m., we observed her on the larboard bow ; we were then steering N.N.E. about ten leagues from Scilly, and nearly calm.

" I immediately set my royals, fore steering-sails, and made all clear for action. At two a.m., when all my endeavours to escape were useless, she being within musket-shot, I addressed my crew, and represented the hardships they would undergo as prisoners, and the honour and happiness of being with their wives and families. This had the desired effect, and I immediately ordered the action to commence, and endeavoured to keep a good offing ; but which he prevented by running alongside, and immediately attempted to board, with a machine I never before observed, which was three long ladders, with points at the end, that served to grapple us to them. They made three desperate attempts, with about twelve men at each ladder, but were received with such a determination that they were all driven back with great slaughter, and formed a heap for the others to ascend with greater facility.

" Finding us so desperate, they immediately, on their last charge failing, knocked off their ladders, one of which they were unable to unhook from our side, and left it with me, and sheered off ; but, I am sorry to say, without my being able to injure them, as they had shot away part of my rudder before they boarded me, and I am sorry to say wounded several of my masts and yards, for it seemed to be their aim to carry away some of my masts, but which, happily, they did not effect. The most painful part of my narrative is the loss of two men and a boy killed, and four wounded ; but the wounded are doing well. Our whole crew amounted, officers and men, to twenty-six men and four boys, and deserve the highest applause that can be bestowed upon them. I arrived off here this afternoon, and, as it is fine weather, I have no doubt of reaching London in safety, as I have but little damage in my hull."

CONCLUSION

WITH this brilliant little incident this account must come to a close.

Are there to be any privateering actions in future naval warfare ? The Declaration of Paris, in 1856, at the close of the Crimean War, lays down that " Privateering is and remains abolished " ; but will this dictum be accounted as holding good, if it should suit any naval power to resort to the practice ?

It cannot be expected that this will be so. The days of the raking, fast-sailing brig or schooner are, indeed, over ; but there remain the swift ocean " greyhounds," admirably adapted, if armed with a few long-ranged, quick-firing guns, for running down and capturing merchant vessels, and showing a clean pair of heels on the appearance of a cruiser. Can it be doubted that some of them will be utilised for the purpose ?

At the recent International Conference it was distinctly suggested that fast merchant vessels may be converted into men-of-war, on the high seas; and though the British delegates refused to recognise the principle, it was not negatived, and remains open.

If a merchant skipper has instructions, upon learning of the declaration of war, to hoist up the guns from his hold and act as a cruiser against the enemy's commerce, the margin between this and privateering is an exceedingly narrow one: moreover, we have had numerous instances lately of the treatment of international treaties and declarations as so much pie-crust; so we must not be surprised if the Declaration of Paris shares the same fate. We may, in fact, in this twentieth century, hark back to the dictum of that shrewd old Admiralty judge, Sir Leoline Jenkins, previously quoted: privateers will probably remain, as " a sort of people that will always be found fault with, but still made use of."

INDEX

Printed by Hazell, Watson & Viney, Ld., London and Aylesbury.